ENEMIES OF INTELLIGENCE

Enemies OF INTELLIGENCE

Knowledge and Power in American National Security

RICHARD K. BETTS

 Columbia University Press   *New York*

Columbia University Press
Publishers Since 1893
New York   Chichester, West Sussex
Copyright © 2007 Columbia University Press
All rights reserved

A Caravan book. For more information, visit
www.caravanbooks.org

Library of Congress Cataloging-in-Publication Data
Betts, Richard K., 1947–
Enemies of intelligence : knowledge and power in American nationalal security /
Richard K. Betts.
p. cm.
Includes index.
ISBN 978–0–231–13888–8 (cloth : alk. paper) —
ISBN 978–0–231–51113–1 (e-book)
1. Intelligence service—United States. 2. National security—United States.
3 . Terrorism—United States—Prevention. I. Title.
JK468.I6B44   2007
327.1273   dc22
2007003937

∞

Columbia University Press books are printed on permanent
and durable acid-free paper.
This book is printed on paper with recycled content.
Printed in the United States of America
c 10 9 8 7 6 5 4 3 2 1

For a very motley crew that, over the years,
helped get me to this book:

Michael I. Handel
Samuel P. Huntington
Robert Jervis
John D. Steinbruner

War is not an exercise of the will directed at inanimate matter, as is the case with the mechanical arts, or at matter which is animate but passive and yielding, as is the case with the human mind and emotions in the fine arts. In war, the will is directed at an animate object that reacts.

—CARL VON CLAUSEWITZ, *ON WAR*

Everyone with experience in decision making knows that the more closely we explore alternative courses of action, the more clearly we become aware of limitations of various kinds which restrict the courses open to us. Sometimes decision making proves to be no more than the painful process of discovering that there is only one thing to do or even "nothing to be done". On the other hand, experience also recognizes situations in which the decision maker can in some degree impose a pattern on the future course of affairs, rather than merely responding to its demands... .
It may be inevitable that we should sometimes expect far more of our governors and even of ourselves than in fact is open to them or to us and suffer in consequence unnecessary agonies of fury or guilt; and should sometimes expect far too little and thus allow a high human function to be abdicated. Yet the extent of such errors might be reduced, if we understood the process better; and it is important that it should be reduced, for at the moment it imperils the whole working of our political system.

—SIR GEOFFREY VICKERS, *THE ART OF JUDGMENT*

Just as the mistakes made in each warning failure are old ones, so are the proposals for doing something about it.

—CYNTHIA M. GRABO, *ANTICIPATING SURPRISE*

CONTENTS

This book puts recent controversies about strategic intelligence into historical and conceptual context. I have toyed with the idea of a book on intelligence off and on since the 1970s. The catalyst for what appears here is the debate over intelligence reform that followed the one-two punch delivered by September 11, 2001, and the mistaken national intelligence estimate a year later concerning Iraq's weapons of mass destruction. The events of September 11 shocked laypeople (and even many professionals in defense policy who should have known better, had they been paying attention to the evolution of terrorism) into a new sense of insecurity. The intelligence estimate provided the justification—though it was not the cause—for the decision to launch an unnecessary and disastrous war.

As citizens and policymakers were shocked into recognizing the importance of intelligence in averting disasters, the natural reaction of many at first was impatience, or disgust, with the apparent incompetence of the American intelligence services that had allowed these catastrophic errors. Much of this reaction reflected the naïveté of those discovering familiar pathologies for the first time. After much controversy, political imperatives forced legislation for a major reorganization of the intelligence system that will take years to shake down. Debate continues, as politicians and bureaucrats grapple with the uncertain results of the reform initiatives.

This book is short, but its roots lie in three decades of thinking about intelligence failures and in participant observation on the periphery of the contemporary U.S. intelligence community. I had the good fortune in the 1970s to be in on the takeoff of the public examination of intelligence processes and I capitalized on that opportunity in my writing. Episodically ever since then and between projects on other subjects, I have combined regular academic research with what I learned from very limited, yet still highly enlightening experiences in the policy world. I was a staff member of the original Senate Intelligence Committee (the Church committee) and the National Security Council in the 1970s, a consultant to the National Intelligence Council and Central Intelligence Agency in the 1980s and in years since, a member of the military advisory and national security advisory panels of the director of central intelligence in the 1990s, and a member of the National Commission on Terrorism (the Bremer commission) in 1999–2000. The melding of policy analysis and theoretical work that I found rewarding from this interaction of research and brief participant observation is out of fashion in contemporary political science, but I continue to believe that separating study-based theory from experience-based policy analysis impoverishes both.

The taproot of the book was my first exposure, in 1975, to real knowledge of intelligence. As I was finishing my dissertation on the role of military advice in decisions to resort to force, the epochal first investigations of the intelligence community by Congress began under Senator Frank Church and Rep. Otis Pike. Originally spurred by a mission to investigate scandals, both committees expanded into more complete examinations of the work of intelligence agencies. Barry Carter, on the ground floor of the Church committee staff as it was gearing up, asked John Steinbruner, then at Harvard, if he knew of budding PhD's who might be recruited for the staff. Having just heard my seminar on my dissertation, John recommended me, and I joined the staff's military intelligence task force. Political conditions at the time, following Watergate and the Indochina debacle, led to unprecedented cooperation between the intelligence community and investigators—to the degree that late in the process, President Gerald Ford fired William Colby, the director of central intelligence (DCI), for allowing so much to be revealed. I have never before or since learned so much in so short a time as I did during those months of 70-hour weeks interviewing intelligence professionals, examining highly classified documents on a wide range of issues, getting briefings on sensitive secret programs, and writing memos, studies, and sections of the committee's final report.

Back then I intended to write a comprehensive book on the role of intelligence in foreign policy, not least because my experience on the Church committee had left the scholar in me frustrated. I could not help thinking that if only the committee's hundreds of file cabinets of secret documents, reports, and interview transcripts could be used as an archive for publishable research, I could write a blockbuster. All but a small portion of the staff's work remained classified, however. The committee's final report, published in seven hefty volumes (on top of six volumes of hearings), was only the tip of the iceberg.

The material in that tip was the beginning of a steadily growing body of officially declassified material and secondary literature based on more reliable information than was ever publicly available in the first half of the Cold War. Before 1975 the genuinely informed literature on intelligence consisted of Roberta Wohlstetter's classic, *Pearl Harbor: Warning and Decision*, based in large part on the thirty-nine volumes of hearings from the congressional investigation of that disaster; a few polemical works by former insiders, such as the partially censored account by Victor Marchetti and John Marks, *The CIA and the Cult of Intelligence*; or memoirs by renegades like Philip Agee's *Inside the Company*. Today there is an ample body of serious work by scholars and practitioners, such as Christopher Andrew, Uri Bar-Joseph, Bruce Berkowitz, Harold Ford, Lawrence Freedman, Roger George, Roy Godson, Alan Goodman, Glen Hastedt, Michael Herman, Robert Jervis, Loch Johnson, Ephraim Kam, Mark Lowenthal, Thomas Mahnken, Ernest May, Timothy Naftali, William Odom, John Prados, Jeffrey Richelson, Richard Russell, Abram Shulsky, Gregory Treverton, James Wirtz, and a number of others, as well as the memoirs of former DCIs (unthinkable before the 1980s). There are also reams of declassified documents from intelligence agencies, hearings and reports from congressional oversight committees, and two good journals, *Intelligence and National Security* and *The International Journal of Intelligence and Counterintelligence*. And this does not count the even more voluminous secondary work by a large number of historians, who usually avoid conceptual generalization but steadily map the record of old cases.

As I completed one book on a particular aspect of intelligence (*Surprise Attack*, published by the Brookings Institution in 1982), other projects led me to different issues in international relations and U.S. defense policy. At the same time, respectable literature on intelligence rapidly began filling the old void. I wrote articles on intelligence from time to time but indefinitely deferred the plan to write a general book on the subject. Then, a couple of years ago, Peter Dimock of Columbia University Press began nudging me to publish a book on U.S. foreign policy. As intelligence policy issues were being splashed across the headlines, this subject seemed appropriate for a book in part because critics who were discovering intelligence pathologies for the first time affirmed my confidence in the relevance of my earlier work.

It quickly became clear that any notion of publishing just an updated collection of old essays would not do. Too much had happened since the end of the Cold War, and especially since 2001. Less than half of the material in this book is drawn from earlier work. Chapters 1, 5, 7, and 8 have never been published. The other chapters incorporate much from earlier articles, but they have been substantially revised, extended, and reorganized. A few unifying themes make the book a coherent argument. That said, readers of my earlier work will find familiar passages. About three-fourths of chapter 2 comes from "Analysis, War, and Decision: Why Intelligence Failures Are Inevitable," *World Politics* 31, no. 1 (October 1978)—the article on intelligence for which I am still best known. Around one-third of chapter 3 originated in "Warning Dilemmas: Normal Theory vs. Exceptional Theory," *Orbis* 26, no. 4 (Winter 1983). A shorter version of chapter 4 appeared first as "Politicization of Intelligence: Costs and Benefits" in *Paradoxes of Strategic Intelligence: Essays in Honor of Michael I. Handel*, edited by Richard K. Betts and Thomas G. Mahnken (London: Frank Cass, 2003). Chapter 6 incorporates pieces of "Fixing Intelligence," *Foreign Affairs* 81, no. 1 (January/February 2002) and "The New Politics of Intelligence: Will Reform Work This Time?" *Foreign Affairs* 83, no. 3 (May/June 2004). Chapter 7 has never been published, but it originated as a lecture to the Yale Political Union on January 24, 2004.

Strategic intelligence involves secrecy, so even with the ample amount of material now available for exploitation, it cannot be studied in the open according to strict standards of social science. This is a book of essays, more than it is new research. No classified information was involved in its preparation. The arguments in these essays come from subjective judgments as well as firm empirical data. And since a substantial piece of the book is about the complex entanglement of intelligence and politics, readers are entitled to know my biases. I am a Democrat; on the right wing of the party during the late Cold War, in its center in recent years. I opposed the invasion of Iraq in 2003. I have usually favored the role of the Central Intelligence Agency as the most objective and important of various U.S. intelligence organizations, a controversial view outside CIA, especially in the Defense Department. And as the book makes clear, I have a cautious view of intelligence reform.

Four very different men helped indirectly and over time to make the book possible, and it is dedicated to them. Michael Handel, one of the principal scholars writing on intelligence in the last quarter of the twentieth century, was a close friend during our years in graduate school and until his death in 2001. His intellectual aggressiveness and tenacity made our frequent debates both exasperating and rewarding. I have profited in many ways from an association with Sam Huntington, one of the few genuine giants of American political science, since my junior year in college, when I responded to a job posting in the student employment office to be his research assistant. Ever controversial, even infuriating to some critics, he has always been an intellectual and personal model of clarity, probity, and loyalty. Bob Jervis, whom I first encountered as a graduate student in his seminar on theories of international politics, is the preeminent academic observer-theorist of intelligence. Bringing me to Columbia, however, is his achievement for which I am most grateful. John Steinbruner and I have profoundly different ideological approaches to national security policy, but he put up with me for a dozen years when he was director of foreign policy studies and I a senior fellow under him at the Brookings Institution—and it was his earlier fortuitous recommendation for the Church committee staff position that got me started combining study and experience to develop the subject of this book.

Too many other people to acknowledge helped along the way, but I must mention a few who provided academic comments or chances to supplement study with intelligence-related experience. Amy Zegart of UCLA and James Wirtz of the Naval Postgraduate School reviewed the proposal and manuscript for Columbia University Press and provided suggestions that improved its focus and coherence. Eric Richard responded unselfishly to a call from an old compatriot on the Church committee staff and reviewed the first version of chapter 7 to check for bloopers that a nonlawyer might make—and found some. My corrections do not satisfy legal standards of analysis (and are not meant to), but the chapter is better than it would have been without his scrutiny. I am also grateful to Alton Quanbeck, director of the military intelligence task force and my boss on the Church committee; Zbigniew Brzezinski, for bringing me briefly to the National Security Council staff to work on Presidential Review Memorandum 10 with Sam Huntington, William Odom, and Catherine Kelleher; John King, Bruce Clarke, and Richard Lehman of CIA and the National Intelligence Council (NIC) for appreciating my first article on the subject and bringing me into the intelligence community as a consultant, a role from which I have profited off and on since 1980; Joseph S. Nye Jr., who as chairman of the NIC arranged my appointment to the DCI's military advisory panel; and Senator Tom Daschle for appointing me to the National Commission on Terrorism. I also thank Tom Lacey for editing the manuscript.

My thanks to my wife, Adela M. Bolet, and our children, Elena, Michael, and Diego, are really not perfunctory. They have had other books dedicated to them, but this one owes them as much. Had any of them caused me even half the amount of anxiety that is normal within families, placed even half the demands on my time to which they have a right, or given love and toleration to just a normal extent instead of so exorbitantly, I would never have gotten this work done.

Richard K. Betts
Teaneck, New Jersey

ENEMIES OF INTELLIGENCE

1 / TWENTY-FIRST-CENTURY INTELLIGENCE

New Enemies and Old

Whatever the foreign policy of the world's leading power should be, it should not be ignorant. Power without knowledge is useless at best, dangerous at worst. Government should know as much as possible about threats and opportunities and in time to do something about them. The intelligence function—the collection, correlation, analysis, and dissemination of relevant information—is integral to national security. Yet Americans seldom think about this until the intelligence system stumbles badly. Then they resolve to shake it up, set it right, and prevent another disaster. These efforts always focus on finding out who or what was responsible for what went wrong on the assumption that, once understood, the sources of error can be fixed.

The mission of fixing the intelligence system became especially salient in the twenty-first century because of the focus on counterterrorism. Intelligence has also continued to be big business: the aggregate budget for all U.S. agencies and activities in 2005 was $44 billion.[1] Confidence in the system, however, has remained low. The stakes are high, but the public view is that scandals are recurrent, performance is often weak, and political manipulation infects the process. Are the problems really so bad? Why do they persist in the face of periodic efforts to fix them?

As serious debate about reform got under way, some critics believed the organization of the system was misconceived from the beginning and never rectified.[2] Others thought that, during a half century of institutional growth and a changing international environment, it had gradually become unwieldy, attuned to obsolete priorities, and outmoded. As Rep. Jane Harman (D-CA) put it, "We are using a 1947 business model to confront a 21st century threat."[3] Transformation, rather than just anodyne reform, became a popular watchword among frustrated insiders.[4] Many politicians and intelligence officers were convinced that business as usual was so intolerable, and the antibodies against change so strong, that a revolution was required to get the system on the right track. For example, just before assuming the position of a top assistant to the director of national intelligence, Deborah Barger wrote a monograph advocating a revolution in intelligence affairs comparable to the Defense Department's much-touted revolution in military affairs.[5]

When a bulky, problematic establishment encrusted with complicated organizations and dubious traditions of operation stumbles in a time of high concern about national security, the idea of a revolution has a natural allure. But real revolutions are dangerous because they are highly destructive. Overturning a thoroughly rotten system with sweeping change makes sense. If a system has redeeming virtues, however, revolution risks throwing out the babies with bathwater. Barger recognizes the risks. She notes that "one of the real downsides of revolutionary change is that it is entirely possible to make a strategic blunder and take the wrong course of action" and cites Richard Hundley's observation that revolutions fail as often as they succeed.[6] (Indeed, when it comes to real revolutions, the principal ones of the past century, engineered by Lenin, Hitler, and Mao, were catastrophes.) If revolution is to be risked, its engineers need to know exactly what they want the result to be, and how actions designed to produce desired change will be sure to do so rather than yield unanticipated consequences. This is a tall order. When concrete initiatives for change get down to the wire, the radical impulse usually falters.

The approach to fixing intelligence that is common among many politicians, pundits, and concerned citizens overlooks some important points:

• In focusing on failures, critics often lose sight of the system's many successes. Thus, the elements of the system that need to be preserved and protected tend to be undervalued. This book focuses on failure, too, but fixates on ensuring that reforms do not break more than they fix.
• Many reformers who respond to the latest scandal or failure have little detailed knowledge of the intelligence process that goes back more

than a decade or two and thus pay little attention to lessons from a longer span of history. This lack of perspective abets facile notions for how to solve deeply rooted problems.

• Everyone agrees that intelligence producers should serve policy but be protected from politics, should speak truth to power, and be immune to corruption by decision-makers' demands to support their policy preferences. Honoring these principles in practice generates tension with the imperative to make intelligence relevant and influential. Yet, not everyone recognizes that the only way to eliminate all risk of political contamination is to remove intelligence so far from the political arena that it loses its place in informing decision making.

The caution this book suggests about radical change flows from a concern with improving American strategic intelligence as intense as any refomer's. It is tempered with skepticism about how much can be expected from reform, but that skepticism should not be mistaken for a counsel of hopelessness or as a brief against change. Limited improvements based on realistic foundations are better than revolutionary changes that founder or make things worse. The essays that follow explore problems in the intelligence process that contribute to this cautionary view. As background, this chapter considers what challenges are new in the landscape of twenty-first-century intelligence, the three sets of enemies that subvert success in intelligence, how to look at the problem of failure with these enemies in mind, and how knowledge and power work together.

A NEW ERA?

The impulse to fix intelligence has burst forth into public debate three times since the United States became a superpower: after the Japanese attack on Pearl Harbor; after the crack-up of the Cold War consensus and the eruption of partisan controversies spurred by the Vietnam War and the Watergate affair; and after the post–Cold War hiatus in concern about security ended with the Al Qaeda attacks of September 11, 2001. The first phase of reform culminated in the National Security Act of 1947, which established the structure of the modern American intelligence community. This community included the new Central Intelligence Agency and the separate intelligence units of the military and cabinet departments. (The array grew to sixteen agencies by 2006: Central Intelligence Agency, Federal Bureau of Investigation, Defense Intelligence Agency, National Security Agency, National Reconnaissance Office, National Geospatial Intelligence Agency, and the intelligence organizations of the army, navy, air force, marine corps, coast guard, Drug Enforcement Administration, and the departments of State, Homeland Security, Energy, and Treasury.). The second phase of reform, in the 1970s, focused less on improving the intelligence function than on disciplining political and legal wrongdoing by intelligence organizations. The changes that resulted were mainly new constraints on domestic intelligence collection and more institutionalized oversight by Congress. The third phase culminated in the Intelligence Reform and Terrorism Prevention Act of 2004, and it is still unfolding. The aim is to fix deficiencies of structure and process that appear to be responsible for the surprise of September 11 and for the mistaken estimate that Iraq possessed weapons of mass destruction, an estimate that gave the president the excuse to launch what turned into a calamitous war.

For a while after the Cold War, two ideas about the new world devalued traditional strategic intelligence work. One was that the demise of a superpower adversary removed the need for strenuous efforts to acquire secrets from other countries. Senator Daniel Patrick Moynihan even proposed abolishing the Central Intelligence Agency. The other idea was that the explosion of communicable knowledge in the information age made open sources the prime means for informing policymakers. In recent times there has been a profusion of reporting and analysis by journalists, think tanks, and academics, and of collection services from nongovernment providers such as commercial satellites. The intelligence community had no comparative advantage in exploiting these open sources. Thus, some intelligence professionals argued for focusing their mission on what was secret and ceding most of the community's work on open sources to nongovernment organizations. For both reasons, the need for a large intelligence establishment spending tens of billions of dollars a year was in question.

The notion that secret intelligence was no longer essential did not survive September 11. The idea that government intelligence should de-emphasize reporting open-source material kept only a bit more appeal. Intelligence agencies in the information age do have more competition for the attention of policymakers. Intelligence analysts have less claim to be unique providers of informed assessments than they did during the first half of the community's existence because officials have more immediate access to raw intelligence and can now act as their own analysts.[7] When looking at the day-to-day duplication of nongovernment sources, some officials do wonder whether the value added from official intelligence is worth the cost. They would be more upset, however, if streamlining the analytic system were to produce lacunae in coverage that catch them up short on some issue.

The volume and complexity of available information from all sources, secret and open, increase the need for a mechanism to assimilate and integrate it so that policy organs can draw on it systematically. Just because unclassified information is available somewhere does not mean it is automatically available to officials who need it, or in the form they need it. For example, what made military planners come to value the research and analysis branch of the Office of Strategic Services was not some secret assessment but an exercise in marshaling material from open sources. In 1942 Sherman Kent used a team of scholars "to produce in record time a series of studies on the ports and railways of North Africa" to support Operation TORCH, the allied invasion. "The military customers . . . couldn't believe so much useful information existed, much less could be written up with authority so quickly."[8] In 2005 an open source center was established under the director of national intelligence to bring together data from the Internet, broadcast and print journalism, "and other unclassified sources around the world."[9] (The value of this addition is questionable if it encourages analysts elsewhere in the intelligence community to think that they need pay less attention to open sources themselves.)

The intelligence community is the logical set of institutions to provide what one might call the library function for national security: it keeps track of all sources, secret or not, and mobilizes them in coherent form whenever nonexpert policymakers call for them. As Gregory Treverton points out, the more information available, the more crucial the problem of verifying it becomes, and this makes policymakers more, not less, dependent on "information brokers." Images "of policymakers surfing the Web themselves, in direct touch with their own information sources, are very misleading. . . . As their access to information multiplies, their need for processing . . . will go up." Nongovernment brokers like CNN compete with intelligence agencies.[10] But policymakers need one place they can go to for full-service correlation of relevant data on whatever issues come across their radar screens.

Even though it is clear that a solid government intelligence system is necessary, some still doubt that there is much to learn from any but recent experience because we have moved into a different world in the twenty-first century. It is popular to assume that the business of intelligence has changed fundamentally in a new millennium, especially since the turn of millennium coincided with the jolt of September 11. This assumption is natural psychologically, but is not logical. There is no objective reason to assume that the changes within the decade from 1995 to 2005 must be more epochal than those between 1985 and 1995, or in any other decade. There have indeed been important changes in the challenges that intelligence faces in recent years, especially in the nature of our adversaries and our capacity to uncover their secrets. The continuities, however, are equally important, especially in the most common sources of intelligence failure.

In any era, intelligence can fail in the collection phase by neglecting to exploit available sources (new surveillance technologies, recruitable agents, relevant open sources), by failing to make stronger efforts or feasible innovations that would increase available sources, or by falling prey to deception and reporting information that turns out to be misleading. Analysis can fail by overlooking or misinterpreting data, by making the wrong prediction, by making no prediction at all (an assessment that does not predict which effects are likely to follow from which actions provides no guidance about what should be done), or by concentrating on excursions of no relevance to policy. Which failures lie in wait from novel challenges and which are rooted in longstanding vulnerabilities of the intelligence process?

The principal challenge to intelligence now is to collect information that adversaries want to keep secret. This is the most important phase of the intelligence cycle, since information that is not collected cannot be used. Collecting strategically relevant information is harder today than in the second half of the Cold War. Then the principal adversary of the United States was the Soviet Union, and the threat it posed was measured primarily in terms of fielded military forces or Marxist allies in other countries. These entities were easier to locate and monitor than are Al Qaeda-inspired cells or the small numbers of weapons of mass destruction that hostile states such as North Korea may hide. During the Cold War about two-thirds of the total U.S. intelligence budget was focused on the Soviet Union and NATO military concerns, and most of that on order-of-battle data—the type, number, location, and weaponry of armed forces. As of 1975 over half of the nation's intelligence budget was allocated to military subjects.[11]

Compared with today, the last three decades of the Cold War was a golden age for intelligence. Technical collection systems—especially reconnaissance satellites and listening posts for interception of communications—matured and proliferated. They proved ideal for finding and tracking major military capabilities. Classic espionage—human intelligence, or HUMINT in the official lexicon—was never as successful as spymasters had hoped, but technical collection provided high confidence in the information needed to inform arms control negotiations and defense planning and to detect attack preparations by large national armies. Its contribution to national security policy then was much greater than that of technical collection systems used against Iraq in the early twenty-first century when, according to an official postmortem by veteran intelligence professionals, they "were able to provide accurate information on relatively few critical issues."[12]

Today the principal adversaries are small groups of terrorist conspirators, irregular resistance groups in the Middle East, and so-called rogue regimes in North Korea and Iran. The threats they pose lie principally in their plans, which are not detectable by satellites, and in the handfuls of instruments of destruction they may acquire that are easier to hide than Soviet missile complexes or armored divisions. It is true, of course, that certain technological innovations have provided significant improvements. The deployment of unmanned aerial vehicles, for example, has enabled quicker and more efficient coverage of some conflict areas. But human intelligence is required to cope with the most crucial aspects of the war on terror more than it was necessary to implement strategies against Moscow.

Intelligence analysis has not gotten any easier than collection. In the Cold War there were big problems in trying to understand and predict political behavior in Communist capitals, and fierce controversies raged constantly, but the ideology, intentions, and behavior of radical Islamists are even harder to divine. It is even more important now, however, to get the right answers. Although the stakes were higher in the Cold War, given the capacity of the main adversary to incinerate American society completely, there was no certainty that the Soviet Union had any desire to attack. It was reasonable to place confidence in deterrence to compensate for lack of certainty. Today, deterrence as a strategy does not offer the same cushion against mistakes in intelligence. There is more reason to doubt the good sense of Kim Jong Il than that of Leonid Brezhnev, and kamikaze hijackers cannot be kept at bay by threatening them with death from retaliation. The good news is that adversaries today are not as capable as those the United States faced in the Cold War; the bad news is that their intentions are more absolutely hostile and that neither their capabilities nor their intentions are well detected. In the Cold War, intelligence targets were easy to find but hard to kill (Soviet military forces); today they are easy to kill but hard to find (terrorists).[13]

The new problems are daunting. Others have not changed, however, and these old problems are likely to be the biggest. If failures that damage national security recur regularly, the challenge is to identify the actors or phenomena that deceive or undermine a big and expensive system and then eliminate or contain these enemies of intelligence. Whatever causes intelligence to fail—intentionally or accidentally, through action or inaction—is an enemy of intelligence. Three sets of enemies have been blamed at various times for disasters. Two are well recognized. If either of these first two is the main problem, the solutions are not hard to pursue (although the pursuit may not always succeed) because they lie primarily in improving the quantity and quality of information and the personnel who evaluate it. The enemies in the third set are less widely understood, the countermeasures against them are less certain, and they are the hardest to defeat.

STRAIGHTFORWARD ENEMIES AND LINEAR SOLUTIONS

The first two sets of enemies get plenty of attention from the public and policymakers.

One set is the most obvious and most clearly fits the normal definition of enemies: the nation's main foreign adversaries, actual and potential. Call these the *outside* enemies. These are governments or groups in conflict with the United States who want to conceal or misrepresent their intentions, capabilities, or vulnerabilities. During the modern intelligence community's first half century, these were Germany, Japan, North Korea, China, and North Vietnam during wartime, and the Soviet Union and its clients and allies in the peacetime phases of the Cold War. More recently they have been revolutionary Islamist terrorists and hostile countries that do not play by American rules—so-called rogue states such as Iraq under Saddam Hussein, Iran, and North Korea. In the future they could be more important countries whose relationship with the United States is satisfactory today but at risk of evolving into a more conflictual one—China, especially.

Those opposed to American policy interests are naturally the enemies of intelligence, since they are seeking ways to conceal information that Washington could use against them or to purvey false information to mislead and deflect U.S. action. In terms of the harm they could do to the United States, today's enemies are far less dangerous than was the old Soviet Union, but as enemies of intelligence they are scarcely less adept at hiding or fabricating what the U.S. government wants to know. Traitors who commit espionage can be counted among the outside enemies.

The second set may be thought of as *innocent* enemies, because they threaten intelligence unintentionally. They are cited by critics who are dismayed by U.S. intelligence failures that so often appear egregious and avoidable in hindsight. Among these are individual intelligence professionals alleged to have fallen down on the job, negligently allowing disasters to happen; the myopic and turf-conscious leadership of intelligence organizations who allow inefficient procedures to block the integration, dissemination, and use of available information; and the politicians or lawyers who deliberately try to constrain intelligence operations that conflict with other values, such as the constitutional rights of citizens. None of these is an enemy in the normal sense of the term because they do not willfully damage American interests. We might even think of some of them as good enemies if they are simply protecting public interests more important than strategic intelligence. Yet, innocent motives do not necessarily excuse damage.

Solutions for dealing with these two sets of enemies are hard to put into practice, but they are straightforward and linear in principle. For the most part they involve increasing the level of effort in both intelligence and counterintelligence, quality of personnel and technology, and rationality of organization. The more that is done in those directions, the better; there is comparatively less risk of counterproductive effects from remedial action than there is with the third set of enemies discussed in the next section. To defeat outside enemies the main solution is to invest in more and better ways to penetrate their secrecy, unmask disinformation, and protect U.S. assets through counterintelligence efforts. For the innocent enemies the main solutions are to fire the dullards and slackers, if stupidity or dereliction are to blame, and replace them with staff that are smarter, more careful, more creative, and harder working; to rationalize the structure and process by improving wiring diagrams and behavioral guidelines, if bad organization and standard operating procedures are the problem; or to repeal or modify the regulations if interference from legal and political constraints is unjustified.

Innocent enemies are a smaller part of the problem than most political debate assumes. Though often fingered in the wake of shocking failures, individual officials are more often the fall guys than the principal culprits. Defects of organizational design are seldom clearly greater than those of alternatives, and legal inhibitions seldom, if ever, caused an otherwise avoidable failure in warning. Nevertheless, innocent enemies are usually the prime target of critics seeking accountability because when shocking failures are investigated they often appear to be "predictable surprises," that is, "events that take an individual or group by surprise, *despite prior awareness of all of the information necessary* to anticipate the events and their consequences."[14] This is a prosecutor's view of intelligence failure: if the persons, process, or guidelines at fault can be identified and replaced, failure can be prevented.

The problem with the prosecutor's view is that it underrates the role of the outside enemies, the forces working to outwit us, and assumes that if our own team is first-rate and unstinting, it should naturally trump the opposition. The prosecutor's view sometimes approaches the challenge of preventing intelligence failures like that of eliminating airplane crashes, space shuttle blowups, nuclear power plant accidents, or floods in New Orleans. The assumption is that if enough resources are invested, protective construction and maintenance optimized, corrections to prevent the recurrence of the latest failure installed, safety mechanisms multiplied and fortified, extraordinary diligence and review institutionalized, and if everything is constantly triple-checked and operations take no chances, failure should be a rare event. This all requires demanding commitment and great cost, but if high cost is accepted, the solution is simply to make the effort heftier, more thorough, more conscientious, and more inventive. This sort of effort is consistent with the traditional American "engineering approach" to solving problems.[15] Indeed, airplane crashes and the wholesale destruction of cities, as occurred with Hurricane Katrina in 2005, *are* very rare events, precisely because of the level of effort made to prevent them and the attention to protective engineering.

National security strategy, however, is not a fight against nature. It is a struggle against conscious counterstrategies. Airplanes, space shuttles, or nuclear power plants do not try constantly to find ways to circumvent safety procedures so that they can crash or melt down, nor are hurricanes relentlessly scheming to outwit the Army Corps of Engineers. Enemy states or hostile groups, however, do exactly that.

Even simple battles against nature can be lost despite major efforts. Weather forecasting, for example, is an analytical task for which there is long experience based on repeated cases and highly developed scientific methods. Yet it still is unreliable more than a few days in advance. Not all potential vulnerabilities are evident in advance, and those that are identified can be minimized but usually cannot be fully eliminated. Mechanisms or procedures introduced to reduce one risk may increase another. Expenditures to guard against dangers that are possible but very improbable must be limited at some point. The psychology of human judgment and the culture of organizations can interfere with rational adaptation and learning.[16] All these sources of risk are compounded in fights against human opponents, when outside enemies scheme about how to block American knowledge of what they are up to. As Robert Jervis points out, "In a system, actions have unintended effects . . . which means that one cannot infer results from desires and expectations. . . . The most obvious reason for this is competition. As actors seek advantage and try to outstrategize one another, some of them—if not all—must be surprised."[17]

Even when lay observers focus on the competitive character of intelligence, they sometimes lose sight of its special limitations. National security strategy is not like a chess game. For diplomats it is more like poker, and for soldiers and intelligence professionals it is more like Kriegspiel—a chesslike game in which the players are unable to see their opponent's pieces or their moves and have only limited information to help them guess what those moves are.[18] Their problems become less straightforward, just as "the engineering approach runs into trouble when there are conflicting ends among which priorities must be established."[19]

INHERENT ENEMIES

Enemies in the third category—*inherent* enemies—grow out of the human condition and the dynamics of the intelligence function itself. They are an amorphous and impersonal group of dysfunctions that, if not quite intractable, are close to it. Solutions for beating inherent enemies are nonlinear and elusive. These enemies are a collection of mental limitations, dilemmas, contradictory imperatives, paradoxical interactions, and trade-offs among objectives in the intelligence process itself that often block proper assessment and judgment and make it difficult to fix one source of failure without creating another. These include defects in organizational design that cannot be changed without risking equally bad results in some other dimension of the process. This motley third set of enemies is less evident to observers outside the intelligence system, and it is reinforced by the outside enemies whose initiatives feed and exploit misjudgment. Inherent enemies pervade the process no matter who is involved, and they intrude time and again. Although not immune to defeat, they are extraordinarily resistant.

Among the inherent enemies are the physical limitations of cognitive processes. Simply because of the physiology of perception and memory, the human brain even at its best apprehends information in ways that are limited and distorted to an extent utterly unappreciated by most officials and critics.[20] Other enemies in this third category include, paradoxically, the complex array of U.S. intelligence needs. Some conflict with each other. Serving one sometimes damages another. These enemies are the contradictions and trade-offs inherent in dealing with uncertainty and complexity, and in working at the nexus of empirical assessment and political decision. They include, as this book will demonstrate, the tensions between the organizational values of centralization and pluralism, the needs to keep secrets from outside enemies and to share information widely to integrate our own knowledge, the conflicting imperatives of accuracy and timeliness, the value of objectivity versus the value of influence, and other good things that do not always go together.

In contrast to the prosecutor's view that goes naturally with a focus on outside or innocent enemies, focusing on inherent enemies produces a tragic view of intelligence failure. Even strong, good-faith efforts can founder because of deeply rooted flaws. Dilemmas dominate the search for counters to this third set of enemies. Used literally here, a *dilemma* is a situation in which there is a "choice between equally unsatisfactory alternatives," or "a problem seemingly incapable of a satisfactory solution."[21] My emphasis on dilemmas has been controversial among critics of intelligence failures because some see it as exaggerated or defeatist or believe that it lets innocent enemies off the hook. If the dilemmas are not confronted, however, hopes for reform will founder no matter how much stupidity or irresponsibility among personnel is eliminated, and defeat will be even more probable.

No one who pays much attention to strategic intelligence is utterly unaware of the inherent enemies. Few observers outside the intelligence community itself, however, face them directly, and when they run up against them they sometimes find themselves leaning against their own recommendations. The Silberman-Robb WMD Commission, for example, recommended creating a new National Counterproliferation Center to follow the massive new National Counterterrorism Center, in a sequence that implies creating yet other special centers outside the regular intelligence agencies to cover important issues. Sixteen pages later in its report, however, the commission points out that "centers run the risk of crowding out competitive analysis, creating new substantive 'stovepipes' organized around issues, engendering turf wars . . . and creating deeply rooted bureaucracies built around temporary intelligence priorities"—a powerful critique of the earlier recommendation! The commission report included other recommendations that pointed in different directions; for example, one was "to integrate the community of analysts while at the same time promoting independent—or competitive—analysis."[22]

The necessary approach to coping with dilemmas is more dialectical than linear. When intellectual or managerial imperatives point in different directions, the natural response is some sort of compromise. For example, the Silberman-Robb commission said of the newly created office of the director of national intelligence, "We fully recognize that the DNI's role calls for a delicate balance. . . . The DNI's analytic cadre must ensure that analytic differences in the Community are not suppressed and, equally important, are not presented to decision makers in a piecemeal fashion that forces senior officials to sort out the differences themselves."[23] This calls for a *really* delicate balance, since revealing a range of views inevitably invites consumers to decide for themselves which ones they like. The delicate balance recommended can work, but only with application of a degree of skill and nuance that does not usually come with the territory of bureaucratic politics, and a delicate solution by definition is not robust.

The process for coping with inherent enemies is necessarily political as well as dialectical. Given the trade-offs between conflicting objectives, choices of how to compromise and which horn of a dilemma to favor emerge from the pulling and hauling of vested interests, priorities, and outlooks. Before investigating how improvements can strike the right balance, however, it is important to think about how intelligence and policy should relate.

KNOWLEDGE, POWER, AND POLICY

The inherent enemies within intellectual and governmental processes are particularly important to confront because the connection between intelligence and policy is not straightforward. Knowledge is power— sometimes. At other times it proves erroneous, irrelevant, or impotent. The power of knowledge depends on who has it, how accurate it is, and how it can be used. Knowledge does not speak for itself. Useful knowledge can be buried or sidetracked or distorted within the complexity of modern government and the hectic pace of work at high levels. To produce power, knowledge must be not only correct but integrated and communicated effectively to the policymakers and implementers in a position to use it productively—the intelligence "consumers." Then those consumers who are in a position to turn the knowledge into power must be sure not to misunderstand or misuse it. Because knowledge is a combination of facts and beliefs intermingled in the minds of decision makers and implementers, ideology and intelligence often prove hard to disentangle.

This reality is in tension with the sacred norm that intelligence should serve policy but be scrupulously separated from the political combat of policymaking. The traditional concept of an intelligence cycle assumes a sequence in which (1) policymakers determine what information they need, and intelligence managers translate these needs into requirements for collection; (2) "tasking" assigns collectors responsibility for seeking the needed data; (3) collectors collect and report the raw data; (4) analysts assess the data in the context of other information and their own broader expertise; (5) "production" converts the analysis into finished reports; (6) products are disseminated to consumers; and (7) the consumers make a policy decision and levy another round of requirements. In the messy political and bureaucratic reality of government, however, these functions often proceed concurrently and autonomously.[24] The actual relationship between intelligence and policy is reciprocal as well as sequential.

For knowledge to be power, it must be ingested and digested by policymakers. This does not happen automatically in a world of overloaded agendas and executive fatigue, especially in a world glutted with information not only from the intelligence community but from the press and other sources as well. To be sure that the intelligence is actually injected into the policy process, producers' presentation must make it speak to consumers and convince them that it provides added value and that absorbing it is worth their time. Thus the power of knowledge sometimes depends on the intelligence producers' knowledge of power. This draws intelligence production closer to the policy maelstrom, raising risks of contaminating the product with policy predispositions.

Instead of the ostensibly rational sequence that subordinates intelligence to policy, circumstances can sometimes make policy serve intelligence. For example, before the Iranian revolution, U.S. policy precluded direct contact between American intelligence personnel and the internal opposition to the Shah's regime. Officials feared that the nervous Shah would suspect a conspiracy and terminate American use of the bases in the country that were collecting technical data on Soviet missile tests.[25] Before the prospects for overthrowing the Shah became evident—knowledge that might have been gained earlier if collection of political intelligence inside Iran had taken precedence—intelligence on Soviet nuclear capabilities appeared to be an obviously higher priority. (Dependence on Iranian territory for technical collection had also increased because the U.S. arms embargo against Turkey after the invasion of Cyprus had caused the shutdown of bases there.)[26] In another example the Bush administration reportedly hosted a visit by Sudan's head of intelligence in 2005, despite his complicity in Sudan's ferocious repression in Darfur, because Sudan had provided helpful intelligence for U.S. counterterrorism projects after September 11.[27] And although intelligence failure is usually tagged with responsibility for policy failure, the reverse can be true, too. Responding to a presidential commission's criticism of poor intelligence on North Korea's nuclear program, Ashton Carter, a former assistant secretary of defense, argued that "policy failure has actually caused intelligence failure in North Korea. From 1994 to 2003 North Korea's plutonium was at a known location, Yongbyon. . . . We could inspect it—or bomb it—at any time." The Bush administration did nothing to stop the North Koreans from ejecting the inspectors and moving the plutonium to a hidden location. As Carter asked, "Are we now supposed to believe it is an 'intelligence failure' that we don't know where it is?"[28]

The ways in which the various enemies interfere with the effective use of intelligence for national security are illustrated in the chapters that follow. Many of the examples are from the Cold War because more reliable documentation and research on that period are available. My emphasis on illustrations from earlier times also puts current problems and proposals for their solution in perspective, highlighting how deep the roots of many problems are.

This book concentrates on a few issues—especially analysis. Though many do not consider this the prime function of intelligence, analysis is the nexus of collection and consumption and links the information that spies and satellites obtain with the process of policy development and judgment. This book is not a study of strategic intelligence in all its aspects; it does not engage many important issues, such as covert political intervention abroad, the means for collecting secret raw data, or the system of legislative oversight. For general surveys, readers may turn to a number of other works.[29]

Chapter 2 surveys the main points. It distills the argument that runs through many of the other chapters and illustrates how outside, innocent, and inherent enemies hobble intelligence in all sorts of times and places. Although the chapter has been updated and revised, its core was written long ago. It holds up even in light of recent circumstances. This underlines my conviction that old knowledge is as important as new, and that reformers who focus on structure and process deductively, without looking at how they have played out historically, risk naïve mistakes in their attempts to fix problems.

Chapter 3 modifies the commonsense assumption that expertise is better than ignorance. The assumption holds true most of the time, of course, but not always—and the exceptions are closely associated with major surprises. Chapter 4 traces the tricky concepts and realities of the politicization of intelligence. Only knowledge of truth can serve policy decision and development. Ideology, faith, or vested interests, however, create incentives to believe certain assertions about what the truth is and to promote those beliefs in policy debate. In essence, politicization is about contending conceptions of the most important truths. It is not only harder to avoid than most assume, but in some very carefully specified respects it should not be avoided. Chapter 5 is a brief comparison of the two most dramatic intelligence failures of recent times and illustrates the incidence of some of the pathologies outlined in other chapters.

Chapter 6 considers various efforts of the latest phase of intelligence reform, the political and organizational context and pitfalls among which they play out, and the odds for their success. Chapter 7 argues that secrecy has more facets than figure in most debates about the relation between intelligence and civil liberties or between sharing information and protecting it. I argue that compromising one element of liberty—privacy—will fortify more important civil liberties and discuss how to keep the compromises of privacy within bounds. Chapter 8 concludes by discussing the good news that should be kept in mind after seven dismal chapters that emphasize how low expectations should be and how enduring the enemies of intelligence are.

Throughout, readers should keep in mind a few arguments:

- For criticism to be realistic, and therefore useful for reform, it should understand that the challenge is not to achieve a "zero defects" standard of performance, but to raise the "batting average" of warning and forecasting.
- Ideas for improving the structure and process of intelligence should be evaluated not just according to what they may fix but what they may break.
- In dealing with the inherent enemies of trade-offs and dilemmas, reform should strike a balance between conflicting imperatives, but because of the difficulty of doing so should be geared to limiting pendulum swings between conflicting solutions.

Like crime or disease, the enemies discussed in what follows can be reduced and suppressed, but not eliminated. The United States will have outside enemies as long as national security exists as an issue and there is any need for strategic intelligence. There will always be innocent enemies in a democracy because of human frailty, disagreements about norms for management, and political contests over which values or missions should take precedence when they conflict. Inherent enemies reside in the nature of human physiology and consciousness, organizational routine, and the complexity of modern government. Their specific forms and strengths will change, but these enemies are all permanent.

Military disasters befall some states, no matter how informed their leaders are, because their capabilities are deficient. Weakness, not choice, is their primary problem. Powerful nations are not immune to calamity either because their leaders may misperceive threats or miscalculate responses. Information, understanding, and judgment are larger parts of the strategic challenge for countries such as the United States. Optimal decisions in defense policy therefore depend on the use of strategic intelligence: the acquisition, analysis, and appreciation of relevant data.

In the best-known cases of intelligence failure, the most crucial mistakes have sometimes been made by the collectors of raw information and the professionals who produce finished analyses, but most often by the decision makers who consume their products. Policy premises constrict perception, and administrative workloads constrain reflection. The available information seldom points unambiguously to the correct conclusion, though there is usually enough of it to alert decision makers to the need for action. Warnings are seldom perfect and failure is rarely complete. At the beginning of the twenty-first century, two disasters—the Al Qaeda attacks of September 11 and the mistaken determination that Saddam Hussein's Iraq possessed stockpiles of chemical and biological weapons—appeared to be exceptions to this proposition. As important as they were, however, they were exceptions only in part.[1]

Observers who see notorious intelligence failures as egregious often infer that disasters can be avoided by perfecting norms and procedures for analysis and argumentation. This is illusory. Intelligence can be improved marginally, but not radically, by altering the analytic system. The illusion is also dangerous if it abets overconfidence that systemic reforms will significantly increase the predictability of threats. The use of intelligence depends less on the bureaucracy than on the intellects and inclination of the authorities above it. To clarify the tangled relationship between analysis and policy, this essay explores conceptual approaches to intelligence failure, differences among intelligence problems, insurmountable obstacles to accurate assessment, and the limitations of solutions proposed by critics.

APPROACHES TO THEORY

Case studies of intelligence failure abound, yet scholars lament the lack of a theory of intelligence.[2] It is more accurate to say that we lack a normative theory of intelligence, or a theory of how to make it succeed. Negative or descriptive theory—the empirical understanding of how intelligence systems make mistakes—is well developed. The distinction is significant because there is little evidence that either scholars or practitioners have succeeded in translating such knowledge into reforms that measurably reduce failure. An affirmative or normative theory of intelligence has not been fully developed because the lessons of hindsight do not guarantee improvement in foresight, and hypothetical solutions to failure only occasionally improve practice.

Intelligence failure can be conceptualized in three overlapping ways. The first is the most reassuring, the second is the most common, and the third is the most important.

Failure in Perspective

A pessimist sees a glass of water as half empty and an optimist sees it as half full. Nonprofessionals usually think about intelligence only when a failure draws attention to it, but they should recognize that the intelligence system is a glass half full. Mistakes happen in any line of work. Failures seem disproportionately significant when considered in isolation rather than in terms of the general ratio of failures to successes; the record of success is less striking because observers will not notice disasters that do not happen. Any academician conducting research would be impressed with a model that predicts outcomes correctly in four of five cases; intelligence analysts must use models of their own and should not be blamed when they miss occasionally.

One problem with this benign view is that there are no clear indicators of the ratio of failure to success in intelligence. Nor is it clear whether many successes on minor issues should be reassuring in the face of a smaller number of failures on more critical problems. Consider the old story recounted by Thomas Hughes: "As that ancient retiree from the Research Department of the British Foreign Office reputedly said, after serving from 1903–1950: 'Year after year the worriers and fretters would come to me with awful predictions of the outbreak of war. I denied it each time. I was only wrong twice.' "[3] In the thermonuclear age, however, just one mistake could have apocalyptic consequences.

Pathologies of Communication

The most frequently noted sources of breakdowns in intelligence lie in the process of amassing timely data, communicating the data to decision makers, and impressing the latter with the validity or relevance of the information. This view of the problem leaves room for optimism because it implies that procedural fixes can eliminate error. For this reason, official postmortems of intelligence blunders always produce recommendations for reorganization and changes in operating norms.

Paradoxes of Perception

The most pessimistic view is that the roots of failure lie in unresolvable trade-offs and dilemmas. Curing some pathologies with organizational reforms often creates new pathologies or resurrects old ones.[4] Perfecting intelligence production does not necessarily lead to perfecting consumption. Making warning systems more sensitive reduces the risk of surprise but increases the number of false alarms, thereby reducing sensitivity. Some of the principles of optimal analytic procedure are incompatible with the imperatives of decision making. Avoiding intelligence failure requires eliminating strategic preconceptions, but leaders cannot operate purposefully without some mental-organizing principles, which amount to preconceptions. Policymakers who would improve the process are often damned if they do and if they don't.

It is useful to disaggregate the problem of strategic intelligence failures in order to elicit clues about which paradoxes and pathologies are pervasive and therefore most in need of attention. The crucial problems in the linkage between analysis and strategic decision can be subsumed under the following three categories:

Attack Warning

The timely prediction of an enemy's immediate intentions and the selling of such a prediction to responsible authorities are the problems here. Major insights into intelligence failure have emerged from strategic surprises, such as Pearl Harbor, the German invasion of the USSR, the North Korean attack and Chinese intervention of 1950, the Middle East wars of 1967 and 1973, the Tet offensive and the Soviet invasion of Czechoslovakia in 1968, the 1979 Soviet invasion of Afghanistan, the Argentinean invasion of the Falkland/Malvinas Islands in 1982, the 1990 Iraqi attack on Kuwait, and other cases.[5] All involve two common problems. First, evidence of impending attack was available but did not flow efficiently up the chain of command. Second, the fragmentary alarms that did reach decision makers were dismissed because they contradicted strategic estimates or assumptions. A comprehensive analysis of the recurrence of variations on these themes makes the success of strategic surprise appear almost overdetermined. Numerous cases exemplify certain principles.

- Surprise is almost always a matter of degree. Victims usually take some protective actions in response to warnings, but almost never enough.
- Procedural obstacles hamper dissemination of warnings. Bottlenecks and proprietary practices limit transmission of data; information is garbled in translation or transmission; salient indicators escape notice because they are buried in a cacophonous clutter of irrelevant data ("noise," as Wohlstetter calls this form of information overload).

- False alarms foster a "cry wolf" syndrome that dulls receptivity of decision makers to subsequent warnings.
- Authorities, racked by uncertainty and tempted to await more information, defer decisions about maximizing response to warnings.
- Enemy deception derails interpretation of warning data.
- The victim fails to anticipate attack options made possible by enemy technical or doctrinal innovations and thus dismisses the operational feasibility of an enemy attack.
- The victim misunderstands enemy calculations because of mirror imaging in assessment or mistaken assumptions that the enemy will be strategically rational and will not start a war that it cannot win.
- The victim empathizes with the defensive fears of the enemy and rejects full countermobilization in order to avoid provoking diplomatic escalation or military preemption.[6]

Operational Evaluation

In wartime the essential problem lies in measuring the results of interacting capabilities and judging their significance. Once hostilities are under way, informed decision making requires assessing tactical effectiveness to adapt strategy and options. Two fundamental points emerge from numerous cases.

First, a glut of ambiguous data allows intelligence officials linked to operational agencies (primarily military) to indulge a propensity for justifying service performance by issuing optimistic assessments, while analysts in autonomous nonoperational units (primarily the Central Intelligence Agency's Directorate of Intelligence) tend to produce more pessimistic evaluations. This was most poignantly demonstrated during the Vietnam War.[7] It was evident even later in the first war against Iraq, which was fought with a much more professionalized force. For example, according to the House Armed Services Committee, "the number of Iraqi naval vessels reported sunk eventually totaled three times the number of naval vessels Iraq possessed" and "the total number of claimed Scud kills was four times greater than the upper end of the intelligence estimates for Iraq's Scud inventory." Preferring the views of his own military intelligence on bomb damage assessment to the more skeptical conclusions of CIA analysts, General Norman Schwarzkopf claimed that the United States destroyed as many as sixteen mobile SCUD launchers. The official gulf war air power survey concluded, however, that there was no evidence that *any* SCUDs had been destroyed by aircraft, and the House investigation determined that Schwarzkopf had also overestimated the number of Iraqi tanks destroyed by up to 134 percent. Ironically, the controversy over bomb damage assessment led to the reduction of CIA's role in military analysis.[8]

Second, in contrast to cases of attack warning, fragmentary tactical indicators of success tend to override more general and cautious strategic estimates. Confronted by differing analyses, a leader mortgaged to a policy tends to resent or dismiss those that are critical, even when they represent the majority view of the intelligence community, and to cling to the data that support continued commitment. Lyndon Johnson, for example, was irked by CIA's pessimistic assessments of the situation in Vietnam. Richard Helms recalled Johnson, with his typically vulgar eloquence, railing at a private White House dinner:

Let me tell you about these intelligence guys. When I was growing up in Texas we had a cow named Bessie. I'd go out early and milk her. . . . One day I'd worked hard and gotten a full pail of milk, but I wasn't paying attention, and old Bessie swung her shit-smeared tail through that bucket of milk. Now, you know, that's what these intelligence guys do. You work hard and get a good program or policy going, and they swing a shit-smeared tail through it.[9]

From the consensus-seeking politician, this was criticism; to a pure analyst, it would have been flattery. But it is the perspective of the former, not the latter, that dominates decision making.

Defense Planning

The main task in using intelligence to develop doctrines and forces for deterrence and defense is to estimate threats posed by adversaries, in terms of both capabilities and intentions, over a period of several years. Here the separability of intelligence and policy, analysis and advocacy is least clear. With regard to how much capability is enough, debates over data merge murkily into debates over options and programs. As in operational evaluation, the problem lies more in data mongering than collecting. The basic points in this category are the reverse of those in the previous one.

First, the justification of a mission (in this case, readiness for future contingencies rather than demonstrating current success on the battle-field) prompts pessimistic estimates by military analysts, while autono-mous analysts without budgetary axes to grind, but with biases simi-lar to those in the intellectual community, tend toward more relaxed predictions.[10] Military intelligence inclines toward worst-case analysis in planning and toward best-case analysis in operational evaluation. (Military intelligence officials such as Lt. Gen. Daniel Graham were cas-tigated by liberals for *under*estimating the Vietcong's strength in the 1960s but for *over*estimating Soviet strength in the 1970s.) Air Force intelligence overestimated Soviet air deployments in the "bomber gap" controversy of the 1950s, and CIA-dominated national intelligence esti-mates (NIEs) underestimated Soviet ICBM deployments throughout the 1960s (overreacting, critics say, to the mistaken prediction of a missile gap in 1960).[11] Most U.S. estimates of enemy military strength and ef-fectiveness in the run-up to the 1991 Persian Gulf War were shown to be excessive by the precipitous collapse of Iraq's defense in the first days of the ground war. In the preparations for the second war against Iraq, U.S. Army plans initially assumed the need for an invasion force much larger than that preferred by Secretary of Defense Donald Rumsfeld, but the conventional phase of the 2003 invasion succeeded easily with the smaller force. On the other hand, Army Chief of Staff Eric Shinseki's estimate that hundreds of thousands of troops would be needed to oc-cupy Iraq effectively was dismissed by civilian authorities, but later was proved prescient.

Second, in peacetime, with domestic claims competing for resources, political leaders have a natural interest in rejecting the most pessimistic military estimates and embracing those of other analysts who justify limiting allocations to defense programs. During the Cold War, debates centered on marginal fluctuations in a high baseline defense budget, and arguments exploited statistical gamesmanship in studies of the military balance to make the case for the necessity of increases or the possibility of decreases. In wartime, as in the early 1950s and after September 11, there is always less incentive to limit military spending, and differing intelligence assessments matter less when decisions are made.

Analysis and Decision

Some chronic sources of error are unique to each of these three general categories of intelligence problems and thus do not clearly suggest reforms that would be advisable across the board. To compensate for the risk of failure in warning of conventional attack, worst-case analysis might seem safest, but in making estimates for defense planning, worst-case analysis mandates economic sacrifices that often prove unnecessary. Removing checks on the influence of CIA analysts and community staffs might seem justified by the record of operational evaluation in Vietnam but not by the record of estimates on Soviet ICBM deployments.[12] It would be risky to alter the balance of power systematically among competing analytic components, giving the "better" analysts more status. Decision makers should instead be encouraged to be more *and* less skeptical of estimates made by certain agencies, depending on the category of analysis.

Some problems cut across all three categories and offer a more general basis for considering changes in the system. But these general problems are not very susceptible to cure by formal changes in process because it is often impossible to disentangle intelligence failures from policy failures. Separating intelligence and policymaking has long been a concern of officials and theorists, who have seen both costs and benefits in minimizing the intimacy between intelligence professionals and operational authorities. The personnel can be segregated, but the functions cannot, unless intelligence is defined narrowly as the collection of data, and analytic responsibility is reserved for decision makers. Analysis and decision are interactive rather than sequential processes.

According to the narrower definition of intelligence, there have actually been few complete failures. When mistakes were made in predicting attacks or in assessing operations, the inadequacy of critical data, or its submergence in a viscous bureaucracy, was at best the proximate cause. The ultimate causes of error in most cases have been wishful thinking, disregard of professional analysts, and above all the premises and preconceptions of policymakers. Fewer fiascoes have occurred during the acquisition and presentation of facts than during interpretation and response. Producers of intelligence have sometimes been culprits, but less often than consumers. Policy perspectives tend to constrain objectivity, and authorities often fail to use intelligence properly. As Ray Cline, former State Department intelligence director, testified in defending his analysts' performance in October 1973 and criticizing Secretary of State Henry Kissinger for ignoring them:

Unless something is totally conclusive, you must make an inconclusive report. . . . By the time you are sure it is always very close to the event. So I don't think the analysts did such a lousy job. What I think was the lousy job was in the bosses not insisting on a new preparation at the end of that week [before war broke out]. . . . The reason the system wasn't working very well is that people were not asking it to work and not listening when it did work.[13]

This charitable view of intelligence is widely accepted among the small corps of scholars who have studied cases of failure, but not among politicians or the public. Eliot Cohen and John Gooch dub the academic consensus the "no-fault" school of surprise.[14] This misunderstands the difference between understanding the probability of frequent failures and absolving players of responsibility for them. Ariel Levite calls the academic consensus the "orthodox" school and claims to refute it by comparing the cases of Pearl Harbor and Midway. He argues that there was no significant warning before the first and that the results in the second prove that excellent warnings do produce response by the defender.[15] This argument is thoroughly wrong, as my detailed review in 1989 demonstrates.[16] These critiques, however, do reflect the natural reluctance of smart people with common sense to believe that the dice are so heavily loaded against the warning system.

Policymakers, with some justification, do not think that partial or ambiguous warnings should exonerate intelligence. For them the function of intelligence is not just to alert them to danger but to give an answer—in effect, to make the strategic decision about how to respond. And for the public the biggest exceptions to the pattern of consumers making more mistakes than producers are very recent and *very* big: September 11, 2001, and the October 2002 NIE on Iraq's weapons of mass destruction. To people oriented to the present rather than to a long historical record, these awful exceptions override other cases.

BARRIERS TO ANALYTIC ACCURACY

Many constraints on the optimal processing of information can be found in the structure of authority and the allocation of time and resources. Harold Wilensky has demonstrated that the intelligence function is hindered most by hierarchy, centralization, and specialization.[17] Yet, precisely these characteristics are the essence of any government. It is fashionable to believe that the way institutions function since the computer revolution has changed radically—to view interaction as shifting from hierarchies to networks—but in a large and complex government, bureaucracies will persist and hierarchy will dominate.

The dominance of operational authorities over intelligence specialists and the trade-off between objectivity and influence are related problems. Operators have more influence in decision making but are less capable of unbiased interpretation of evidence because they have a vested interest in the success of their operations; autonomous analysts are more disinterested and usually more objective, but they lack on-the-scene knowledge and, especially, influence. Senior generalists at the policy level often distrust or discount the judgments of analytic professionals and place more weight on reports from operational sources.[18]

In response to this phenomenon, legislating the requirement that decision makers consider analyses by the CIA's intelligence directorate before establishing policy was once suggested.[19] Such a requirement, however, would offer no more than wishful formality because statutory fiat cannot force human beings to value one source above another. "No power has yet been found," Richard Helms, the former director of central intelligence (1966–73), testified, "to force presidents of the United States to pay attention on a continuing basis to people and papers when confidence has been lost in the originator."[20] Moreover, principals tend to believe that they have a wider range of view than middle-level analysts and are better able to draw conclusions from raw data. That belief underlies their fascination with current intelligence and their impatience with the reflective interpretations in finished (meaning analyzed) intelligence.[21] For example, the Church committee (the original Senate investigation of the intelligence community) deplored the tendency of decision makers to focus on the latest raw data rather than on refined analyses, a practice that contributed to the intelligence failure in the 1974 Cyprus crisis. The failure in the 1973 Middle East War, however, had been largely due to the opposite mistake—disregarding tactical warning indicators because they contradicted finished intelligence that minimized the possibility of war.[22]

The dynamics of decision are also not conducive to appreciating analytic refinement. In a crisis, both data and policy outpace analysis, the ideal process of staffing and consultation falls behind the press of events, and careful estimates cannot be digested in time. As Winston Churchill recalled of the hectic days of spring 1940, "The Defence Committee of the War Cabinet sat almost every day to discuss the report of the Military Co-ordination Committee and those of the Chiefs of Staff; and their conclusions or divergences were again referred to frequent Cabinets. All had to be explained or reexplained; and by the time this process was completed, the whole scene had often changed."[23] In recent times the prominence of "real-time" news reporting via CNN further draws policymakers away from carefully processed intelligence.

When there is ample time for decision, on the other hand, bureaucratic impediments gain momentum. "Where the end is knowledge, as in the scientific community, time serves intelligence," says Wilensky. "Where the end is something else—as in practically every organization but those devoted entirely to scholarship—time subverts intelligence, since in the long run, the central institutionalized structures and aims (the maintenance of authority, the accommodation of departmental rivalries, the service of established doctrine) will prevail."[24] Just as information processing is frustrated by constraints on the time that harried principals can spend scrutinizing analytic papers, it is also constrained by the funds that a government can spend. To which priorities should scarce resources be allocated? The Schlesinger report of 1971, which led to President Nixon's reorganization of U.S. intelligence, noted that criticisms of analytic products were often translated into demands for more extensive collection of data but that "seldom does anyone ask if a further reduction in uncertainty, however small, is worth its cost."[25] Authorities do not always know, however, which issues require the greatest attention and which uncertainties harbor the fewest potential threats. Beyond the barriers that authority, organization, and scarcity pose to intelligence lie more fundamental, and less remediable, intellectual sources of error.

Ambiguity of Evidence

Intelligence veterans have noted that "estimating is what you do when you do not know,"[26] but "it is inherent in a great many situations that after reading the estimate, you will still not know."[27] These observations highlight an obvious but most important obstacle to accuracy in analysis. It is the role of intelligence to extract certainty from uncertainty and to facilitate coherent decision in an incoherent environment. (In a certain and coherent environment there would be less need for intelligence.) To the degree they reduce uncertainty by extrapolating from evidence riddled with ambiguities, analysts risk oversimplifying reality and desensitizing the consumers of intelligence to the dangers that lurk within the ambiguities. To the degree they do not resolve ambiguities, analysts risk being dismissed by annoyed consumers who see them as not having done their job.

Uncertainty reflects inadequacy of data, which is usually assumed to mean a *lack* of information. But ambiguity can also be aggravated by an *excess* of data. In attack warning, there is the problem of "noise" and deception; in operational evaluation (particularly in protracted unconventional wars such as Vietnam and Iraq), there is the problem of overload from the high volume of finished analyses, battlefield statistics, reports, bulletins, reconnaissance, and communications intercepts flowing upward through multiple channels at a rate exceeding the capacity of officials to absorb or scrutinize them judiciously. During the Vietnam War the White House regularly received from the CIA current intelligence dailies, weekly reports, daily intelligence information cables, occasional special reports and specific memoranda, analyses from the CIA Vietnam working group, and other materials. In estimates for defense planning, there is the problem of innumerable and endlessly refined indices of strategic capability and balances of power, and the dependence of assessments of capabilities on complex and variable assumptions about the doctrine, scenarios, and intentions that would govern their use.

Because it is the job of decision makers to make decisions, they cannot react to ambiguity by deferring judgment.[28] When the problem is an environment that lacks clarity, an overload of conflicting data, and lack of time for rigorous assessment of sources and validity, ambiguity abets instinct and allows intuition to drive analysis. Intelligence can fail because the data is too permissive for policy judgment rather than too constraining. When a welter of fragmentary evidence offers support to various interpretations, ambiguity is exploited by wishfulness. The greater the ambiguity, the greater the impact of preconceptions. Cognitive theory suggests that uncertainty provokes decision makers to separate rather than integrate their values, to deny that inconsistencies between values exist, and even to see contradictory values as mutually supportive.[29] (These points should be distinguished from the theory of cognitive dissonance.)[30]

There is some inverse relation between the importance of an assessment (when uncertainty is high) and the likelihood that it will be accurate. Lyndon Johnson could reject pessimistic NIEs on Vietnam by inferring more optimistic conclusions from the reports that came through command channels on pacification, interdiction, enemy casualties, and defections. Observers who assumed Soviet malevolence focused on analyses of nuclear forces that emphasized missile throw weight and gross megatonnage (Soviet advantages); those who assumed more benign Soviet intentions focused on analyses that emphasized missile accuracy and numbers of warheads (U.S. advantages). In assessing the naval balance, Secretary of Defense Rumsfeld (in his first tour in the job) focused on numbers of ships (Soviet lead), and Rep. Les Aspin, then a critic of the Pentagon, focused on total tonnage (U.S. lead).

Ambivalence of Judgment

Where there are ambiguous and conflicting indicators (the context of most failures of intelligence), the imperatives of honesty and accuracy leave a careful analyst no alternative but ambivalence. There is usually some evidence to support any prediction. For instance, the CIA reported in June 1964 that a Chinese instructor (deemed *not* "particularly qualified to make this remark") had told troops in a course on guerrilla warfare, "We will have the atom bomb in a matter of months."[31] Several months later the Chinese did perform their first nuclear test. Had the report been the only evidence, should analysts have predicted the event?

If they do not make a leap of faith and ignore the data that do not mesh, analysts will issue estimates that waffle. In trying to elicit nuances of probability from the various possibilities not foreclosed by the data, cautious estimates may reduce ambivalence, but they may become delphic or generalized to the point that they are not informative guides to decision. (A complaint heard several times in conversations with U.S. officials during the Cold War was that the name of any other great power in history—imperial Rome, sixteenth-century Spain, Napoleonic France—could have been substituted in estimates of Soviet objectives and they would have sounded equally valid.) Hedging is the legitimate intellectual response to ambiguity, but it can be politically counterproductive if the value of the intelligence is to shock consumers out of wishfulness and cognitive insensitivity. A wishful decision maker can fasten on the part of an ambivalent analysis that supports his predisposition.[32] A more objective official may escape this temptation but may then consider the estimate useless because it does not provide "the answer."

Atrophy of Reforms

Disasters always stimulate organizational changes designed to avert the same failures in the future. In some cases these changes work. In many instances, however, they persist formally but erode substantively. Standard procedures are constant. Dramatic failures occur only intermittently. If the reforms in procedure which they have provoked do not fulfill day-to-day organizational needs—or if, as often happens, they complicate operations and strain the organization's resources—they fall into disuse or become token practices. The downing of the U-2 spy plane over the Soviet Union in 1960 and the capture of the intelligence ship *Pueblo* in 1968 occurred in part because the risk assessment for specific collection missions, primarily the responsibility of overworked middle-level officers, had become ponderous, sloppy, or ritualized.[33] Efforts to increase responsibility in the process did not take hold. With the postmortem of North Korea's downing of a U.S. EC-121 intelligence collection aircraft in 1969 came a great emphasis for several months on risk assessments for intelligence collection missions. Generals and admirals personally oversaw new procedures for making the assessments. Six months later, majors and captains were doing the checking. "Within a year the paperwork was spot-checked by a major and the entire community slid back to its old way of making a 'quick and dirty' rundown of the JCS criteria when sending in reconnaissance mission proposals."[34]

Periodically, intelligence analysts have been criticized for failing to specify odds in their predictions or for confusing their estimates of odds by using vague prose. In 2005, for example, one wrote, "It's time to require national security analysts to assign numerical probabilities to their professional estimates." As the critic himself noted, however, this had already been tried in the 1960s and '70s when particular words were assigned particular ranges of probability—"almost certain" meant odds of at least 93 percent, "probable" meant 75 percent or more, and so on. The injunction was not followed. Efforts a couple decades later to make analysts specify probabilities also foundered.[35]

One perennial suggestion for reform is to get senior officials more involved in setting the agenda and priorities for intelligence and in checking on professional compliance, but efforts to do this have been generally unsuccessful. At the highest level, a National Security Council intelligence committee was established in 1971 to improve responsiveness of intelligence staff to the needs of policymakers. But since the sub-cabinet consumers who made up the committee were pressed by other responsibilities, it lapsed in importance and was eventually abolished.[36] A comparable NSC committee that *did* serve tangible, day-to-day needs of consumers to integrate intelligence and policy—the verification panel that dealt with the Strategic Arms Limitation Talks—was more effective, but it was focused on arms control issues rather than designed to oversee the intelligence process itself. The reorganization legislation of 2004 established a new joint intelligence community council as a high-level mechanism for consumer participation. It includes a half-dozen cabinet members in addition to the director of national intelligence.[37] History suggests that it will be an uphill battle to make this council perform in more than pro forma ways.

Organizational innovations will not improve the role of intelligence in policy unless they flow from the decision-makers' views of their own needs and unless they provide frequent practical benefits. None of these barriers is an accident of structure or process. They are inherent in the nature of intelligence and the prosaic dynamics of work. As such they constitute severe constraints on the efficacy of structural reform.

ELUSIVE SOLUTIONS

If they do not atrophy, most solutions proposed to obviate intelligence dysfunctions have two edges: in reducing one vulnerability they increase another. After the seizure of the *Pueblo*, the Defense Intelligence Agency (DIA) was reprimanded for misplacing a message that could have prevented the incident. The colonel responsible developed a careful microfilming operation in the message center to ensure a record of cables transmitted to authorities in the Pentagon. This check, however, created a three- to four-hour delay—another potential source of failure—in getting cables to desk analysts whose job was to keep reporting current.[38] September 11 led to numerous security measures and new technologies, which did not all function well enough to outweigh the problems they introduced. For example, customs officials sometimes allowed trucks to pass through new radiation monitors too quickly and reduced the monitors' effectiveness by turning them down because they produced too many false alarms.[39]

Thus, procedural solutions often are two steps forward and one back; organizational fixes often cannot transcend the basic barriers. The lessons of Pearl Harbor led to the establishment of a watch committee and the National Indications Center in Washington. Although this solution eliminated a barrier in the communication system, it did not prevent the failure of a timely alert to the Chinese intervention in Korea or the 1973 October war because it did not eliminate the ambiguity barrier. In later years the watch committee was replaced by the DCI's strategic warning staff and then by a national intelligence officer for warning. Surprises continued periodically despite the adjustments in the system. DIA was reorganized four times within its first ten years (and a number of times in the decades following), yet it continued to leave most observers dissatisfied.

Ideas for organization that seem to be logical improvements are some-times promoted without considering empirical evidence about them. The Agranat commission's review of Israel's 1973 intelligence failure produced proposals for institutional reform that are striking because they amount to copying the American system of the same time—*which had failed in exactly the same way as the Israeli system.* These propos-als, with their U.S. analogues noted in parentheses, were to appoint a special intelligence adviser to the prime minister (director of central intelligence) to supplement the military chief of intelligence; reinforce the foreign ministry's research department (State Department Bureau of Intelligence and Research); provide more autonomy for nonmilitary intelligence (CIA); amend rules for transmitting raw intelligence to re-search agencies, the defense minister, and the prime minister (routing of signals intelligence from the National Security Agency); restructure military intelligence (creation of the Defense Intelligence Agency in 1961); establish a central evaluation unit (National Intelligence Coun-cil).[40] Reform is not hopeless, but hopes placed in the solutions most often proposed—such as the following—should be limited.

Assume the Worst

A common reaction to traumatic surprise is the recommendation to cope with ambiguity and ambivalence by acting on the most threaten-ing possible interpretations. If there is any evidence of threat, assume it is valid, even if the apparent weight of contrary indicators is greater. In hindsight, when the point of reference is an actual disaster attribut-able to a mistaken calculation of probabilities, this response is always justifiable, but it is impractical as a guide to standard procedure. Acting on worst-case analysis requires extraordinary expense, risks being coun-terproductive if it is effective (by provoking enemy countermeasures or preemption), and is likely to be ineffective because routinization will discredit it. Many Israeli observers deduced from the 1973 surprise that defense planning could rest only on the assumption that no attack warning will be available and that precautionary mobilization should always be undertaken even when there is only dubious evidence of impending Arab action.[41] American hawks argued that if Soviet intentions were uncertain, the only prudent course was to assume they were seeking the capability to win a nuclear war.

The norm of assuming the worst poses high financial costs and potential risks increasing political friction that could make crises escalate unnecessarily. Frequent mobilizations strain any country's economy, and countermobilization can defeat itself. Three times between 1971 and 1973, the Egyptians undertook exercises similar to those that led to the October attack. Israel mobilized in response, but nothing happened. It was the paradox of the self-negating prophecy.[42] The Israeli chief of staff was sharply criticized for the unnecessary cost. The Israeli command estimated a higher probability of attack in May 1973 than it did in October. Having been proved wrong in May, Chief of Staff David Elazar lost credibility in challenging intelligence officers, then complained that he could no longer argue effectively against them, and consequently was unable to influence his colleagues when he was right.[43] The opposite problem of hypersensitivity appeared in 1977, when Chief of Staff Mordechai Gur believed that President Anwar Sadat's offer to come to Jerusalem was a camouflage for an Egyptian attack.[44]

Precautionary escalation or weapons procurement may act as self-fulfilling prophecies, either through a catalytic spiral of mobilization (à la World War I), an arms race that heightens tension, or military doctrines or deployments that frighten the adversary and provoke preemption (although, in reality, preemption—as distinct from preventive war—rarely occurs). A surprise attack or defeat makes the costs of underestimates obvious and dramatic; the unnecessary defense costs due to overestimates can only be surmised since the minimum needed for deterrence is uncertain. Worst-case analysis as a standard norm would also exacerbate the cry wolf syndrome. Unambiguous threat is not an intelligence problem. The challenge lies in the response to fragmentary, contradictory, and dubious indicators because most turn out to be false alarms. Analysts who reflexively warn of disaster are soon derided as hysterical. Gen. William Westmoreland recalled that warnings issued before the 1968 Tet offensive were ignored. Each year, U.S. headquarters in Saigon had predicted a winter-spring offensive, "and every year it had come off without any dire results. . . . Was not the new offensive to be more of the same?"[45] Likewise, the American public soon became jaded about the color-coded alert system instituted after September 11.

Within two years the system was changed to preserve the credibility of warnings by reducing them.[46]

Given the experience of intelligence professionals that most peace-time indicators of suspicious enemy activity lead to nothing, which colonel who has the watch some night will risk lighting up the board in the White House on the basis of weak apprehension? How many staffers will risk waking a tired president, especially if they have done so before and found the action to be needless? How many distracting false alarms will an overworked president tolerate before he makes it clear that aides should exercise discretion in bothering him?

Even if worst-case analysis is promulgated in principle, it will be compromised in practice. Routinization corrodes sensitivity. Every day that an expected threat does not materialize further dulls receptivity to the reality of danger. As Roberta Wohlstetter wrote of pre–Pearl Harbor vigilance, "We are constantly confronted by the paradox of pessimistic realism of phrase coupled with loose optimism in practice."[47] Seeking to cover all contingencies, worst-case analysis loses focus and salience. By providing a theoretical guide for everything, it provides a practical guide for very little.

Multiple Advocacy

Blunders are often attributed to the inattention of decision makers to unpopular viewpoints or to a lack of access by dissident analysts to higher levels of authority. To reduce the chances of such mistakes, Alexander George proposed institutionalizing a balanced, open, and managed process of debate so that no relevant assessments will be submerged by unchallenged premises or the bureaucratic strength of opposing officials.[48] The goal is unobjectionable, and formalized multiple advocacy certainly would help. But confidence that it will help systematically and substantially should be limited.

In a loose sense there has usually been multiple advocacy in the U.S. policy process, but it has not prevented mistakes in deliberation or decision. Lyndon Johnson did not decide to pursue limited bombing and gradual troop commitment in Vietnam in 1965 because the system failed to present him with extensive and vigorous counterarguments.

He considered seriously (indeed, he solicited) Undersecretary of State George Ball's analysis, which drew on NIEs and lower-level officials' pessimistic assessments that any escalation would be a mistake. Johnson was also well aware of the arguments by DCI John McCone and the air force from the other extreme—that massive escalation in the air war was necessary because gradualism would be ineffective.[49] The president simply chose to accept the views of the middle-of-the-road opponents of both Ball and McCone. Furthermore, there is no necessary reason that increasing the range of arguments heard by a chief executive will guarantee that a better choice is made. Two decades after Johnson's ill-fated decision to commit combat forces to South Vietnam, Ronald Reagan authorized the disastrous initiative to trade arms for hostages with Iran, despite the adamant dissent of both his secretary of state and secretary of defense,[50] perhaps because multiple advocacy gave the lower-ranking enthusiasts for the idea equal standing in the president's consideration.

To the extent that multiple advocacy works, and succeeds in maximizing the number of views put forth and in supporting the argumentative resources of all contending analysts, it may simply highlight ambiguity. In George's ideal situation, the process would winnow out unsubstantiated premises and assumptions about ends-means linkages. But because of data overload, uncertainty, and time constraints, multiple advocacy may in effect give all of the various viewpoints an aura of empirical respectability and permit leaders to choose whichever accords with their predispositions.[51]

George stipulates that multiple advocacy requires "no major maldistribution" of power, influence, competence, information, analytic resources, and bargaining skills.[52] But except for resources and the right to representation, these subjective factors can rarely be equalized by design. If they are equalized, in the context of imperfect data and time pressure, erroneous arguments as well as accurate ones will be reinforced. Nonexpert principals have difficulty arbitrating intellectually between experts who disagree. The efficacy of multiple advocacy (which is greatest when data is manageable and ambiguity low) may vary inversely with the potential for intelligence failure (which is greatest when data is confusing and uncertainty high). The process could, of course, bring to the surface ambiguities where false certainty had prevailed; in these cases it would be as valuable as George believes. But if multiple advocacy increases ambivalence and leaders do not indulge their instincts, it risks promoting conservatism or paralysis. Dean Acheson saw danger in presidential indecisiveness aggravated by debate. "I know your theory," he grumbled to Richard Neustadt. "You think presidents should be warned. You're wrong. Presidents should be given confidence."[53] Even Clausewitz argued that deference to intelligence can frustrate bold initiative and squander crucial opportunities. Critics charged Kissinger with crippling U.S. intelligence by refusing to keep analysts informed of his intimate conversations with foreign leaders.[54] To have done so, however, would have created the possibility of leaks and might thereby have crippled his diplomatic maneuvers. It is doubtful that Nixon's initiative to China could have survived the full bureaucratic play of debate, dissent, analysis, and leaks.

It is unclear whether more managed multiple advocacy would yield markedly greater benefits than the redundancy and competitiveness that have long existed. At best it would improve the marketplace of ideas, combining the benefits of centralization and regulation on one hand and decentralization and pluralism on the other. The first major reorganization of the American intelligence community in 1946–47 emphasized centralization in order to avert future Pearl Harbors caused by fragmentation of authority. Later reorganizations—such as the creation of DIA in 1961, Jimmy Carter's extension of authority of the director of central intelligence over military intelligence programs in 1977, or the most recent creation of the director of national intelligence—have emphasized centralization to improve efficiency and coherence. Yet, decentralization has always persisted in the overlapping division of labor among numerous agencies. Some theorists of bureaucracy see such duplication as beneficial because competition exposes disagreement and presents policymakers with a wider range of views. Redundancy inhibits consensus and impedes the herd instinct in the decision process, thus reducing the likelihood of failure due to unchallenged premises or cognitive errors. To ensure that redundancy works in this way, critics oppose a process that yields coordinated estimates that are negotiated to the least common denominator and cleared by all agencies before they are passed to the principals. George's "custodian" of multiple advocacy could ensure that this does not happen.

There are, of course, trade-off costs for redundancy. Maximizing competition limits specialization. In explaining the failure of intelligence to predict the 1974 coup in Portugal, William Hyland, then the director of the State Department's Bureau of Intelligence and Research, pointed out that "if each of the major analytical components stretch their resources over the same range, there is the risk that areas of less priority will be superficially covered."[55] The main problem with arguing that the principals themselves should scrutinize numerous contrasting estimates in their integrity, however, is that they simply will not. They do not have the time, being constantly overwhelmed by administrative responsibilities and demands for meetings; they cannot read, ponder, and digest so much material. Most intelligence products, even NIEs, are never read by high-level policymakers. At best, they are used by second-level staffers as background material for briefing their seniors.[56] Consumers want previously coordinated analyses in order to save time and effort. The practical imperatives of day-to-day decision contradict the theoretical logic of ideal intelligence.

Consolidation

According to the logic of estimative redundancy, more analysis is better than less. Using this line of reasoning, Senate investigators noted critically that as of fiscal 1975 the U.S. intelligence community still allocated 72 percent of its budget for collecting information, 19 percent for processing technical data, and less than 9 percent for producing finished analyses. (Since the era of huge expenditures for technical intelligence collection began well before then and has not abated, there is no reason to assume that those percentages have changed radically.) On the other hand, according to the logic of those who focus on the time constraints of leaders and the confusion that results from innumerable publications, quantity counteracts quality. The size of CIA's intelligence directorate and the complexity of the production process "precluded close association between policymakers and analysts, between the intelligence product and policy informed by intelligence analysis."[57] For the sake of clarity and acuity, in this view the intelligence bureaucracy should be streamlined.

This view is consistent with the development of the Office of National Estimates (ONE), which was established in 1950 and designed to coordinate the contributions of the various organs in the intelligence community for the director of central intelligence. DCI Walter Bedell Smith envisioned an operation of about a thousand people. But William L. Langer, the scholar Smith imported to organize ONE, wanted a tight group of excellent analysts and a personnel ceiling of fifty. Langer prevailed, and though the number of staff members in ONE crept upward, it probably never exceeded one hundred in its two decades of existence.[58] Yet ONE could not eliminate the complexity of the intelligence process; it could only coordinate and integrate it for the production of national intelligence estimates. Other sources found conduits to decision makers (to cabinet members through their own agencies or to the president through the National Security Council). And some policymakers, though they might dislike the cacophony of multiple intelligence agencies, were suspicious of the consolidated NIEs, knowing that there was pressure to compromise views to gain agreement.

Over time the dynamics of bureaucracy also blunted the original objectives of ONE's founder. From a cosmopolitan elite corps it evolved into an insular unit of senior careerists from the CIA. The national intelligence officer system that replaced ONE reduced the number of personnel responsible for coordinating NIEs but was initially criticized on other grounds, such as its greater vulnerability to departmental pressures. Bureaucratic realities have frustrated other attempts to consolidate the intelligence structure. The Defense Intelligence Agency was established in 1961 to unify Pentagon intelligence and reduce duplicative activities of the three service intelligence agencies, but these agencies regenerated themselves. In less than a decade they were larger than they had been before DIA's inception.[59]

The numerous attempts to simplify the organization of the analytic process thus have not solved the major problems. Either the streamlining exercises were short-lived and bureaucratization crept back in, or the changes had to be moderated to avoid the new dangers they entailed. Contraction is inconsistent with the desire to minimize failure by plugging holes in intelligence, since compensating for an inadequacy usually requires *adding* personnel and mechanisms. Pruning the structure that contributes to procedural sluggishness or complexity may create lacunae in substantive coverage. Ironically, the net effect of structural changes after September 11 was not to make the system simpler but to increase the number of units and layers within it.

Devil's Advocacy

Multiple advocacy ensures that all views within the analytic system will be granted serious attention. Some that should receive attention, however, may not be held by anyone within the system. Virtually no analysts in Israel or the United States believed the Arabs would be "foolish" enough to attack in 1973. Virtually no one with any standing in 2002 believed that Saddam Hussein might not have weapons of mass destruction. Therefore, many observers have recommended institutionalizing dissent by assigning to someone the job of articulating apparently ridiculous interpretations to ensure that they are forced into consideration.

Establishing an official devil's advocate would probably do no harm, although some argue that it may perversely facilitate consensus building by domesticating true dissenters or providing the illusory comfort that all views have been carefully examined.[60] Worse, it might delude decision makers into believing that uncertainties have been resolved. But in any case, the role is likely to atrophy into a superfluous or artificial ritual. The devil's advocate is likely to be dismissed by decision makers as a sophist who makes an argument only because he is supposed to, not because of its real merits. Institutionalizing devil's advocacy is likely to be perceived in practice as institutionalizing the cry wolf problem; "there are limits to the utility of a 'devil's advocate' who is not a true devil."[61] She becomes someone to be indulged and disregarded. Given its rather sterile definition, the role is not likely to be filled by a prestigious official who will prefer more "genuine" responsibility. It will therefore be easier for policymakers to dismiss the arguments. To avert intelligence failures, an analyst is needed who tells decision makers what they don't want to hear, dampening the penchant for wishful thinking. But since it is the job of devil's advocates to do this habitually, and since they are most often wrong (as is inevitable, since otherwise the conventional wisdom would eventually change), they dig their own graves. If the role is routinized, and thus ritualized, it loses impact; if it is not, there can be no assurance that it will be operating when it is needed.

Despite the last point, which is more important in attack warning than in operational evaluation or defense planning, there is a compromise that offers more realistic benefits: the ad hoc utilization of real devils. This selective or biased form of multiple advocacy may be achieved by periodically giving a platform within the intelligence process to minority views that can be argued more persuasively by prestigious analysts outside the bureaucracy. This is what the President's Foreign Intelligence Advisory Board and DCI George H. W. Bush did in 1976 by commissioning the "Team B" critique of NIEs on Soviet strategic objectives and capabilities. (See the lengthier discussion of this case in chapter 4.) Dissenters within the intelligence community who were skeptical of Soviet intentions were reinforced by a panel of sympathetic scholars, with a mandate to produce an analysis of their own. This controversial exercise, even if it erred in many of its own ways, as dovish critics contend, had a major impact in promoting the reexamination of premises and methodology in U.S. strategic estimates. The problem with this option is that it depends on the political biases of the authorities who commission it. If it had been balanced by a comparable Team C of analysts at the opposite extreme (who would have been more optimistic about Soviet intentions than the intelligence community consensus), the exercise would have been like regular multiple advocacy, with the attendant limitations of that solution.

Another variant would be the intermittent designation of devil's advocates in periods of crisis, when the possibility of disaster is greater than usual. Since the role would then be fresh each time, rather than ritualized, the advocate might receive a more serious hearing. The problem here is that the receptivity of decision makers to information that contradicts preconceptions varies inversely with their personal commitments and that the commitments grow as a crisis progresses.[62]

Sanctions and Incentives

Some critics attribute intelligence failures to dishonest reporting or the intellectual mediocrity of analysts. Suggested remedies include threats of punishment for the former and inducements to attract talent to replace the latter. Others emphasize that, will or ability aside, analytic integrity is often submerged by the policymakers' demands for intelligence that suits them; "the NIEs ought to be responsive to the evidence, not the policymaker."[63] Holders of this point of view would institutionalize the analysts' autonomy. Unobjectionable in principle (though if analysts are totally unresponsive to the consumer, they will be ignored), these implications cannot easily be operationalized without creating as many problems as they solve.

Self-serving operational evaluations from military sources, such as optimistic reports on progress in the field in Vietnam or pessimistic strategic estimates, might indeed be obviated if analysts in DIA, the service intelligence agencies, and command staffs were credibly threatened with firing, nonpromotion, reprimand, or disgrace. Such threats theoretically could be a countervailing pressure to the career incentives which analysts have to promote the interests of their services. But, except in the most egregious cases, applying such standards without arbitrariness and bias is difficult given the problem of ambiguity, which simply encourages an alternative bias or greater ambivalence. Moreover, military professionals would be placed in an untenable position, pulled in opposite directions by two sets of authorities. To apply the sanctions, civil authorities would have to violate the most hallowed military canon by having civilian intelligence officials interfere in the chain of command. And then they would also be charged with politicization, since their judgment of the analyst would reflect their own beliefs about the subject. In view of these dilemmas it is easier to rely on the limited effectiveness of redundancy or multiple advocacy to counteract biased assessments.

Critics concerned with attracting better talent into the analytic bureaucracy have long proposed raising salaries and providing more high-ranking positions to which analysts can aspire. This has been done to some degree over the years (in the creation of senior intelligence service positions), and folklore that attributed a difference in quality between CIA and DIA analysts to a difference in grade structure that disadvantaged the latter has not always been borne out by data.[64] Moreover, American government salaries have been reasonably high by average standards in academia or journalism, the main competing professions for analysts. That those who want the highest-paying positions normally have to move from research to administration also is as true in the world of scholarship as in government.

Raising pay and status always helps recruit more and better personnel in any line of work. Doing so is no more nor less advisable for intelligence agencies than for any other public or private institutions. One valid criticism, though, is that military personnel systems and promotion standards traditionally do not reward intelligence officers, thus discouraging the best from seeking intelligence assignments.[65] This situation was improved, but only partially, halfway through the Cold War, but intelligence is still not a good career choice for anyone seeking high rank.

Nonmilitary analysts, or high-ranking soldiers with no promotions to look forward to, have fewer professional cross-pressures to contend with than military intelligence officers have. But analysts' autonomy varies inversely with their influence, and hortatory injunctions to be steadfast and intellectually honest cannot ensure that they will be. Richard Helms once noted that "there is no way to insulate the DCI from unpopularity at the hands of presidents or policymakers if he is making assessments which run counter to administrative policy. That is the built-in hazard of the job. Sensible presidents understand this. On the other hand they are human too."[66]

Integrity untinged by political sensitivity courts professional suicide. If the analyst insists on perpetually bearing bad news, he is likely to be beheaded. Helms himself succumbed to pressures from policymakers in compromising estimates of the MIRV capabilities of the Soviet SS-9 missile in 1969 and the prospects for Cambodia in 1970.[67] The same practical psychological constraints are reflected in the incident in which Chief of Naval Operations Elmo Zumwalt, who had already infuriated Nixon and Kissinger several times with his hawkish assessments of the U.S.-Soviet balance of power, was determined to present yet another unwelcome analysis. Secretary of Defense James Schlesinger dissuaded him, saying, "To give a briefing like that in the White House these days would be just like shooting yourself in the foot."[68]

Cognitive Rehabilitation and Methodological Consciousness

The intertwining of analysis and decision and the record of intelligence failures due to mistaken preconceptions and unexamined assumptions suggest the need to reform the attitudes, awareness, and modes of perception of intelligence consumers. If leaders were made more self-conscious and self-critical about their own psychologies, they might be less vulnerable to cognitive pathologies. This approach to preventing intelligence failure is the most basic and metaphysical. If policymakers focus on the methodologies of competing intelligence producers, they would be more sensitive to the biases and leaps of faith in the analyses passed to them. "In official fact-finding . . . the problem is not merely to open up a wide range of policy alternatives but to create incentives for persistent criticism of evidentiary value."[69] Improvement would flow from mechanisms that force decision makers to make explicit rather than unconscious choices, to exercise judgment rather than engage in automatic perception, and to enhance their awareness of their own preconceptions.[70]

 Unlike organizational structure, however, cognition cannot be altered by legislation. Intelligence consumers are political animals who have risen by being more decisive than reflective, more aggressive than introspective, and confident as much as cautious. Few busy activists who have achieved success by thinking the way they do will change their way of thinking because some theorist tells them to do so. Even if they could be forced to confront scholarly evidence of the dynamics of misperception, it is uncertain that they could consistently internalize it. Preconception cannot be abolished; it is in one sense just another word for model or paradigm—a construct used to simplify reality, which any thinker needs in order to cope with complexity. There is a grain of truth in the otherwise pernicious maxim that an open mind is an empty mind. Moreover, the line between perception and judgment is very thin, and consumers cannot carefully scrutinize, compare, and evaluate the methodologies of competing analyses for the same prosaic reason (the problem of expertise aside) that impedes many proposed reforms: they do not have the time. Solutions that require principals to invest more attention than they already do are conceptually valid but practically weak. Ideally, perhaps, each principal should have a special assistant for rigor enforcement.

Although failures occur more often at the consuming than the producing end of intelligence, it is impractical to place the burden for correcting those faults on the consumers. The most realistic strategy for improvement would have intelligence professionals anticipate the cognitive barriers that limit decision makers' use of their products. Ideally, the director of national intelligence and the director of CIA should have theoretical temperaments and personal skills in forcing unusual analyses to the attention of principals; they might act as George's "custodian" of the argumentation process.[71] To fulfill this function they should be not only intellectually sharp analysts but also skilled as bureaucratic politicians. These qualifications seldom coincide. Indeed, of the nineteen individuals who have held the position of DCI or DNI as of 2007, only three—James Schlesinger, John Deutch, and Robert Gates—met those combined criteria. Their combined service totaled only about three years out of the nearly six decades since the National Security Act, and despite their skills all three proved highly controversial.

The DNI's coordinating staff and National Intelligence Council should be adept at detecting, making explicit, and exposing to consumers the idiosyncrasies in the assessments of various agencies—the reasons that the focus and conclusions of the State Department's Bureau of Intelligence and Research tend to differ from those of DIA, or of naval intelligence, or of CIA. For such a procedure to work, the consumers would have to favor it, as opposed to negotiated consensual estimates that would save them more time. There is always tension between what facilitates timely decision and what promotes thoroughness and accuracy in assessment. The fact that there is no guaranteed prophylactic against intelligence failures, however, does not negate the value of incremental improvements. The key is to see the problem of reform as one of modest refinements rather than as a systematic breakthrough.

Living With Fatalism

Organizational solutions to intelligence failure are hampered by three basic problems. Most procedural reforms that address specific pathologies introduce or accent other pathologies; changes in analytic processes can never fully transcend the constraints of ambiguity and ambivalence; and more rationalized information systems cannot fully compensate for the predispositions, perceptual idiosyncrasies, and time constraints of political consumers. Solutions that address the psychology and analytic style of decision makers are limited by the difficulty of changing human thought processes and day-to-day habits of judgment by exhortation. Most theorists have thus resigned themselves to the hope of marginal progress, "to improve the 'batting average'—say from .275 to .301—rather than to do away altogether with surprise."[72]

There is some convergence of the implications for all three ways of conceptualizing intelligence failures. Mistakes should be expected because the paradoxes are not resolvable; minor improvements are possible by reorganizing to correct pathologies; and despair is unwarranted because, seen in perspective, the record could be much worse. Marginal improvements have, in fact, been instituted episodically since World War II. Although many have indeed raised new problems, most have yielded a net increase in the rationalization of the system. Chapter 6 examines recent moves for reform at length. Here let us briefly scan how much was done previously.

The diversification of sources for assessments of adversaries' military power grew consistently after the establishment of the intelligence community, obviating the necessity to rely exclusively on military staffs, although this trend unfortunately was reversed at the end of the Cold War, as the Pentagon reclaimed most of the responsibility. The resources and influence of civilian analysts of military data, principally in CIA's Office of Strategic Research and Directorate of Science and Technology from the 1950s through the '70s, were unparalleled in any other nation's intelligence system. The DCI's mechanism for coordinating the activities of all agencies (the intelligence community staff, subsequently the community management staff) grew and became more diverse and representative, less an extension of CIA, as more staffers were added from the outside. In 1972, a separate product review division was established within the staff to appraise the "objectivity, balance, and responsiveness" of intelligence studies on a regular basis. It conducted postmortems of intelligence failures on the Yom Kippur war, the Cyprus crisis of 1974, the 1976 Indian nuclear test, the seizure of the *Mayaguez,* and other cases.[73] Previously, postmortems were conducted by the analysts who had failed. Such a procedure hardly guaranteed objectivity. The product review division lapsed for some time, but its functions were performed episodically by other units.

Within the Pentagon, capabilities for estimates relevant to planning were enhanced with the establishment of the Office of Net Assessment to analyze the significance of foreign capabilities in comparison with U.S. forces. CIA, DIA, and national intelligence estimates normally estimate only foreign forces. (The Office of Net Assessment evolved into a sponsor of studies on various topics rather than a unit focused consistently on net assessment. The importance of net assessment as a function also declined after the Cold War, since the military balance of power between the United States and any other country is not a crucial question under unipolarity.) Civilian direction of military intelligence was reinforced at various times by an assistant secretary of defense for intelligence after the 1970 recommendation of the Fitzhugh commission, a deputy secretary for intelligence briefly in 1976, an undersecretary for policy since 1978, and an undersecretary for intelligence in the administration of Bush the Younger. The dominance of operators over analysts within the intelligence community also waned for some time after the phasing out of paramilitary operations in Southeast Asia and the reductions in size and status of CIA's covert action branch that began in 1973. Clandestine activities bounced back as the Cold War was reborn at the end of the Carter administration, more so under Reagan, and especially after September 11. Dysfunctions in the military communications system, which contributed to crises involving intelligence collection missions in the 1960s (the Israeli attack on the USS *Liberty* and North Korea's seizure of the *Pueblo*) were alleviated, though not cured, by new routing procedures and by instituting an "optimal scanning system" in the Pentagon.[74] They were improved further with the evolution of technology. Statistical analyses of military power became more rigorous and comprehensive. As staffs outside the executive branch—such as the Congressional Budget Office—became involved in the process, they also became more competitive.[75]

Few of the changes in structure and process generated more costs than benefits, but it is difficult to prove that they significantly reduced the incidence of intelligence failure. For attack warning, for instance, sophisticated coordination mechanisms have been introduced over time. After the 1974 Cyprus crisis, DCI "alert memoranda"—"brief notices in a form which cannot be overlooked"—were instituted.[76] No major warning failure occurred for a while. Even when such memoranda were issued, however, they failed to keep policymakers from feeling surprised by the Soviet invasion of Afghanistan or the Iraqi invasion of Kuwait.

Regarding operational evaluation, it is clear that there was greater consciousness of the limitations and cost ineffectiveness of aerial bombardment during the Vietnam War than there had been during the Korean conflict, due largely to the assessments made by the offices of systems analysis and international security affairs in the Pentagon and Secretary of Defense Robert McNamara's use of CIA estimates and contract studies by external analytic organizations.[77] Yet this greater consciousness did not prevail until late in the war because it was not a consensus; air force and naval assessments of bombing effectiveness contradicted those of the critical civilian analysts. Similar controversies persisted even into the era of precision targeting with disagreements over bomb damage assessment in Iraq and Kosovo.

In defense planning, elaborating and diversifying analytic resources for strategic estimates also did not clearly reduce the potential for erroneous decisions. Determining the salience and proper weight of conflicting indicators of military power and objectives or of the comparative significance of quantitative and qualitative factors in politically charged assessments of the U.S.-Soviet military balance was inextricable from the fundamental debate over foreign policy. Uncertainties always remained, leaving the individual's visceral fears or hopes to tilt the balance of judgment in arguments over détente and arms control.

Although marginal reforms may reduce the probability of error, the unresolvable paradoxes and barriers to analytic and decisional accuracy make some incidence of failure inevitable. Concern with intelligence failure then coincides with concern about how policy can hedge against the consequences of analytic inadequacy. Covering every hypothetical vulnerability would lead to bankruptcy, and hedging against one threat may aggravate a different one. The problem is thus one of priorities, and hedging against uncertainty is hardly easier than resolving it. Any measures that clarify cost-benefit trade-offs in policy hedges will mitigate the danger of intelligence failure.

In principle, one reasonable rule would be to survey the hypothetical outcomes excluded by strategic premises as improbable but not impossible, to identify those that would be disastrous if they were to occur, and then to pay the price to hedge against them. This is no more practicable, however, than the pure form of worst-case analysis because it requires willingness to bear and inflict severe costs for dubious reasons and risks counterproductive results. Escalation in Vietnam, after all, was a hedge against allowing China to be tempted to devour the rest of Southeast Asia, and attacking Iraq in 2003 was meant to eliminate a source of terrorism, although it turned out to spawn one instead. Analytic uncertainty and decisional prudence compose a vicious circle that makes the absolute segregation of descriptive intelligence and prescriptive policy an unattainable, Platonic ideal.

In the simplest situation, the intelligence system can avert policy failure by presenting relevant and undisputed facts to nonexpert principals who might otherwise make decisions in ignorance. But these simple situations are not those in which major intelligence failures occur. Failures occur when ambiguity aggravates ambivalence. In these more important situations—Acheson and Clausewitz to the contrary—the intelligence officer may perform most usefully by not offering the answer sought by authorities but by forcing questions on them, acting as a Socratic agnostic, nagging decision makers into awareness of the full range of uncertainty and making the authorities' calculations harder instead of easier, as those authorities wish. Sensitive leaders will reluctantly accept and appreciate this function. Most will not. They will resent such attempts as an unhelpful waste of their time, they will make some mistakes that more careful consideration of analysis might have avoided, and they will continue to share responsibility for so-called intelligence failures.

Two general values, which sound wistful in the context of the preceding fatalism, remain to guide the choice of reforms: whatever facilitates effective dissent and access to authorities by intelligence producers and whatever facilitates skepticism and scrutiny by consumers. These are synergistic. One will not improve the use of intelligence without the other. A third value, but one nearly impossible to achieve, would be anything that increases the time available to principals for reading and reflection.

Intelligence failures are not only inevitable, they are natural. Some are even benign, if a success would not have changed policy. Scholars cannot legitimately view intelligence mistakes as egregious because they are no more common or less excusable than academic errors. They are not as forgivable only because they are more consequential. Error in scholarship is resolved dialectically, as deceptive data is exposed and regnant theories are challenged, refined, and replaced by new research. If decision makers had but world enough and time, they would rely on this process to solve their intelligence problems. But the press of events precludes the luxury of letting theories sort themselves out over a period of years, as in academia. My survey of the intractability of the inadequacy of intelligence, and its inseparability from mistakes in decision, suggests one final conclusion that is perhaps most outrageously fatalistic of all: a tolerance for occasional disaster in foreign policy. Not an indifferent, lazy, or resigned tolerance, to be sure, but a readiness to absorb once in a while the tragic consequences of assault by the powerful coalition of outside, innocent, and inherent enemies of intelligence.

3 / THEORY TRAPS:

Expertise as an Enemy

Intelligence can't live with theory and can't live without it. This is the fundamental problem in using analysis to anticipate threats, to prompt a response from policymakers, and to avoid surprise. Theories are necessary for judging the meaning of data, but they are also the source of mistaken judgments of evidence. The obvious source of this problem is the imperfection of all theories about social phenomena. A less obvious source is that theories that are ideal for some analytical functions turn out to be dangerous for others. In fact, theories that are normally best because they have a good track record can maximize vulnerability to surprise in a particular crisis. Paradoxically, sometimes the more one knows about a subject, the worse one's judgment of it. Knowledge can become an innocent enemy of intelligence.

NORMAL THEORY VS. EXCEPTIONAL THINKING

Experts usually are better predictors than those who know less about a question, but in unusual situations the nonexpert may do better. Intelligence and policy certainly cannot live without experts. But when and how can we know when their odds of error go up and when comparatively uninformed hypotheses should get more respect?

Theories and Threats

Disentangling types of theories is complicated because policymaking elites and intelligence bureaucracies are not naturally inclined to deal with theories in a conscious, rigorous, or sustained manner. Within the intelligence community, particularly CIA, there have been substantial moves in recent years to sensitize analysts to theoretical and methodological issues, as training programs have become longer and more careful and internal organizations like the CIA University and the Sherman Kent School for Intelligence Analysis have developed programs to grapple with clarifying assumptions and conceptual problems in the production of finished intelligence. In the world of intelligence consumers, however, officials do not realize most of the time that a theoretical presumption is at issue because they are busy deliberating about what they think are only matters of fact. Indeed, hardly anyone in government likes to dwell on theory because it seems soporific and sophomoric, a naive or misleading distraction from serious business. Many operators are actively hostile to what they think is theory.

Consumers, nevertheless, are every bit as theoretical as anyone else even if they don't realize it, since they make assumptions all the time about how patterns of experience demonstrate general propositions about the way the world works. Theory makes sense of numerous pieces of information by explaining or predicting relationships among things and by clarifying which causes of various effects are essential and which are peripheral.[1] Academics are comfortable with theory and deal with it explicitly because they relish abstraction and especially because they are not burdened with the responsibility to produce outcomes in public policy. Except for ideologues, who do sometimes come to power, political decision makers and bureaucrats are uncomfortable with explicit theory because the hard knocks of experience have made them distrust abstraction and because they are responsible for getting concrete results. When they use theories they do so implicitly and unsystematically, in a manner that assumes theories to be simple common sense. Much as they would like to, officials cannot avoid generalizations, and generalizations are theoretical. Officials' theories are usually the generalizations they have derived from personal experience and from institutional folklore and doctrine.

Threat assessment poses two tasks: collecting facts and interpreting their implications. Interpretation cannot avoid theory—whether it concerns axioms about an adversary's objectives, capabilities, or constraints. If facts could speak for themselves there would be no intelligence problem because there would be no need for further search or judgment. The problem for the policy process is how to know when the theories are weaker than the facts and which contradictory risks are greatest. (When there are no risks or when they all point in the same direction, there is no decision problem.) The dilemma is that, while too little introspection risks premature decision about what to do, too much second-guessing paralyzes deliberation.

Two types of threat assessment pose two different analytical problems. One aims to project the adversary's objectives, capabilities, and typical propensity for risk—to estimate the likely incidence of conflict and crisis over time. This sort of estimate provides guidance for choices in defense spending, alliance diplomacy, and degrees of regular peacetime military readiness. The second type aims at guessing what the enemy will do about a specific issue in the short term or in a crisis, when one occurs. This sort should guide immediate action, such as alerts, mobilization, and crisis diplomacy.

Two Tracks for Warning

The first task—projecting developments over time—must emphasize probabilistic thinking and making the best possible estimates about behavior in numerous incidents of international competition. It puts a premium on those powerful theories that account for typical enemy action—those that explain behavior in the largest percentage of cases. This might be called normal theory. For example, an analyst in 1960 might have been asked, "What are the odds that the Soviet Union will risk war to achieve gains in the next ten years?" Judging by the record, she should properly have responded that Moscow was likely to limit risks to those below the danger of war. The theory behind this estimate, based on typical cases, was indeed accurate in the sense that it accounted for most instances of behavior.

If asked more particularly in 1962 whether Khrushchev would put missiles in Cuba, however, analysts using this intellectual approach would (and did) produce the wrong answer. The Soviet Union had seldom acted recklessly or taken high risks of direct confrontation in previous Cold War maneuvering, and it seemed obvious to American analysts that provoking the United States in such a manner would bring the two countries to the brink. The special national intelligence estimate, issued less than a month before the missiles were discovered, rested on "indicators derivable from precedents in Soviet foreign policy."[2] The estimate noted that Moscow "could derive considerable military advantage" from putting medium- or intermediate-range missiles or a submarine base in Cuba. "Either development, however, would be incompatible with Soviet practice to date," it reported, and such action "would indicate a far greater willingness to increase the level of risk in US-Soviet relations than the USSR has displayed thus far."[3]

Critics and postmortems have emphasized the need to avoid making a single prediction of behavior. For example, a prominent assessment done by the DCI's senior review panel argued in 1983 for presenting judgments in terms of probabilities rather than categorical guesses.[4] It did not get much farther, however, since the surprises most often of concern were over events that had been low in probability. An assessment that flags the possibility of a dangerous event but still rates it as very unlikely is not likely to prompt a response. To get policy operators to act, an assessment has to show plausibly why an event that was improbable in terms of normal theory has become more probable.

Since crises are rare, and war even more so, they represent aberrant behavior—that is, if the adversary handles international disputes diplomatically 99 percent of the time and forcibly only 1 percent, the forcible cases are deviations from an otherwise powerful theory. Thus, in contrast to long-range projections, which must rely heavily on explanations of past behavior, specific crisis-oriented predictions must be more concerned with exceptions to a powerful theory, with potentially deviant cases more than with typical ones, and with worst-case possibilities as well as best estimates of probability. Severe consequences of low probability threats take precedence over the higher probability of less intense threats. Whereas normal theory derives its power from categorical simplifications and parsimony, crisis predictions must dwell more on complexity, contingent propositions, and the residual risks within a usually accurate normal theory. In social science terms the second approach is almost atheoretical; I will call it exceptional thinking.[5] The theory for this approach is waiting to be found since there is not yet an established, compelling formulation of how to go about predicting discontinuity. Exceptional thinking will include whatever ideas make the case for acting on the basis of improbable contingencies. For good reasons, this is always an uphill battle.

ANTICIPATING IRRATIONALITY

A crucial component in any type of exceptional thinking must be a scheme for predicting apparently nonrational behavior. The concept of rationality is a minefield in political science, but it need not be settled here if we focus on the qualifier *apparently*. Apparently nonrational behavior is that which the observer sees as counterproductive to the interests and objectives of the observed government or group. One of the principal reasons that policymakers often dismiss indications that an adversary may strike is that it seems obviously suicidal. Indeed, some of the most successful strategic surprises have been followed by the defeat of perpetrators by the victims or by allies who came to their aid. Germany lost after stunning initial successes against the Soviet Union; Japan was conquered after Pearl Harbor; the Soviet Union withdrew its missiles from Cuba; Egypt and Syria were roundly defeated on the battlefield in 1973; Iraq was expelled from Kuwait.

Predicting Suicide

It is hard to believe that countries would deliberately cut their own throats and that any would not know when attacking would amount to doing just that. To some intelligence professionals it appears impossible to avoid this sort of mistake. As the head of the office that produced the mistaken estimate about Soviet missiles in Cuba put it:

It is when the other man zigs violently out of the track of "normal" behavior that you are likely to lose him. If you lack hard evidence of the prospective erratic tack and the zig is so far out of line as to seem suicidal, you will probably misestimate him every time. No estimating process can be expected to divine exactly when the enemy is about to make a dramatically wrong decision. We were not brought up to underestimate our enemies. We missed the Soviet decision to put missiles into Cuba because we could not believe that Khrushchev would make such a mistake.[6]

This phenomenon is unusual, but it is more common than leaders expect. Something similar to the 1962 mistake happened seventeen years later. U.S. intelligence estimators evaluating Soviet mobilization around Afghanistan at the end of 1979 believed that Moscow might either intervene with a few battalions or with a multidivision force much larger than what was being prepared, but they ruled out the option between these extremes since it would get them in trouble without providing enough to win. Yet, that excluded, intermediate option was the one executed in the Soviet invasion at the end of December. As Douglas MacEachin said, "One of the dark humor jokes circulating around CIA in the months after the invasion was that the analysts got it right, and it was the Soviets who got it wrong."[7]

Pessimism rests on the assumption that estimates will naturally follow normal theory. A process that injects some form of exceptional thinking—for example, applying contrary hypotheses and reasoning backward from the improbable outcome to make the case for how it could happen—might mitigate the risks in relying on probabilities based on long experience. This can never replace the application of normal theory but should supplement it.

In recent years, managers of analytic production have developed training programs to prompt more careful use of assumptions and logic and have fostered numerous mechanisms to overcome normal theory. One impressive manual surveys a range of diagnostic techniques, such as "Key Assumptions Check, Quality of Information Check, Indicators of Signposts of Change, Deception Detection, Analysis of Competing Hypotheses"; contrarian techniques, such as "Devil's Advocacy, Team A/Team B, High-Impact/Low-Probability Analysis, 'What If' Analysis"; and imaginative thinking techniques, such as "Brainstorming, Outside-In Thinking, Red Team Analysis, Alternative Futures Analysis."[8] These efforts are positive but difficult to institutionalize.

These two approaches—normal theory and exceptional thinking—require different analytical instincts, attitudes, and styles. Yet it is usually the same individuals who have to deal with both by virtue of their responsibility for certain subjects over time. An intelligence official or policymaker cannot easily shift mental gears and consciously apply different standards of evaluation from day to day. This is especially true for the majority of officials who use theory unconsciously rather than explicitly, and even more so for those at the highest level who are too busy and have too broad a scope of responsibility to spend time in epistemological reflection. Evaluation—especially in a collective process—more often approximates simple binary formulations and choices than a comprehensively integrated calculation.[9]

The basic problem is that both analytic specialists and political generalists often apply normal theory (though their theories may differ from each other) in cases where unusual possibilities may turn out to be more relevant. This promotes a bias toward assuming continuity rather than deviance. Normally, the best estimate of behavior at $t + 1$ is behavior at t, or at $t - 1$, $t - 2$, or $t - 3$. Since this is true most of the time, experts find themselves impatient with others who are too easily impressed by apparently threatening facts taken out of the context they know so well. Mark Lowenthal, someone with experience from several vantage points in the intelligence system, observes, "Given a choice between appearing jaded or naive on a given subject, the average intelligence professional will choose to appear jaded. . . . Few situations are treated as being truly new."[10]

The psychological bias toward continuity is not just some emotionally driven irrationality. It results from the physiology of human cognitive processes that are often quite functional. Memory mechanisms reinforce particular channels in the brain. "Once people have started thinking about a problem one way, the same mental pathways or circuits get activated and strengthened each time they think about it. This facilitates the retrieval of information. These same pathways, however, also become the mental ruts that make it difficult to reorganize the information mentally so as to see it from a different perspective."[11]

This is not wishful thinking, but an unconscious human tendency to see what one expects to see, which distorts the analytical handling of evidence. The most common cognitive bias identified in anthropologist Rob Johnston's study of intelligence professionals was *confirmation bias*, "the tendency of individuals to select evidence that supports rather than refutes a given hypothesis." This is reinforced institutionally by the orientation process, the research inventory, and incentives to produce a corporate product. Johnston quotes an analyst who says, "I've looked at our previous products, and I've got a good idea of the pattern; so when I sort through the traffic, I know what I'm trying to find."[12] Experienced analysts do not try to connect dots on a tabula rasa, especially when there is a wealth of data that can be sorted in various ways: "Instead of a picture emerging from putting all the pieces together, analysts typically form a picture first and then select the pieces to fit it."[13] Psychologically, the threshold is higher for discrediting information inconsistent with the dominant hypothesis than for confirming it, and impressions persist even after the evidence on which they were based is discredited. When strategic assumptions about enemy aims and behavior are consistent with tactical indicators of impending action, threats are perceived and precautionary actions are taken. When there are discrepancies between the strategic assumptions and tactical indicators, strategic assumptions prevail.[14]

A bias toward continuity does not necessarily imply unwarranted optimism. Hawks who interpret enemy behavior as more threatening than doves do can derive dire predictions from a normal theory. But erroneous worst-case estimates can be as damaging as optimistic ones,[15] especially if they foster the cry wolf syndrome. False alerts discredit alarm by highlighting probability of occurrence (which runs counter to unusual behavior such as resort to force) at the expense of severity of consequences. The maxim "When in doubt, assume the worst" may be seen as congenial by intelligence officials who worry about failing to anticipate a threat, but it is of little help to policymakers who must worry about the financial and political costs of responding to numerous ambiguous dangers or to commanders who cannot get their troops to take frequent alerts seriously.

Simply substituting exceptional thinking for normal theory is no solution. Normal theory is indispensable because it usually produces the right conclusion. Most of the time, government works on the edges of long-standing problems. The diversity and complexity of foreign-policy issues demand probabilistic thinking—the only alternative is rudderless intellectual confusion and policy incoherence or immobility. Indeed, in many instances the system fails because it does not develop enough expertise to generate good normal theory. The Silberman-Robb WMD Commission concluded that few analysts in the U.S. intelligence community were left working on any account long enough to become truly expert.[16] This problem is far worse than having too many experts.

The problem is how to reduce the chances that good normal theories will go unchallenged in a crisis. The neophyte can have an advantage here. When experienced analysts feel they have enough information to make a judgment, getting more does not usually increase the accuracy of their judgment. But having additional information does tend to increase their confidence in that judgment. Experimental research also shows that analysts who follow a problem from an early stage are handicapped perceptually compared with others who first encounter it at a later stage because all people tend to rely too much on images they form early in the process of dealing with a problem. Analysts who started at the beginning had their images formed when information was sparser and murkier than that available to those who formed theirs in a later phase.[17] It is especially hard to discipline these mental processes according to standards of the scientific method in the many difficult cases where evidence is complex and uncertainty is high; in these cases, people rely even more on their mind-sets.[18]

Ways to get at this problem involve changes in structure, so that nonspecialists can be involved in the search for indicators of danger, and changes in process, to manage the interaction between generalists and specialists within the intelligence community's warning apparatus. (At the political level, crisis decisions will always be made by generalists.) Analytical specialists will (and should) always have the primary estimating role because they have the expertise about the region or function at issue. Because they deal with that subject day in and day out, however, and because they see so well how normal theory explains the problem over time (and because the normal theory is *their* theory), they are less likely to shift gears and contemplate exceptional theories. The normal theory, in fact, is integral to their expertise. A nonspecialist, by virtue of his comparative ignorance of all the powerful reasons to bet on continuity, is more susceptible to exceptional thinking. The expert knows the adversary's character—sometimes too well. The nonexpert may naively view the enemy as a generic chess player or as a mirror image of our own way of thinking—views that normally prompt misunderstanding but are more open to the possibility that a normally predictable enemy will act out of character.

This is not an argument for devil's advocates but for taking a new broom to problems. In some instances a nonspecialist might function as an idiot savant, raising questions about established bases of prediction, introducing naive ideas which, in exceptional circumstances, could prove correct. Think about the notorious misestimate of Iraq's weapons of mass destruction in fall 2002. If someone had been involved in the process who knew nothing about the history of inspections by the UN Special Commission on Iraq (UNSCOM) and all the circumstantial evidence pointing to Saddam Hussein's continuing concealment of chemical and biological stockpiles, she might have challenged the conclusions of the estimate that were based on deduction from accumulated circumstantial evidence rather than direct evidence. As it was, since no one was that ignorant, no one could take seriously the possibility that Iraq did not have the weapons (see chapter 5).

In most cases, exceptional thinking can best be done by a seasoned generalist who applies lessons from other cases and wider experience. To be more than a reticent nonparticipant or a gadfly nipping at the edges of an estimate, however, such a generalist (or a specialist from another area) needs to have an institutionalized status in the process. To a certain extent this had been done in the United States through various mechanisms such as the watch committee, then later by the strategic warning staff and the national intelligence officer for warning, all of which were designed to complement, not substitute for, the warning responsibilities of regional and functional specialists. The challenge is to tread a line between having too many people involved (creating a parallel bureaucracy that could generate so much day-to-day activity that the crisis role could be obscured) and too few.

Linking the Tracks

To see how the differences can be integrated, consider the warning process in the summer of 1990. Most intelligence experts on the Middle East believed that Iraq's military mobilization was only coercive muscle flexing. The national intelligence officer specializing in Near East and South Asia sensed that although some military action was likely if Kuwait did not make concessions, a major attack to conquer all of Kuwait was unlikely. Charles Allen, however, as the generalist national intelligence officer for warning, issued a "warning of war" on July 25 that estimated the chances of attack as over 60 percent, and another on August 1 that raised the odds to 70 percent. "Allen was not on a first-name basis with the Egyptian or Saudi leaders the Bush administration relied on to gauge Iraqi intentions. He just kept thinking about the Iraqi forces that had taken up positions near the Kuwaiti border."[19] He was better positioned to give credence to tactical indicators that contradicted strategic assumptions.

To be influential the exceptional thinker also needs to avoid being placed in the position of devil's advocate (which makes his assessment forced and thus easier to dismiss) and must avoid unstructured argument or rapid-fire, random hypotheses (which suggest aimless flailing). One way to help is to direct the exceptional thinker's challenge of a normal theorist's estimate in two directions. First, she should focus on discrepant circumstances or uncertainties that leave room for doubt about the normal theory's application to a case. Such differences would include particular indicators and hypotheses that could be consistent with a more pessimistic estimate and pieces of data that might bear on the interpretation but that are missing from the pile of what has been collected. Second, she should construct the case for an enemy miscalculation. That is, when normal theory suggests that an enemy attack (or whatever dangerous action) would be irrational or uncharacteristic, the critic would assume the enemy's decision to take such action and reason backward to postulate the differences in the enemy interpretation of the stakes, risks, and alternatives that could yield a calculation that going to war is less unthinkable than the consequences of not doing so.

The consultation process between intelligence managers and political leaders should involve explicit, simultaneous consideration of a high-consequence/low-probability estimate of enemy action with the possible range of low-cost response options that offer a hedge against such action. Decision makers will be less prone to cognitive dissonance, paralysis, or reluctance to consider threatening possibilities if they are offered a solution that does not pose grave difficulties. The danger is that their response might be insufficient, but that is better than no appreciable response at all—which is more likely if the threat is ambiguous and no such exercise has been undertaken.

The Right Average?

The biggest mistake would be to take the argument here too far. Recognizing the occasional limitations of expertise must not be mistaken for a dismissal of its importance. That would oppose the essence of intelligence and provide a disastrous excuse for policymakers to give free rein to their instincts and prejudices whenever those with real knowledge pointed to a different conclusion.

None of the suggestions here offers a pathbreaking solution because the dilemmas are inherent in the intellectual and political problems of intelligence analysis and policy decision. The collection of intelligence is not so hampered, although sometimes it faces hard choices in resource allocation. Predicting dire threats that are not highly probable is a tricky business because acting against them may require expensive or unpleasant hedges, such as military alerts or mobilizations that will prove controversial if they come to be seen as unnecessary, and such predictions will indeed often be wrong. If analysts strive to minimize the incidence of predictive error, however, they will rely on assumptions that have the best track records—that is, on dominant concepts and normal theories—and thus increase the chances that by being right most of the time they will be wrong in rare but critical instances.

Normal theory is the most important way to deal with intelligence on a daily basis—providing that it is good, properly derived normal theory based on the fullest feasible integration of data and experienced observation. Normal theory should be challenged periodically, in the same way that academic theories are challenged in the play of revisionism and debate in journals. But nonexpert gadflies cannot be given equal attention all the time. Outside-the-box thinking will produce lots of wild swings, and it makes no sense over time to give hitters with low averages equal status. Whenever tactical indicators of danger contradict the benign predictions of the normal theory's strategic assumptions, however, it is time to give exceptional thinkers a chance at bat.

For warning officers applying exceptional thinking, the best batting average is not the highest. They risk swinging and missing more often than do those who get lots of singles and walks. Babe Ruth struck out a lot. If a warning officer strikes out all the time, he should be sent back to the minors, but if he hits enough home runs and does so in the clutch, his slugging percentage should earn him forgiveness for his mediocre batting average. A team needs to rely primarily on consistent hitters who get to first base often—solid experts applying the best normal theories—rather than erratic sluggers. The best team will be one that has a stable of both types. Even then their fates will depend heavily on the quality of the pitching they face—on the outside enemies of intelligence.

4 / INCORRUPTIBILITY OR INFLUENCE?

Costs and Benefits of Politicization

Why should taxpayers spend their money on intelligence? Because the public servants who make and implement policy should be informed. Intelligence serves policy. The basic responsibility of intelligence professionals is to find the truth about what goes on in the important byways of the world, and why and how it does, and to communicate that truth to policymakers, letting the chips fall where they may. For policymakers, however, knowing the truth is a means, not an end—a means to getting the right things done. What the right things are depends less on what is than on what should be, less on the truth than on what should be made to become true. As pragmatists, officials know they must bound their aims within the limits of what is possible, but the ultimate aims are matters of values.

The main challenge to intelligence professionals, therefore, is to get enough information and assess its real implications dispassionately, while the main challenge to operators at the highest levels is to recognize when a proper understanding of reality confirms the feasibility of their aims, or compels them to change course. These functions are not easy to keep separate, and the difference in responsibilities between analysts and policymakers fosters different perspectives, attitudes, priorities, and behavior. A few people can straddle these differences and work effectively in both functions. Many however, do not fully grasp the difference in their responsibilities, and they are easily frustrated when their counterparts in the other camp march to a different drum.

The first section of this chapter surveys the differences that make the relationship between analysts and policymakers at different times one of love, hate, or indifference. Later sections explore the concept and practice of politicization. *Politicization* is a fighting word, usually invoked as a charge of simple bad faith. In reality, however, it is a complicated phenomenon, which in a few limited respects offers benefits as well as costs. It can be bad or good, and it can flow down or up. The popular conception of the term focuses only on the bad form and the top-down direction. Politicization is bad when it suppresses or distorts the truth to promote a political agenda; it can be good when it does not misrepresent but packages information in a way that prevents it from being shunted aside as irrelevant. It can be exerted from the top down if officials try to make intelligence conform to policy. It can also flow from the bottom up if professionals imbue analysis with their own political biases.

THE TWO TRIBES

Observers who have worked in both worlds have sometimes likened intelligence professionals and policymakers to two tribes speaking different languages.[1] For issues on which their differences in orientation are complementary, intelligence and policy collaborate smoothly. But it is often on the most important issues, those involving controversial policy choices, that the working relationship between the tribes falters. Policymakers are often dissatisfied with what they get from intelligence analysts, while analysts are frustrated when what they produce is apparently misused or not used at all. Conflicting constraints and incentives shape the work of people in both groups. When tension emerges, the issue of politicization is close behind.

Accuracy or Influence?

The best analysis is useless if those with authority to act on it do not use it. One longstanding problem that members of a large intelligence establishment face is that much of what they produce is ignored by policymakers. In World War II, the research and analysis branch of the Office of Strategic Services produced work of "exceptionally high quality," but there was "precious little evidence that the reports, analyses, and forecasts churned out in the branch figured decisively in the determination of military or diplomatic policy."[2] Half a century later the situation was scarcely better and was in some ways worse, since the volume of available information had increased. The nonuse of intelligence is a problem even for governments with bureaucracies smaller than those in the United States. In the Middle East War of 1973, for example, the Israeli public was shocked to see the Egyptians using precision-guided antitank munitions to knock out counterattacking Israeli armored units, and many wondered why this tactic had not been anticipated. It *had* been anticipated. Israeli military intelligence produced a report well before October 1973 warning in detail of the threat posed by the Egyptian antitank missiles, but tacticians and the high command did not respond to it. The nonuse of this warning should not seem egregious to those who give any thought to the loads of information we do not digest, or even find time to ingest, in our own lives. As Amos Kovacs reminds us, "Our walls are lined with books we should have read." For policymakers especially, "attention is a scarce resource."[3]

Other warnings fail to register where it matters. In the Carter administration, for example, policymakers ignored warnings that the Somoza regime in Nicaragua might fall. White House staff later claimed that the intelligence community had not alerted them, while intelligence professionals could cite a paper trail to show that they had.[4] In a sense, both were probably right, since the highest officials are awash in what Roberta Wohlstetter called "noise" and are too busy or exhausted to read much. As Joseph Nye, a scholar who became chairman of the National Intelligence Council noted, officials at high levels "spend their days drinking from a fire hose of information. The basic paradox of government is that it rests on a sea of paper, but the higher you go, the more it becomes an oral culture."[5]

At the top, intelligence is conveyed at best in briefings or simply in conversation. In stark contrast to carefully crafted papers, conversation is haphazard and subjective. For example, "In the case of Iraq, daily briefings and other contacts at the highest levels undoubtedly influenced policy in ways that went beyond the coordinated analysis contained in the written product. Close and continuing personal contact, unfettered by the formal caveats that usually accompany written production, probably imparted a greater sense of certainty to analytic conclusions than the facts would bear."[6] Briefings are a step up, but dependence on them saps intellectual acuity. It takes much longer to hear a given presentation than to read it, further reducing the effective use of limited time, and mediocre analysis seems better than it should when dressed up with PowerPoint, a confident voice, and an entertaining manner. Dependence on briefings is inevitable, however, not just because they are ingrained in official culture but because they require less energy from the consumer, in the same way that watching television requires less energy than reading.

Different responsibilities promote different inclinations. Policymakers tend toward optimism, since whatever they do is futile or worse if desirable results are not achieved. Analysts tend toward pessimism, if only because the risk to their reputations is greater for failing to predict a negative development than from issuing a warning that turns out to be fortunately wrong.[7] Policymakers tend to leave options open and hold onto their goals even if they are not achieving them, and they are comfortable juggling what analysts perceive to be incompatible aims. "The policymaker . . . avoids as long as possible the notion that he has to trade off one goal for another."[8]

The roots of controversy over politicization lie deep within the contradictions between the dynamics of the analytical process and the decision process, of professional norms and political utility, and of the qualities required for accuracy in analysis and for influence on policy.[9] The analyst's imperative is intellectual: to produce a paper that conveys the truth. To do this without arguing beyond what the evidence supports means producing a paper that faithfully reflects reality in all its complexity and ambiguity, does not distort the facts by oversimplifying them, and clarifies the range of possible futures left open by circumstances. The policymaker's imperative is political: to make decisions and produce results, to act quickly and with confidence. Complexity and uncertainty impede decision, and digesting careful analysis increases the time and thought involved. A policymaker is more likely to prefer papers that are simple, punchy, and conclusive. Attention will focus on the question "What's the bottom line?" A careful analyst will be more like Hamlet; an effective operator, more like Patton.

Accurate analysis should be balanced, distinguishing facts from their implications and admitting as many reasonable interpretations as the facts allow. Balance in this sense promotes papers or estimates of two types, neither of which is ideal from the policymaker's viewpoint. One is lengthy and ambivalent, tries to include all relevant arguments, and bobs back and forth between majority interpretations and registered dissents. The other type suppresses those qualities by coordinating the draft down to the mushiest least common denominator. The former is too much for busy officials whose in-boxes are piled high; the latter tells them little that they do not already know. They are likely to prefer papers that are short and decisive, that offer "the answer"—and such papers may be more tendentious than balanced.

Careful, balanced, accurate papers usually take a long time to produce—they need extra time at each stage for writing, criticism and coordination, and revision. Such delays do not harm a long-range estimate. Policymakers, however, are more interested in papers that are turned out fast, that offer quick responses to help them put out fires. They care about the long term and wish they had more time to think about it, but a kind of temporal Gresham's law normally operates in decision making: immediate problems drive out distant ones.

There are, of course, exceptions to this characterization of style at high levels. The dominant problem for policymakers in using intelligence, however, remains *time*. However interested they may be in accurate or long-term estimates, they never have enough time to read as much as they would like. Only rarely is this due to laziness (although that phenomenon is not unknown at the top). The higher one rises in the policy hierarchy, the wider the range of issues for which one is responsible, and the greater the proportion of each working day and night spent in meetings, on the phone, traveling, and providing diplomatic hospitality.

Ideally, officials should be bicultural, understanding the inclinations and limitations of each other's tribes. Few in policy leadership positions, however, have much experience in the intelligence world. Nor is biculturalism easily developed at working levels in the intelligence community, where outreach and marketing do not come naturally to personalities who have chosen what is, in government, the life of the mind. As an analyst told Gregory Treverton, "If I'd wanted to sell shoes, I'd have done that. I became an analyst because I wanted to reflect, not hawk my wares in downtown Washington."[10] An understanding of both sides of the divide is more commonly developed among top managers in the intelligence community who, unlike their counterparts among consumers in policy departments, interact frequently in both worlds. If intelligence managers bear primary responsibility for making their products useful or even used, however, their vulnerability to charges of politicization increases.

Who Should Drive the Process?

Because the purpose of intelligence is to serve policy, there is general agreement in principle that the consumers of it should determine requirements and priorities for getting it and that the producers should respond. A consumer-driven process should maximize relevance and minimize wasted or misdirected effort. What is agreed in principle, however, is problematic in practice. Policymakers often complain that the intelligence community does not give them the type of information they need, but they have trouble giving meaningful guidance for collection and analysis. For some purposes, moreover, it is good for the professionals to take the lead.

Desire for better integration of intelligence requirements and policy concerns goes back years. In 1971, for example, after a review by the Schlesinger study group at the Office of Management and Budget found that the intelligence community was getting almost no direction from policymakers, the Nixon administration attempted to institute a guidance mechanism at the highest level, a National Security Council intelligence committee. This committee had one thirty-minute meeting and then did not convene again for more than two and a half years, when it met for barely an hour.[11] The next two presidents upgraded the membership of the group charged with making recommendations on collection (as well as covert action) by vesting responsibility in units with cabinet-level members—the Operations Advisory Group for Ford, and the NSC's Special Coordination Committee for Carter. Previous units with this responsibility had often been at the level of undersecretary. But Ford's and Carter's executive orders continued to recognize the time constraints of top leaders by providing that the cabinet members could send designees to meetings if necessary.[12] Two decades later the Aspin-Brown commission flagged the same old problems:

In practice, the NSC's structures created to perform such functions have foundered. Senior officials . . . usually have little or no background in intelligence and are inundated by the press of other duties. . . . Subordinates are increasingly sent to meetings in place of principals, and meetings become progressively less frequent. As a result, a true "consumer driven" intelligence process has never fully evolved within the NSC, regardless of the administration in office.[13]

When consumers abdicate, intelligence managers try to provide policy-relevant guidance themselves. In the mid-1970s the director of central intelligence established the key intelligence questions (KIQs) to "identify topics of particular interest to national policymakers." Departmental intelligence agencies set comparable mechanisms for determining requirements.[14]

The fate of the KIQs illustrates the frustration of many innovative attempts to set requirements. They were designed to get all intelligence agencies to respond to the needs of policymakers rather than just to the parochial requirements of their departments. DCI William Colby said that he intended a KIQ to do what the acronym (pronounced "kick") sounded like it would do: jolt collectors into responsiveness. But Colby faced a problem typical of DCIs—insufficient authority to enforce his community-coordinating responsibility. He could not compel genuine response from State and Defense Department agencies. Although the National Security Agency made some good efforts, other Defense Department agencies did not give priority to nonmilitary questions posed by the DCI. Colby even had trouble enforcing the guidance on CIA, the agency directly answerable to him. Even without the problem of departmental independence, the KIQs did not work well for clarifying priorities. Almost every topic was embodied in them in some form. James Schlesinger called them "aggregated wish lists."[15]

The obstacles to effective direction by policymakers are hefty but not immutable. By the late 1990s there was actually much progress toward making the process of collection and analysis more responsive to them. This was mainly because intelligence managers decided to give higher priority to current intelligence over long-range assessments and honor demands from the Pentagon to privilege support to military operations over other intelligence missions. Both of these adaptations were reasonable but were taken too far. Events suggested the limitations of an excessively consumer-driven process.

Few would deny that support to military operations—providing timely tactical intelligence on enemy military strength, unit disposi- tions, and communications to facilitate combat by U.S. forces—must take precedence among the responsibilities of the intelligence com- munity, at least in wartime or periods of national danger. Military commanders never have as much high-quality tactical intelligence as they want. It was peculiar, however, for the Clinton administration to *increase* this priority in the 1990s, after the Cold War had thoroughly ended and the only military operations were minor peacekeeping for- ays or humanitarian interventions. The shift was consistent with Clin- ton's general inclination to avoid confronting the professional military whenever possible.

Downgrading long-range research was a natural response to the feel- ing of policymakers that they had much more need for up-to-the-min- ute support in putting out fires. In the early decades of the Cold War, CIA had a separate unit, the Office of Current Intelligence (OCI), de- voted to such reporting. Subsequently, OCI was abolished and current intelligence became the responsibility of practically all units—a respon- sibility that steadily crowded out work on long papers looking beyond immediate problems. Owlish analysts complained about the trend, but there was no effective challenge to the notion that nothing was as im- portant as servicing the daily needs of consumers. This consensus was derailed by the shock that followed the mistaken assessment of Iraq's weapons of mass destruction and the surprise in the wake of insurgent resistance after the 2003 invasion. A torrent of complaints gushed out about the tyranny of current intelligence and the need for more in- depth research and reflection on difficult questions.

A process that subordinated consumers' directions to the preferences of producers would make no sense. Occasionally, however, it is appro- priate for intelligence professionals to grab policymakers by the lapels and insist that they consider festering problems that are not on their plates at the moment but are at risk of blowing up in the future. This means not just doing the research and sending a paper over the tran- som but actively marketing it to avoid the situation in which intelli- gence warned the White House about Somoza but did not do so loudly enough for the warning to register. Savvy marketing, however, blurs the line between pure intelligence and policy advocacy and highlights the complexity of the dreaded phenomenon of politicization.

FACES OF POLITICIZATION

Everyone knows politicization is bad.[16] It is assumed to damage the credibility of intelligence. Some believe that it is not much of a problem, but virtually no one believes it is a *good* thing. For the most part this view is correct—especially when we think only in terms of the popular understanding of the concept. Depending on the definition of the term, however, politicization is to some degree inevitable and in some forms necessary. To deal with the problem it is first necessary to consider the term afresh, without the pejorative presumption.

The strict definition of *politicize* is not ipso facto pejorative. It is "to give a political tone or character" or "to bring within the realm of politics."[17] And policy—which is, after all, where intelligence is used—is squarely in the realm of politics. In foreign policy only simple facts, or explanations of minor matters about which policymakers know or care little, are uncontroversial. *Assessments* of facts on matters of much importance are always controversial. Most of what is seen as illegitimate politicization is only the reflection of what is considered normal controversy in other arenas. It is seen as evil because of the sacred norm that intelligence judgments be more objective, nonpartisan, and scientific than other judgments. The real world of policy makes politicization in one form the worst thing that can happen to intelligence; in another form, however, it is the best. The pejorative presumption obscures this point and makes navigating away from the worst and toward the best forms more difficult.

The prevalent conception behind the pejorative connotation is that politicization fabricates or distorts information to serve policy preferences or vested interests.[18] This view covers a multitude of sins, some blatant and crude, some subtle and artful. Such corruption can be deliberate or unconscious and can happen when operators intent on making a policy work put pressure on intelligence producers to state conclusions that confirm the validity of the policy, or when analysts manipulate information to undermine a policy of which they disapprove. When manipulative politicization is deliberate it is sinful, but it is usually motivated by the best of intentions—to serve what is seen as a good higher than intellectual probity. When it is unconscious it is more innocent but also more insidious because it is harder to pin down and expose.

A more forgiving view is that politicization is not simply a malign choice or intellectually sloppy but a nearly unavoidable condition. For issues of high import and controversy, any relevant analysis will perforce be politically charged because it will point at least implicitly to a conclusion about policy—whether it will work, whether it addresses the right issue, whether it will have negative side effects, and so on. Various disputes—which elements of information are correct, ambiguous, or false; which are important, incidental, or irrelevant; in which context they should be understood and against which varieties of information pointing in a different direction they should be assessed—are in effect, if not intent, disputes about which policy judgment stands or falls. The latter view of the problem is more realistic in its approach to making intelligence serve policy, but it entails much greater risks in keeping boundaries straight. In one sense, intelligence cannot live with politicization but, in another, policy cannot live without it. The more intelligence matters, the more politicized it will appear to some faction in a policy debate. Grappling with the problem is frustrated by the unwillingness of anyone, on any side of the debate, to admit that their own approach might be politicized.

Before proceeding I will stipulate one simple standard to which intelligence analysis must adhere, and let none of what follows confuse the sanctity of that standard. The irrevocable norm must be that policy interests, preferences, or decisions must *never* determine intelligence judgments. As I will argue, there is a difference between corruption of that sort and another form of bringing intelligence within the realm of politics—the presentation and packaging of assessments in ways that effectively *engage policymakers' concerns*. Keeping the difference straight is difficult, and skeptics will think that it should not be attempted lest the attempt slide down a slippery slope to corruption. Nothing in what follows, however, should be read as challenging the principle that intelligence serves policy badly if it panders to it.

Types of Politicization and Intelligence-Policy Interaction

The prevalent concept is that politicization is the top-down dictation of analytical conclusions to support preferred policy. This view dominates discussion of the problem, but examples are seldom seen in stark form. The more forgiving view sees politicization as a subtle contamination of analysis by policy predispositions. This concept is manifested far more frequently, but there is no consensus about what should be done to cope with it. Politicization in either sense exists in the eye of the beholder whose political preferences are inconsistent with the implications of the analysis.

Much confusion and rancor about what constitutes politicization flow from different models of how the intelligence process should relate to policymaking. These might be considered the Kent and Gates models.[19] The Kent model derives from Sherman Kent, the legendary Yale historian who wrote the first major postwar treatise on intelligence and headed the Office of National Estimates in its formative years. Kent warned about the danger of letting intelligence personnel get too close to policymaking circles, lest their objectivity and integrity be compromised.[20] The view that objectivity takes precedence over everything dominated the culture of the Central Intelligence Agency (although not of all other intelligence organizations in the cabinet) for at least its first three decades.

The Gates model—after Robert Gates who, long before he became secretary of defense, was deputy director for intelligence at the Central Intelligence Agency in the Reagan administration and DCI in the administration of Bush the Elder—arose from critiques of ineffective intelligence contributions to policymaking and from the view that utility is the sine qua non. (The earliest critique in this vein, by Willmoore Kendall, argued for an explicitly prescriptive role for intelligence in policymaking.)[21] To be useful, intelligence analysis must engage the concerns of policymakers who need studies that relate to the objectives they are trying to achieve. Thus, analysis must be sensitive to the policy context, and the range of options available, to be of any use in making policy. (As Robert Jervis says, "Intelligence is also easier to keep pure when it is irrelevant.")[22] Jack Davis poses the notion most forthrightly: "Effective analysis requires the analyst to intrude into the policymaking process—to organize the available information and assumptions on contentious issues and to assist in implementing goals."[23]

The Gates model emerged in the 1980s and was ascendant until 2003.[24] Its partisans saw the earlier orthodoxy as a prescription for irrelevance and their own approach as contextualization, or as the realistic management of policymakers' cluttered radar screens. Adherents to the Kent model see the Gates approach as a prescription for politicization in the prevalent, pejorative sense. (Full disclosure: I have always leaned, with ambivalence, toward the Gates model.[25] That ambivalence intensified with the post-2003 controversies discussed below.) Packaging intelligence to be productive makes it harder to draw sharp lines between what is relevant and what supports a particular policy choice. Maintaining the distinction determines whether and how honesty and utility can be preserved at the same time.

The form of politicization that evokes the most direct protests is the top-down variety, whereby policymakers dictate intelligence conclusions. The reverse form—bottom-up coloration of products by the biases of the working analysts who produce intelligence—is frequently charged by the policymakers. Traditionally, liberal policymakers have suspected analysts in the intelligence agencies of the military services and the Defense Intelligence Agency of hawkish predispositions. Conservative policymakers have suspected analysts in CIA and the State Department's Bureau of Intelligence and Research (INR) of dovish inclinations. These images highlight a problem for the Kent model because unacknowledged prejudices allow the autonomy of analysts to foster politicization in the name of objectivity, and enable them "to pass off opinions as facts."[26]

A variation between these two forms is one that operates in both directions, mediating between the contrasting mind-sets of policymakers and analysts. This involves the shaping of intelligence products by analysts' managers in their capacity as editors or institutional brokers and in ways that original drafters sometimes consider inconsistent with evidence and motivated by policy concerns. If done properly, managers' editing should be the benign form of politicization, bringing intelligence "within the realm of politics" without corrupting it. Heavy editorial management, however, is easily seen by working analysts as pandering. Accusations of politicization flow when unconscious bottom-up bias and bias in editorial management collide.

Contrasting Functions and Thin Lines

In principle, no one can be against maximizing either credibility or utility in intelligence analysis. So why must a choice between them ever be made? The main reasons lie in the contrasting responsibilities for analysis and action and the resulting trade-offs between accuracy and impact. There are thin lines between packaging that is sensitive to policy context and political pandering and between editorial management and distortion. And the managerial need to render consensus judgments competes with the intellectual need to highlight disagreements.

Professionals optimize their analysis and let the chips fall where they may, even if they fall into a hole and are never noticed by anyone who could use them. As Uri Bar-Joseph puts it, "The quality of the intelligence product is more important than its marketing."[27] Indifference to the reception that analysis gets, however, is a form of goal displacement as irresponsible as any other parochial bureaucratic tendency to let means become ends. Taxpayers hire intelligence analysts not to produce truth for its own sake but to produce useful truth. If analysts or managers compromise quality in order to improve receptivity, however, they also vitiate the purpose, since informed judgment depends on accurate knowledge. Analysts worry most about truth; operators worry most about utility. But neither truth nor utility matters unless they are joined.

Often the main issue in compromising quality is the danger of haste or oversimplification. Avoiding those problems leads analysts to take longer to produce and makes their papers longer when they do. As Arthur Hulnick's surveys have indicated, "Policymakers value research work . . . on the basis of brevity, timeliness and relevance *in that order*. Intelligence producers tend to reverse those priorities."[28] Analysis that undermines a policy option is most useful if it arrives before a decision to choose that option is made. It may be discomfiting or unwelcome even then, but it has more of a chance of affecting choice. Once policymakers move from decision to implementation, however, their interests become vested. Revisiting a policy choice is not impossible but is likely only in the face of outright failure. "We've fallen into the same pattern of mistakes as the French," George Allen of CIA told dissident analyst Sam Adams during the controversy over estimating the number of Communist forces in Vietnam. "They didn't begin by faking intelligence; they merely assumed success in the absence of clear proof of failure."[29] Negative analysis has a higher hurdle to surmount if it is to figure in the implementation phase.[30]

Analysts' awareness of the complexity of the issues they deal with makes them sensitive to the reasons policies will not work. Analysts who complicate and equivocate do not compete as effectively for the limited attention of consumers as those who simplify and advocate—but the latter politicize their product more egregiously. "Advocacy is always not only more simple, but more fun, than intelligence assessment," writes Harold Ford, a former head of the National Intelligence Council. "The latter has to be all-seeing, responsible, free from any taint of being 'cooked.' The former can pick, choose, and skew its facts and arguments. This is not a fair fight: advocacy will always look more attractive to a harassed policymaker than will the usually more sober facts of life."[31]

Outright pandering clearly crosses the line. But what about a decision simply not to poke a policymaker in the eye, to avoid confrontation, to get a better hearing for a negative view by softening its presentation when a no-compromise argument would be certain to provoke anger and rejection? Paul Pillar, a veteran of bruising battles with policy officials, counts the sugarcoating of unwelcome news among the bad types of politicization.[32] But therein lies the fine line between corruption and counterproductive honesty. On some crucial questions, like Iraq perhaps, intelligence professionals should fall on their swords. But intelligence managers who operate at high levels get to know that there are times and issues when it serves no purpose to do that, and when it is more sensible to live to fight another day—even if it means caving in on a hopeless issue. "We live out our lives with families, friends, bosses, allies, and opponents (who may become allies)," Loch Johnson observes. "How we deal with them at time t_a will influence how they deal with us at t_b, as every legislator who practices logrolling and compromise understands."[33] On the other hand, Kent warns, "When intelligence producers realize that there is no sense in forwarding to a consumer knowledge which does not correspond to preconceptions, then intelligence is through. At this point there is no intelligence and the consumer is out on his own with no more to guide him than the indications of the tea leaf and the crystal ball."[34]

Consider a couple of examples of this dilemma.

Almost two weeks before the U.S. invasion of Cambodia in 1970, the Office of National Estimates drafted a memorandum, "Stocktaking in Indochina: Longer Term Prospects," which noted that denial of North Vietnamese base areas in Cambodia would hurt the Communist military effort but not cripple it. DCI Richard Helms did not forward the memo to the White House immediately. He had been told about the impending attack on the condition that he not inform his analysts, and he considered it unwise to forward an assessment that had been drafted in ignorance of the plan.[35] His caution was reasonable given the political realities of the situation. The draft did not contain blockbuster conclusions that forcefully invalidated the president's reasons for deciding to invade, and the decision was so far advanced that last-minute reconsiderations were nearly inconceivable. The memo would probably only have provoked the president's wrath, especially since Nixon already had a strong distrust of CIA, which he saw as "staffed by Ivy League liberals who behind the facade of analytical objectivity were usually pushing their own preferences."[36] Indeed, it would have been counterproductive, poisoning the reception for the next and possibly more important contrarian estimate that might be sent up. Nevertheless, withholding in this case effectively rejected the principle that analysis should never bow to the prejudices of consumers.

In 1991, military intelligence analysts in Central Command (CENTCOM) clashed with CIA analysts in the battle damage assessment (BDA) process during the initial six-week phase of air strikes in the first war against Iraq. CENTCOM estimated much greater Iraqi tank losses from coalition air attacks than did CIA. The difference mattered because the U.S. plan was to wait to launch the ground war until half of Iraqi armor had been destroyed from the air. CIA and army observers believed that high claims were due to overreliance on pilot reports, double- or triple-counting the number of tanks struck, and the general disposition of air forces to overestimate their own performance. CENTCOM believed that analysts in Washington relied too much on satellite photos that could not reveal all the destruction. As General Schwarzkopf later quipped, "If we'd waited to convince the CIA, we'd still be in Saudi Arabia." More to the point, Schwarzkopf believed that intelligence agencies outside the theater were positioning themselves to put the blame on him in case the U.S. ground attack failed by establishing a record of warning that the BDA did not support the decision. Arbiters at the highest level sided with CENTCOM in order to avoid undercutting the military leadership with a vote of no confidence, and Chairman of the Joint Chiefs of Staff Colin Powell worked to get CIA out of the BDA process. After the war, however, army observers claimed that most Iraqi tanks destroyed were hit by ground forces during the last four-day phase of the war rather than from the air. The House Armed Services Committee concluded that the final evidence showed CIA to have been correct and that Schwarzkopf's claims of the number of Iraqi tanks destroyed may have been overstated by 134 percent.[37] Both sides of the BDA argument suspected each other of politically motivated manipulation of data, but each was relying on different methods of estimation that each considered an honest basis for judgment.

Avoiding the opposing pitfalls of corruption and irrelevance takes the analytical process to the thin line between managerial responsibility and political manipulation. Intelligence products are supposed to represent the best judgments of whole organizations, not single authors. Thus, as managers point out, "There is an inherent tension between the intellectual autonomy of the analyst and the institutional responsibility for the product"[38] and "If you are a manager, you are responsible for the product. You have to satisfy yourself that you can stand behind those judgments."[39] As Robert Gates himself put it in a message to analysts after his bruising confirmation battle and the report of a task force on politicization that he established:

Unwarranted concerns about politicization can arise when analysts themselves fail to understand their role in the process. We do produce a corporate product. If the policymaker wants the opinion of a single individual, he or she can (and frequently does) consult any one of a dozen outside experts on any given issue. Your work, on the other hand, counts because it represents the well-considered view of an entire directorate and, in the case of National Estimates, the entire intelligence community. Analysts . . . must discard the academic mindset that says their work is their own.[40]

These are reasonable responses to the frequent complaints of working analysts that their work is massaged and distorted by higher-ups before it is disseminated. The issue is joined when editorial managers are suspected of tilting the corporate product to their own interpretations.

The next sections discuss cases involving allegations of politicization. Each also involved policy issues of the highest priority. These cases illustrate the importance of whether coordinated estimates should attempt to provide a single consensus conclusion or should instead array evidence systematically behind contending views.

Bald-Faced Politicization:
The Vietnam Order-of-Battle Estimate

The long war in Vietnam provided many instances of dishonesty motivated by the need of those waging the war to convince audiences (and themselves) that they were winning.[41] The most publicized case was the 1967 dispute over the estimate of Communist military strength in South Vietnam. CIA was arguing for higher numbers in the order-of-battle (O/B) estimate, and the Military Assistance Command, Vietnam (MACV), for lower numbers. CIA wanted to count a wider range of irregular forces (including organizations with marginal roles in supporting military operations) and to attribute higher numbers than the military did to those forces. Most public accounts of the dispute come from those who sided with CIA and who saw MACV's behavior as intellectually corrupt.

Even this case is more ambiguous than the common conception of politicization implies. There are some grounds on which to argue that MACV's overall judgments turned out to be better than CIA's. For example, the number of Communist forces used in the Tet offensive was substantially lower than even MACV's strength estimate.[42] Most importantly, the dispute over the proper numbers was not hidden from top policymakers at cabinet level and in the White House. The officially published special national intelligence estimate (SNIE 14.3-67), which settled more or less on the military's lower numbers as the best estimate, also included discussion of the disputed categories of forces and higher estimated figures, although it did not include this material in the introductory summary of conclusions.[43] Although this made the exercise technically honest, it did not neutralize the impact of the lower figures. Unlike academics, policymakers are not attuned to careful scrutiny of qualifications and footnotes: "Prose caveats buried deep in the SNIE . . . could not compete among senior readers with the impression created by the tabulation of ostensibly hard numbers up front in the Conclusions section."[44]

Whichever methods of estimation were correct in their ultimate implications, there were instances of raw politicization, especially in connection with the conference between CIA and MACV to thrash out the figures before the SNIE. For example, the military applied methodological double standards in counting. All casualties from Communist irregular forces, whether marginal in combat roles or not, were included in the body count, which was then compared with the aggregate strength figures that did not include those forces from the beginning, thus inflating the apparent progress in attrition. In another instance, military representatives in one conference insisted that a CIA estimate was invalid because it was based on a sample of districts—twenty-eight—that was too small, yet they defended an estimate of their own that was based on a single district.[45]

Military personnel involved in the negotiations confessed privately that the O/B figure should be higher but that there had been a command decision to keep the number below three hundred thousand.[46] This was implicitly confirmed in a cable from Gen. Creighton Abrams (then Westmoreland's deputy) to Earle Wheeler, the chairman of the Joint Chiefs of Staff, three weeks before the conference. Abrams suggested dropping two categories of Vietcong irregular organizations to keep the number at the previous level because, he said, "We have been projecting an image of success over the recent months," and the press would draw "an erroneous and gloomy conclusion. . . . All those who have an incorrect view of the war will be reinforced."[47] At the time of the O/B conference, Robert Komer, the highest civilian in MACV, lobbied against coming up with a higher number for similar reasons: "Komer concluded that there must not be any quantifying of the enemy's irregular forces, on the grounds that so doing 'would produce a politically unacceptable total over 400,000.'"[48] George Allen quoted Komer as saying, "You guys [CIA] simply have to back off. Whatever the true O/B figure is, is beside the point."[49]

The honest answer would have acknowledged that the categories of analysis had been changed and that earlier estimates were therefore too low in the new terms of reference. Estimates that were higher than the old ones could therefore be consistent with the position that Communist strength had declined. Political and military leaders naturally feared that such an explanation, even if true, would either be overlooked, misunderstood, or seen as disingenuous, leading the press to ignore the methodological issue and trumpet the upward change in the estimated number, thus creating a false impression that would undermine policy.[50] When MACV gave a press briefing in November, the new O/B figures were lowered further to 242,000, but in line with advice from Ellsworth Bunker no mention was made that the figures were the result of dropping categories of units from the count. The announced estimate, therefore, was not only questionable in terms of overall accuracy. It purveyed incommensurate data in order to manipulate impressions of military progress not supported by accurate comparisons with earlier data.[51] The change in categories counted was admitted later, but after the press had moved on.

There were three linked problems in this imbroglio. First, the subject of the estimate was centered on the issue of the single greatest priority in U.S. foreign policy at the time: the success of strategy in the Vietnam War. The conclusions could not be insulated from political passions. Second, the conclusions as a result had to be made public in a press conference. Sensitivity about misinterpretation or leaps to the wrong conclusions by opinion makers could not be assuaged by the comfort of secrecy. Policy leadership that could have afforded a thoroughly honest analysis if it was to remain classified could not possibly accept one that would be seen by opinion leaders and voters as striking at the heart of the policy.[52] Third, policymakers were no longer using intelligence to make basic choices about strategy. The die had long been cast in Vietnam policy, implementation was well under way, and reevaluation of alternatives would subvert the effort. These points do not excuse the politicization, but they do explain it.

The main problem, however, was that the intelligence dispute could not be depoliticized because it could not be kept secret—a prime example of the view that politicization flows from the opening of intelligence to democratic debate.[53] If the O/B controversy could have remained hidden from public view, the political dynamite latent in the analytical problem

might have been handled by turning the estimate into a carefully refer-
eed *debate*, where contention would make clear which assertions were
known for sure to be true, which were deduced, and which were simply
assumed. All points of view can be held to the fire and the reasons for
differing judgments smoked out, rather than trying to provide a single
answer that had to carry so much political freight. Biases may not be
purged by making the exercise a debate, but they can compete on a level
playing field. This solution is intellectually attractive and is sometimes
necessary in practice, although mostly for midlevel consumers or other
readers in the intelligence community. Harried authorities at the top will
most often consider such exercises academic and unhelpful.

In most instances, policymakers want analysis that gives them the
consensus, or the best single estimate, of the intelligence community.
The way to keep a single best estimate depoliticized, however, is to split
differences and reduce judgments to lowest common denominators—
which transmutes analysis into mush. This renders the product useless
and is a form of distortion in its own right—just one that is politically
neutral. If there is to be a single best estimate and it is not to be soporific and spineless, there will be competition over what is to represent the
institutional view.[54] That maneuvering, and the victory of one group
over another, can politicize the result. That is what happened in the
O/B controversy.

The one adjustment that could and should have been made to minimize manipulation would have been to highlight the disagreement in the
conclusions section of the estimate, which everyone reads, rather than
relegating the discussion to the main text, which high-level consumers
ignore. This would have made the exercise more of a competitive analysis, rather than a single best estimate. But on a matter of such priority, so
fraught with high political stakes, it is an illusion to believe either that
a single best estimate is meaningful when there is no actual consensus
among analysts or that a depoliticized estimate is realistically possible.

Competitive Politicization? Team B and the Soviet Estimate

In 1976, at the behest of the President's Foreign Intelligence Advisory
Board (PFIAB), the director of central intelligence undertook an explicit

exercise in competitive analysis, doing something closer to what should have been done in the 1967 Vietnam O/B dispute. Two separate estimates reflecting different assumptions were to be arrayed together. Like the O/B controversy, this case concerned the issue that was the highest priority in U.S. foreign policy at the time—in this case, the assessment of Soviet strategic capabilities and objectives. In addition to the regular national intelligence estimate (NIE 11-3/8) on Soviet nuclear capabilities, three parallel studies were commissioned to be done by a prestigious panel of outsiders—Team B—under the leadership of Harvard historian Richard Pipes. The membership of Team B was selected from among those known to have views on the subject more hawkish than that which the PFIAB considered the general orientation of the regular NIE. In effect, this turned out be a sort of open and balanced politicization—giving two fundamental attitudes toward the nature and extent of the Soviet threat a chance to make their best case.

The emphasis here is on "in effect." The regular estimators (Team A, as it were) did not initially consider the exercise to be adversarial, nor did they realize to what extent it had been consciously organized to criticize and counter previous NIEs, nor would they admit that they had a particular bias themselves. In the end, the Team B report presented a sharp contrast in tone and content to the NIEs of the previous decade, and the whole exercise involved reciprocal charges of bad judgment and unsupported assertion. Defenders of the regular NIEs charged Team B with setting out to support preconceived conclusions and to use the study to undermine détente.[55] The leader of Team B charged that the problem with earlier NIE 11-3/8s was that "politicized scientists and uncritical devotees of arms control had misconstrued the Soviet strategic threat."[56]

In the initial stage of the exercise, some objected to including the nontechnical subject of Soviet objectives.[57] (The issue of objectives dominated public reports and controversy about the Team B report, although much of the entire project consisted of technical panels on Soviet programs.) Pipes refuted objections by arguing that "it is not possible completely to divorce an assessment of capabilities from the judgment of intention: the significance of a person's purchasing a knife is different if he is a professional chef or the leader of a street gang, although the technical 'capability' which the knife provides is the same in each case."[58]

After the Team B report, the drafters of NIE 11-3/8 revised the final estimate in a manner that made statements about Soviet intentions more consistent with Team B's views. The changes were mainly deletions of statements not based on hard evidence.[59] The Team B report on Soviet objectives, however, focused primarily on criticism of "mirror imaging" and underestimation of offensive aims, rather than adducing evidence to justify its own assumptions about Soviet motives. Team B's interpretation was essentially an essay asserting the difference in the Soviet worldview and a quest for military superiority as the driving force in Soviet programs and diplomacy.[60]

In a public article that was in effect an unclassified version of Team B's report on Soviet objectives, Pipes did cite a number of sources for his interpretation, including articles in the classified Soviet journal, *Soviet Military Thought*.[61] Soon thereafter, Raymond Garthoff published an article drawing on the same Soviet sources—but citing different passages—which refuted the view propounded by Pipes. Garthoff's article was implicitly a defense of the record of estimates attacked by Team B.[62]

The underlying problem, which was never made clear in public debate, was a confusion about which level of analysis was at issue—an implicit blurring together of Soviet *political objectives* and *military strategy*. At the level of what might be called *strategic* intent (how to approach war if it came), Soviet military doctrine was indeed clearly offensive and aimed at securing maximum advantage. Virtually no one challenged this point. Team B and Pipes focused on this but did not distinguish the military strategic orientation clearly from *political* intent (objectives to be achieved), on which there were many more indications of Soviet commitment to avoiding nuclear war at nearly all costs. Team A and Garthoff focused on this point. Pipes compared apples and oranges—American political intent with Soviet strategic intent, and American public rhetoric (emphasizing mutual assured destruction) with Soviet operational doctrine. He criticized American acceptance of assumptions about mutual deterrence, which were articulated at the policy level, but failed to note that in operational planning at the strategic level, the U.S. military engaged energetically in counterforce targeting and developed options for the preemptive launch of offensive forces. He mistook the change in emphasis in PD-59 (President Carter's 1980 directive to emphasize planning for counterforce targeting, prolonged nuclear war, and attacks on command-and-control structures) for a revolutionary shift.[63]

The confrontation of interpretations by teams A and B reflected the essential debate of the 1970s between hawks and moderates over the nature and extent of the Soviet threat. (Doves were not represented in the exercise; that would have required a Team C staffed by Soviet apologists.) The real driving force was the question of Soviet political intent—whether Moscow aimed for peaceful coexistence or military aggression. This was a question of high politics (and for most in the policy world, articles of faith) on which it would have been utterly futile to attempt a single best intelligence estimate. Once the issue for assessment was cast in terms of Soviet capabilities and objectives, and arms control negotiations had energized hawks, moderates, and doves to focus on indices of power and policy that would support their views, there was no way to keep such assessments free of policy predispositions. Complexity of data meant that any selectivity in presentation of evidence, any emphasis, could be seen as manipulation to support policy preferences. Data could not help but be political ammunition, and attitudes toward data analysis naturally paralleled attitudes on the high politics of U.S.-Soviet relations. Indeed, as Jim Klurfield concluded, when Ronald Reagan defeated Jimmy Carter, "Team B, in essence, became Team A."[64]

Unconscious Politicization? The Gates Revolution and Reaction

Allegations of politicization come up periodically. Since the Vietnam War they have been most prominent during Republican administrations, if only because Republicans have controlled the executive branch for seven of the ten administrations since 1968. There were complaints about the Carter administration's manipulation of intelligence on Central America and about NIEs in the Clinton administration that allegedly downplayed the threat from North Korean missiles, but the controversies in those Democratic administrations never reached the same intensity as under Reagan and the two Bushes.

At the end of the Cold War, grumblings inside the intelligence community burst into public view in the confirmation hearings for the nomination of Robert Gates to be director of central intelligence. One major, long-serving analyst charged that as head of the Directorate of Intelligence under DCI William Casey, Gates had politicized intelligence to support the extreme anti-Soviet policies of the administration by

the imposition of intelligence judgments without adequate evidence, often over the protests of the consensus in the Directorate of Intelligence and even in the entire Intelligence Community . . . the suppression of intelligence that didn't support the Casey agenda . . . the use of the Directorate of Operations to slant intelligence of the Directorate of Intelligence . . . the manipulation of personnel or what I call judge-shopping in the courthouse, finding someone to do your bidding . . . to reach your conclusions.[65]

Other junior and senior analysts testified in a similar vein. Views of this sort led some to conclude that "never before in the history of the CIA was the intelligence process so systematically corrupted" as in the Reagan-Casey-Gates era.[66] Allegations against Gates were countered by testimony that denied the charges and interpreted acts in dispute differently. The differences in view depended to some extent on whose ox was being gored ideologically. As Mark Lowenthal notes, some who charge politicization are simply the "'losers' in the bureaucratic battles."[67]

Where analysts saw corruption of the process, Gates and other leaders of the intelligence bureaucracy in the 1980s believed they were using managerial discretion to improve rigor and relevance. Their concern was not just about their responsibility for the corporate imprimatur; it was with the biases of analysts themselves. Politicization can operate unconsciously from the bottom up if analysts let their own policy biases contaminate their writing. Indeed, the fear of some policymakers that professional analysts share a common bias and politicize their conclusions to undermine alternative policies had been the reason behind the Team B exercise. When National Intelligence Officer Graham Fuller defended Gates in the 1991 confirmation hearings, he raised countercharges, in effect, of unconscious politicization simply from the naïveté of the analysts who were attacking Gates, analysts who came primarily from the Office of Soviet Affairs (SOVA) in the Directorate of Intelligence:

Because of the strongly felt Casey position, I am afraid a counterculture seems to have sprung up among SOVA analysts. . . . SOVA seemed to bend over backwards to compensate. . . . In my own personal observation [SOVA] seemed inclined towards, yes, a highly benign view of Soviet intentions and goals. . . . SOVA analysts may perhaps have been expert on the Third World . . . but few of them had gotten their feet dirty, so to speak, in the dust of the Third World, and had not watched Soviet embassies work abroad.[68]

Where does the line lie between editing and distortion, when both original analysis and revision by editors involve decisions about proper scope, emphasis, and selection of relevant data? When evidence is mixed, as it always is on difficult issues, choices about emphasis are political choices—whether made by dovish analysts or hawkish managers. One charge against Gates was that in 1981 he and National Intelligence Officer Jeremy Azrael rewrote the key judgments section (the summary of conclusions at the beginning of a study) "to suggest greater Soviet support for terrorism, and the text was altered by pulling up from the annex reports that overstated Soviet involvement."[69] Who should decide what information should go in the main text or the annex, or which data overstates or understates evidence?

Initial versions of the latter study concluded that there was scant support for the view that Moscow was a major instigator of terrorism. In a subsequent redraft by Lincoln Gordon, a member of the DCI's senior review panel, the scope of the study was broadened to include revolutionary war, which led to more evidence of Soviet support. One of the analysts involved considered this politicization because it allowed the paper to "avoid definitions of terrorism" and to suggest "that the Soviet Union, by providing support for revolutionary violence, supported international terrorism."[70] This exemplifies the problem that the very terms of reference for an analysis can be heavy with political bias. There has never been a consensus on how to define terrorism, primarily because it is a highly pejorative and politically loaded term. Narrow definitions are favored by those who wish to exclude actions by groups whose cause they approve; broad definitions, by those who wish to tar groups whose cause they abhor. Assessments of terrorism yielded another story about policy contamination of intelligence, via blowback

from covert action. According to Washington folklore, Casey was energized to prove that the Soviets supported terrorism because of claims to
that effect in Claire Sterling's book, *The Terror Network*.[71] He discovered
only later that Sterling's information had come from a disinformation
project by the CIA's own Directorate of Operations. In the only account
of this that I have seen in print, Lincoln Gordon said that "a small part"
of the Sterling information had come from such blowback.[72]

Another example of difficulty in disentangling editing from politicization was an estimate on Mexico produced in the mid-1980s. The
national intelligence officer for Latin America, John Horton, believed
that the Reagan administration was exerting pressure to emphasize in-
stability in the country. His superior, Herbert Meyer, maintained that
Horton revised the draft done by a CIA Mexico expert, and Meyer in
turn revised Horton's revisions to reinstate the other analyst's conclusions. Horton charged that the estimate that emerged from Meyer's action "was full of unsubstantiated allegations. What Meyer was doing
was putting in what Casey wanted."[73] When a high manager supports
an analyst against a middle manager, who is winning? Autonomous
analysts or coercive management? Episodes like this demonstrate that
editorial disagreements can amount to dueling politicization.

The Nadir: 2002 and On

The controversies during the modern intelligence community's first
half century were bruising, but none proved as bitter and destructive
as those after September 11, 2001. With the new sense of urgency
about security, concern about where and how to draw the red line
between policy and intelligence declined, as the imperative to collaborate in supporting the war against terror took precedence.[74] Within
a year, however, the movement to initiate war against Iraq brought
back tension in relations, and with a vengeance. Bitter charges of corruption and subversive politicization flew in opposite directions. A
number of intelligence professionals saw the Bush administration at-
tempting to make intelligence judgments conform to the anti-Iraq
agenda, while Republican political leaders came to see the professionals, especially at CIA, as out to undermine the administration. Accusa-

tions of politicization were aired with more shrillness and publicity than ever before.[75]

The charge of the most blatant top-down pressure on intelligence in the administration of Bush the Younger was that John Bolton, then an undersecretary of state, tried to force official assessments to support hard-line policies toward Cuba and Syria. Bolton tried to have the national intelligence officer for Latin America and the main biological weapons expert in the State Department removed from their positions because their analyses did not conform. Democrats in Congress were denied when, in the midst of Bolton's confirmation hearings for appointment as UN ambassador, they sought documents on this and other allegations about Bolton's demands for names of Americans monitored by the National Security Agency.[76]

The war against Iraq provoked numerous accusations of administration deception, manipulation, and damage to the intelligence system. President Bush and Prime Minister Tony Blair denied the so-called Downing Street memo written by Blair's aide, Matthew Rycroft, which in July 2002 noted reports by the chief of British intelligence that Bush had decided to overthrow Saddam Hussein and that "the intelligence and facts were being fixed around the policy."[77] Another charge was that top officials kept the claim that Iraq tried to buy uranium from Niger in the president's State of the Union speech, even though it had been discredited. Next came charges that top officials "outed" the identity of Valerie Plame Wilson as a CIA operations officer under cover to discredit the public refutation of the uranium claim by her husband, Ambassador Joseph Wilson, who had been sent to investigate it.[78]

One frequent complaint of politicization by policymakers was that administration spokesmen often used intelligence selectively in public arguments, "cherry-picking" bits and pieces that supported the case for war against Iraq and not revealing contradictory information or the fact that most intelligence professionals disagreed with the interpretation. This charge is telling in principle but impossible to police in practice. For one thing, selection of some sort is the essence of analysis; the issue is the choice of what should be emphasized, not whether anything should be. One partisan's cherry-picking is another's focusing or connecting dots. Moreover, selective presentation of evidence, or spin control, pervades the political process. Nothing can force a partisan to give equal time to an array of facts or to views favored by the opposition. This political reality poses two big problems.

First, if politicians use intelligence selectively but deny professionals the right to reveal contradictory interpretations, the politicians' arguments benefit deceptively by bearing the imprimatur of intelligence.[79] This can happen when officials at the highest level declassify pieces of information informally, while professionals cannot. For example, Vice President Dick Cheney, Secretary of Defense Rumsfeld, and Condoleeza Rice, then the assistant to the president for national security affairs, publicly discussed the majority view that aluminum tubes imported by Iraq were part of a clandestine nuclear weapons program, but intelligence officials or government scientists who disputed that view of the tubes could not air their disagreements. Democratic Senators Bob Graham and Richard Durbin revolted when the partially declassified NIE on Iraq's WMD that the administration made public in October 2002 omitted the reservations and the nonconforming evidence that had been in the classified full text, but they were told by CIA that the White House had ordered DCI George Tenet not to release anything further.[80]

Second, selective attention to congenial information can become egregious. Critics charged that political leaders of the Bush administration pressured intelligence analysts to affirm their belief in a linkage between Al Qaeda and Saddam Hussein's regime through relentless demands to focus on certain indications and questions. Vice President Cheney made several unusual trips to CIA to review and discuss the search for intelligence on this question, and a special unit, the Policy Counterterrorism Evaluation Group, was established in the Office of the Secretary of Defense (OSD) under the aegis of Undersecretary of Defense Douglas Feith to scrutinize raw intelligence independently and to suggest alternatives to interpretations provided by the regular intelligence community. Cheney and Rumsfeld's status allowed them to blunt the claim to authority made by the official intelligence community consensus and to push dissident views with equal force so that "whenever the principals of the National Security Council met with the president and his staff, two completely different views of reality were on the table."[81]

To some analysts who believed there was no evidence of significant cooperation between Al Qaeda and Saddam, these attempts to second-guess them constituted harassment of professional experts in order to gain political support for the administration's agenda against Iraq. The fact that the OSD unit presented its conclusions to the White House without coordinating them with or even informing DCI Tenet struck critics as improper.[82] Democratic Senator Carl Levin issued a report detailing machinations by Feith to communicate views contradicting the intelligence community consensus without presenting the intelligence professionals' factual corrections of his unit's drafts.[83] Those supporting the Cheney and Feith initiatives argued that it is healthy to challenge any consensus and force more careful attention to alternate possibilities and that neither Cheney nor the staff in OSD attempted to suppress what the regular analysts produced when they did agree.

The Silberman-Robb WMD Commission found no evidence of politicization because its criterion was that "no analytical judgments were changed in response to political pressure to reach a particular conclusion." The commission argued the benefits of Cheney's and OSD's forays thus: "Good faith efforts by intelligence consumers to understand the bases for analytic judgments, far from constituting 'politicization,' are entirely legitimate. This is the case even if the policymakers raise questions because they do not like the conclusions or are seeking evidence to support policy preferences."[84] Secretary of Defense Rumsfeld himself said that he valued Feith's special unit because it helped him to question his daily CIA briefings: "What I could do is say, 'Gee, what about this? Or what about that? Has somebody thought of this?'" This sort of challenge is reasonable, as long as the prodding does not turn into browbeating, but some of the analysts involved believed that the prodding crossed that line. Vincent Cannistraro described the pressure as demoralizing and thus subtly corrupting: "The analysts are human, and some of them are also ambitious. What you have to worry about is the 'chill factor.' If people are ignoring your intelligence, and the Pentagon and NSC keep telling you, 'What about this? What about this? Keep looking!'—well, then you start focusing on one thing instead of the other thing, because you know that's what your political masters want to hear."[85] As a top terrorism expert and national intelligence officer for the Middle East, Paul Pillar also tangled with the administration over this relentless insistence on focusing efforts against particular hypotheses. He wrote that

on any given subject, the intelligence community faces what is in effect a field of rocks, and it lacks the resources to turn over every one. . . . In an unpoliticized environment, intelligence officers decide which rocks to turn over based on past patterns and their own judgments. But when policymakers repeatedly urge the intelligence community to turn over only certain rocks, the process becomes biased. The community responds by concentrating its resources on those rocks, eventually producing a body of reporting and analysis that, thanks to quantity and emphasis, leaves the impression that what lies under those same rocks is a bigger part of the problem than it really is.[86]

Where should the line be drawn between reasonable second-guessing and nudging by consumers to consider alternate interpretations seriously, on one hand, and harassment on the other? Postmortems of intelligence failures always criticize professionals for not having rigorously challenged their own assumptions. In principle, special units like Feith's contribute to checks and balances in the process. The issue should be when and how they may go too far. The main problem arises after the final coordination process, in which such challenges from outside the normal intelligence bureaucracy should be included. Disagreements from the handful of kibitzers may legitimately be noted but should not be tabled at the highest level as if they have equal standing with finished collective estimates. Critics claim that this is what Rumsfeld did in National Security Council meetings, forcing DCI Tenet to make an inappropriate scene were he to challenge the propriety of the ploy. (Tenet did counter criticism from Senator Ted Kennedy about reticence in internal discussions by assuring him that "you have the confidence to know that when I believed that somebody was misconstruing intelligence I said something about it.")[87]

Abuses of proper procedure should be prevented. But how? No reform can be legislated that can keep a presidential lieutenant from saying something the president wants to let him say. The most common and least remediable form of politicization is the fast-and-loose conversational exchanges through which intelligence is conveyed and judged at the highest levels. Compared with this problem, politicization of wording in formal written estimates is small potatoes. The only safeguards at the top are the character and stolidity of the intelligence officers interacting with the politicians.

If political leaders believe that intelligence is politicized from below, activism to push different questions, assumptions, and approaches to assessment onto the professional agenda is legitimate. Challenging mind-sets should be a two-way street. Unless taken unreasonably far, such measures of goading from policymakers should be borne without complaint. When political leadership is composed of zealots, however, wishful challenges to intelligence professionals do easily go too far. Zealots are not preoccupied with finding the truth because they are confident that they already know what it is. What they seek from intelligence is ammunition, not truth. There is no solution to this problem apart from ousting the zealots.

Outrage in the other direction, against intelligence professionals, was equally heated at this time. By the time of the 2004 presidential election, Republican politicians and pundits were convinced that disloyal, liberal, or anti-Semitic CIA personnel were out to undercut the administration's Middle East policy and help put Senator John Kerry in the Oval Office.[88] They cited two books published by an anonymous CIA analyst (later revealed to be Michael Scheuer), Ambassador Wilson's op-ed article charging administration deception on the Niger uranium question, as well as press stories about National Intelligence Council studies that predicted negative results from an invasion of Iraq.[89] After Lewis Libby, Vice President Cheney's assistant for national security, was indicted for revealing the identity of Valerie Plame Wilson, embarrassed Republicans countered by pointing to the firing of Mary McCarthy, a high CIA official, for allegedly revealing classified information (a charge she denied). Right-wing radio personality Rush Limbaugh cited McCarthy, a veteran bureaucrat through many administrations, as a "Clinton person."[90] Danielle Pletka, a former Republican congressional staffer, said, "If the CIA had spent less time leaking its opinions, throughout the 1990s, opposed to any conflict with Iraq, and more time developing assets inside Iraq, the agency would have more credibility and better intelligence."[91]

When Porter Goss moved from chairmanship of the House Permanent Select Committee on Intelligence to become the last DCI before the reform legislation of 2004, he brought four Republican staffers with him, a move seen by some professionals as an attempt to clean house politically at CIA. In November 2005, Republicans charged Democrats on the Senate Intelligence Committee with pulling a publicity stunt when they forced a closed-door session of the full Senate to discuss allegations about the Bush administration's misuse of intelligence to justify the war in Iraq. Democrats claimed that the Republican majority on the committee had failed to fulfill an agreement to follow up the Silberman-Robb commission with an investigation of the consumer end of the Iraq intelligence controversy, while the Republicans countered that the committee staff was working on the issue.[92]

This imbroglio marked the low point of the principle of nonpartisanship in intelligence oversight. The system of House and Senate oversight committees introduced in the 1970s had been remarkably free of politicking in its first decade, frayed only a bit in the 1980s, unraveled more in the '90s, and fell into stark politicization of the bad sort thereafter. Democrats pushed for investigations of the misuse of intelligence on Iraq and for requiring new estimates on Iran. Republican members of the committees resisted, and the Senate Republican Policy Committee was brought into the fray, issuing a broadside against criticism of administration use of intelligence.[93] Analysis became a political football once again as Democratic politicians touted press accounts of a national intelligence estimate from April 2006 according to which the war in Iraq was increasing the threat from terrorism. The Bush administration countered by declassifying the estimate's key judgments section to show that the point about Iraq was a small part of the assessment.[94]

The good news, perversely, is that the attacks on the intelligence community in the past three decades have come from both the right and the left. Criticism from the left was most often about covert action and from the right about analysis, but over time there was no consensus that the intelligence establishment in general was identified with a single political bias. The bad news, however, was the same—dissatisfaction came from across the board. Especially in the twenty-first century, beliefs that both competence and impartiality had been lost left the intelligence establishment's credibility weakened with much of the public, rather than with just one side of the spectrum.

Navigating the Thin Lines

The challenge remains to make intelligence relevant without making it dishonest by pulling punches in a way that lets policymakers believe what they want. In practical terms, if intelligence is to be useful, its politicization will be a continuum from more to less, with the least being the aim for which professionals strive, zero being unattainable without denuding an analysis of all connection with political reality. Minimal contamination by political bias, or open and balanced competition between analysis from different predispositions, must be the norm, but enforcing it may generate just as many charges of politicization as it averts. Much depends on the artful straddling of thin lines by intelligence managers—something not easily done—or on signals sent in the choice of managers.[95]

There was less concern that intelligence was politicized in the first half of the Cold War, mostly because of greater secrecy and because of a greater consensus among the players about the context of basic policy objectives. But the care given to symbolic protections, such as the appointment of professionals unassociated with political parties to the top positions in the intelligence community, was also a factor. Until the post–Watergate era and the congressional investigations of the 1970s, eight of ten DCIs were not identifiable partisans of the administrations they served. They were military officers (Sidney Souers, Hoyt Vandenberg, Roscoe Hillenkoetter, Walter Bedell Smith, William Raborn), career intelligence officers (Richard Helms, William Colby), and a member of the opposition party (Republican John McCone under Kennedy and Johnson). Only Allen Dulles and James Schlesinger were political appointees in the mold of cabinet members. In a period in which there have been more public controversies about politicization, however, leadership has been more typically political. Only two of the last nine DCIs since Colby were ostensibly nonpolitical (Adm. Stansfield Turner and Judge William Webster). Two were as visibly partisan as one could possibly imagine (George Bush the Elder, who had been chairman of the Republican National Committee, and William Casey, Ronald Reagan's campaign manager). The others were a former career intelligence officer who made his reputation serving near the top of the White House and who had earlier been accused of trying to co-opt analysts for the Reaganite worldview (Gates), and three standard cabinet-like political appointees from the president's own party (James Woolsey, John Deutch, and Tenet under Clinton).[96] The last DCI, Porter Goss, was a member of Congress from the president's party who came to office with an audible mandate to discipline disloyal professionals. The first DNI, John Negroponte, was a career diplomat but one who rose to prominence because of his close association with Republican policies in Central America in the 1980s and Iraq after the U.S. conquest. Two other nominees who had to withdraw from confirmation battles were visible partisans of the president's party (Theodore Sorensen in 1977 and Anthony Lake in 1997).

Should norms about choice of intelligence leadership bear much of the weight of these problems, it would be desirable for the top intelligence manager to be from the opposition party, or to be a nonpolitical career professional from the military or intelligence community itself. It would also help to make the DNI a terminal office for elder statesmen who are not suspected of seeking further advancement in the military or the policy world. At the least, these symbolic criteria would dull suspicions of politicization when intelligence seemed to support administration policy, since they would provide prima facie reasons to believe that the DNI had no vested interest in pandering. This would complicate the process of choosing an effective DNI, however, because the sine qua non should be to have rapport with the president. Otherwise, all the good intelligence in the world will have less entrée to decisions. Since the 1970s, in any case, there has been no constituency of any consequence for instituting a rule against normal political appointment to the top intelligence office.

Despite complaints from some analysts and intellectuals, moreover, the Gates model continued to dominate in the management of intelligence analysis until the imbroglio over Iraq's WMD. Policymakers were scarcely bothered by the danger of politicization, and many in the foreign policy establishment who genuflected to the danger of politicization still endorsed closer connections between intelligence and policy.[97] Indeed, DCI Tenet was called on at several points to function as a diplomat, brokering delicate elements of negotiation in the Israeli-Palestinian peace process during the Clinton administration.

If the dissatisfaction across the board could be depolarized and made bipartisan, moves back to the Kent model would become politically feasible. The appeal of structural safeguards might then grow. One model recommended by some is the Federal Reserve Board, an organization with institutionalized independence of the president that is governed by a board whose members have lengthy, fixed terms of office. Or for legislative oversight, the function could be shifted to a congressional agency similar to the Government Accountability Office or Congressional Budget Office.[98] Such changes might insulate intelligence from pressure from political leadership, although they would not prevent bottom-up politicization from the biases of the staff or commissioners of such organs. As chapter 6 will elaborate, they could not make intelligence any more useful or influential because they could not force presidents to rely on their judgments or legislators to act on their recommendations. These recommendations are not promising.

Some of the ill effects of accentuated politicization that have come with increased publicity may be softened by the natural dynamics of constitutional pluralism as it already exists, which fosters a dueling politicization and some rough balance. The institutionalization of oversight in Congress contributes to this. After the Team B exercise, for example, the Senate Select Committee on Intelligence issued a staff report examining and criticizing it, essentially from the point of view of Team A. Thus, a Republican PFIAB countered alleged CIA bias with Team B, and Senate Democrats countered alleged Team B bias with their own assessment. In turning intelligence disputes into public controversies, intelligence may be damaged, but policy may be served by forcing important issues onto the table. Protracted battles between intelligence and policy, as in the history of bleak estimates on the Vietnam War, become less possible because congressional oversight would bring them "quickly to the surface and thus cause them to be resolved."[99] This check via institutional pluralism, however, has been strongest in periods of divided government, when different parties controlled the executive and legislative branches.

Within the executive branch, where policy is made and implemented in a hectic rush every day, there is still a tension between objectivity and influence. As Lawrence Freedman describes the paradox, "There is a direct relationship between the potential importance of the estimates in critical policy debates, and the difficulty faced within the community in forging an agreed consensus and in preventing estimates being misused by the political masters."[100] In no small part, however, this is because of the struggle to produce *a single best estimate* on the most fundamentally controversial disputes—indeed, they are in effect theological disputes—about threats to national security. Single best estimates can be useful, and often uncontroversial, on secondary matters or when leaders do not have well-formed views of their own already, and when their convictions are not already invested. On matters of high politics, however, producing a consensus estimate is likely to be meaningless because it either rests on negotiated mush or will be bloodily contested, in which case politicization in some measure is the essence of the enterprise.

In the second type of cases, futile attempts to combine quality and consensus make less sense than a conscious process for the careful presentation of contrasting views. The organizational pluralism of the intelligence community is the best defense against deceptive and damaging politicization, and that defense may best be provided by unmasking and setting up a competition between predispositions, rather than letting biases sneak into products striving for ideal objectivity. SNIE 14.3-67 could have done this better on the Vietnam order-of-battle controversy by giving equal time in the summary conclusions to the analyses that yielded higher strength figures for Communist forces. The Team B exercise was a more explicit step in the direction suggested, but an incomplete one—and the incompleteness severely marred the result.

Consensus estimates are ideal when they emerge naturally or when they convey basic information rather than interpretations of its implications for a matter of political controversy. On matters that are more politically fraught, the adversarial approach, organized more like contending presentations and questioning of evidence in court proceedings, makes sense. The best way to tell which cases warrant a single best estimate and which require casting the estimate as a debate is to find out whether such an estimate can be obtained without splitting differences. If undiluted key judgments that are not obvious can be agreed on with negligible dissent, such a consensus can be useful. Otherwise, a lengthier product that lays out the alternatives may be unwelcome to policymakers, but it is better to make clear the limits of intelligence than to obscure them. This puts the ball in the consumers' court. It puts them on notice that intelligence cannot solve their problem or bless their policy. They must either make the effort to look harder at the bases for disagreement among the experts or forthrightly accept that they are operating on the basis of their own articles of faith, rather than a complex reading of divided expert opinion.

All contamination of analysis by policy predispositions will never be fully purged from the process. Every analyst's ideas and assumptions, and those of managers or competing analysts, will be politicizing forces, however muted or constrained professional standards of rigor may make them. Analysis that remains trenchant, rather than descending into negotiated mush, will never be politically neutral. Bias can be minimized, however, by enforcing rigorous standards of evidence and comparison, and the effects of bias can be mitigated or made productive by organizing the confrontation of views in as systematic a manner as possible. As long as this is not done through a ponderous and deadening belaboring of methodological formulas that make the product unreadable, the process will involve artful management and walking dangerous lines. Managers must strive for the right balance. If it proves too delicate to maintain, they must then tilt clearly toward the imperative of accuracy rather than toward influence. It is better for intelligence to be useless than to be corrupt, but such a choice should be a last resort.

Robert Gates and George Tenet may have strayed too far from the Kent model, but Gates's message to analysts after the chastening of his confirmation hearings for the DCI post in 1991—a message that he composed by drawing on competing drafts supplied by a variety of analysts—charts the right course among pitfalls. According to Gates, "We must draw a line

• Between producing a corporate product and suppressing different views;
• Between adjusting stylistic presentation to anticipate your consumer's predilections and changing the analysis to pander to them. . . .
• Between viewing reporting critically and using evidence selectively."[101]

Gates's message also noted that the main entrance to CIA headquarters is dominated by a chiseled inscription from the Bible: "And ye shall know the truth and the truth shall make you free."[102] To many cynical observers, especially those lay critics whose image of the CIA derives from Hollywood or from the history of dirty tricks by the Directorate of Operations, that inscription is ironic, paradoxical, or disingenuous. But for working analysts, intelligence managers, and policymakers who place any value on knowledge as a basis for making and implementing decisions, no other rationale can give the enterprise meaning.

Al Qaeda's surprise attacks on the World Trade Center and the Pentagon were a second Pearl Harbor for the United States. The shocks jolted Americans out of the complacency about national security that they had enjoyed during the dozen years after the Cold War and launched them into a worldwide war against terrorists. When this was followed by the failure to find weapons of mass destruction (WMD) after the invasion of Iraq, recriminations over the intelligence failures provoked the most radical reorganization of the intelligence system since the post–Pearl Harbor National Security Act. In the first case, the intelligence community failed to provide enough warning; in the other, it failed by providing too much.

The discussions that follow are not complete case studies of the two failures; lengthy examinations are available in definitive official investigations.[1] This chapter uses the main points concerning the two most prominent intelligence failures of recent times to illustrate the barriers to success and the dilemmas discussed in other chapters. Both cases were more complex dramas than is generally understood and included much good intelligence work despite the failures at the bottom line. In both, hindsight reveals mistakes that could have been avoided as well as mistakes that were tragic yet natural.

These cases reflect the ample roles of all the enemies of intelligence. Most of all, the outside enemies—Al Qaeda and Saddam Hussein's government—concealed their capabilities and strategic intentions and misled the American intelligence system. Their deception was compounded by innocent and inherent enemies within the U.S. system. At a few points, law enforcement officials concerned about their legal backing held back maximally intrusive domestic intelligence collection; at others, political officials with strong views tried to make the interpretation of data match those views. As always, bureaucratic confusion, breakdowns in communication, the wayward cognitive processes of analysts and policymakers, and difficult choices between opposing risks got in the way.

LIMITS OF WARNING: SEPTEMBER 11, 2001

Conventional wisdom after the strikes on the World Trade Center and the Pentagon was that U.S. intelligence had failed egregiously. One CIA retiree described the failure as worse than Pearl Harbor because in 1941 we "did not have a director of central intelligence or 13 intelligence agencies or a combined intelligence budget of more than $30 [billion] to provide early warning of enemy attack."[2] True. Yet, before September 11, 2001, as before December 7, 1941, the U.S. intelligence system did succeed in providing timely warning of a sort, though the sort of strategic warning that was given proved absolutely useless. The system had detected and trumpeted a raft of indications that a major attack was imminent weeks before it happened. However, the system could not get beyond that stage to the level of tactical warning because it did not uncover or link specific information that might have made it possible to intercept the strikes. The system warned clearly about *whether* an attack was coming and that it would be soon, but it could not determine *where*, *how*, or *exactly* when. The warning was too vague to be "actionable."

In the mission to provide a usable warning, performance before September 11 failed in all phases of the intelligence cycle. The system failed in collection, since it did not discover the perpetrators, plans, or means of attack that lay beneath the "chatter" in signals intelligence that indicated an imminent action. It failed in processing and dissemination, as some pieces of information were not correlated in ways that would have raised the odds of identifying individuals involved in the plot or the instruments they planned to use. It failed in analysis by not finding the right pattern by which to connect the dots within the array of clues that was both incomplete and full of clutter. And policymakers also failed. The administration of Bush the Younger had not made terrorism as high a priority as either the intelligence community or the preceding Clinton administration had. The position of national coordinator for counterterrorism on the NSC staff was downgraded, the deputies committee (one notch below the top level of interagency coordination) did not meet to discuss counterterrorism until three months into the administration, and the principals committee (the top level) met for the first time on the subject four months after that, only one week before the attacks occurred.[3]

Errors of Omission

Before the bombings of U.S. embassies in Kenya and Tanzania in 1998, the intelligence community was slow to focus on Al Qaeda. A 1995 national intelligence estimate on terrorism and a 1997 update barely mentioned Osama bin Laden. After 1999 the Counterterrorism Center of the director of central intelligence had some success in penetrating Al Qaeda, but the agents were not at a high level in the organization.[4]

Nonetheless, throughout 2001, attention to Al Qaeda and warnings of action by the group escalated precipitously. There were more than forty articles relating to bin Laden in the president's daily brief (PDB) in the first eight months of the year; in the spring, reporting on terrorist threats reached its highest level since the alert before the turn of the millennium. In May there were several reports of attacks planned within the United States, and in June and July other reports poured in, although they indicated action in the Middle East or Rome. At the end of June, the official on the staff of the National Security Council (NSC) who was in charge of counterterrorism warned Condoleeza Rice, the assistant to the president for national security affairs, that indications of attack planning "had reached a crescendo." Most attention focused on probable strikes abroad, but several times in mid-2001 President Bush asked "whether any of the threats pointed to the United States." CIA answered on August 6 with an article in the president's daily brief titled "Bin Laden Determined to Strike in US." As DCI Tenet later described the situation in the summer, "the system was blinking red"[5] and he was running around Washington with his hair on fire. Two months before September 11, an official briefing said that bin Laden "will launch a significant terrorist attack against U.S. and/or Israeli interests in the coming weeks. The attack will be spectacular and designed to inflict mass casualties."[6]

Technical intelligence collection through photographic reconnaissance could not uncover Al Qaeda attack preparations, as it could have against a conventional military assault that requires the mobilization, loading, and movement of large forces. Signals intelligence, however, could detect many communications, and an upsurge of chatter among suspected terrorists was much of the reason for the intense sense of urgency during the summer. On the day before the attacks, the National Security Agency (NSA) intercepted messages "in which suspected terrorists said, 'The match is about to begin' and 'Tomorrow is zero hour.'" These messages were not translated until September 12. In themselves, they would not have made a crucial difference because they did not mention details of where a strike might occur, that airplanes would be used, or what the targets might be. The director of NSA at the time, Lt. Gen. Michael Hayden, "also noted that more than 30 similar cryptic warnings or declarations had been intercepted in the months before 9/11 and were not followed by any terrorist attack."[7]

If this collection of strong but nonspecific warnings could have been supplemented by detection and tracking of the plotters, the odds of blocking the attack would have gone up. The discovery that might have been most telling was shunted aside. Two months before the attacks, an FBI agent who had noticed the "inordinate number of individuals of investigative interest" attending flight schools in Arizona wrote the so-called Phoenix memo, which warned that bin Laden might be orchestrating a project, and recommended closer investigation of the situation at the flight schools. The memo was sent to a single field office. Although it also went to the units at FBI headquarters that were focused on bin Laden and radical fundamentalism, investigators there did not see it until after September 11.[8] Intelligence discovered some travel patterns of two of the future hijackers, Khalid al Mihdhar and Nawaf al Hazmi, but organizational boundaries and differences in procedure prevented piecing together some of the meetings of the two and handing off the job of monitoring from CIA to FBI when they entered the United States from Southeast Asia. CIA took too long to put al Mihdhar on the State Department watch list for suspected terrorists and did not notify FBI that he had a visa allowing repeated travel to the United States. FBI did not give CIA the Phoenix memo, and CIA did not effectively publicize al Mihdhar and al Hazmi's connections to Al Qaeda, which might have alerted other agencies to check on connections to flight schools.[9]

FBI fell down the most. In its normal priorities the bureau focused overwhelmingly on investigating for criminal prosecution rather than for general intelligence gathering, and confusion about legal requirements blocked sharing of information between those involved in the two missions. FBI failed to mount a full investigation of Zacarias Moussaoui, a student at a Minnesota flight school. Agents found that he had jihadist beliefs, a large amount of money in the bank, and a suspicious record of travel in and around Pakistan. Reports from the French government provided evidence of his association with Chechen rebels. Nevertheless, FBI agents did not obtain a warrant to conduct a search of Moussaoui's computer because they could not find probable cause sufficient to meet what they thought were required legal standards. Their understanding of legal limitations was later revealed to be incorrect. FBI headquarters also believed that Minneapolis agents were exaggerating the danger posed by Moussaoui. The chief of the bureau's international terrorism section did not even know that agent Harry Samit had sent a report three weeks before September 11 which warned that Moussaoui might be involved in a hijacking plot.[10] An unlimited effort to investigate Moussaoui might have uncovered his ties to the other plotters and forced immediate concentration on the potential for an attack involving airliners.[11]

The intelligence community's organization was not optimized for coordinating efforts on counterterrorism. NSA, for example, analyzed communications among several suspected terrorists who they thought might be up to something, but the agency did not attempt to establish the identities of the individuals in detail. NSA assumed that it was supposed to respond to requests from consumers or analytical agencies such as CIA. If the identities had been researched, the odds would have gone up that more dots would have been accurately connected.[12] Overall management of the community did not designate a single point of responsibility for coordinating efforts; instead, all involved were assumed to have that responsibility, the field units more than others. As a result, in the view of the 9/11 commission, CIA "headquarters never really took responsibility for the successful management of this case."[13]

Mistaken Priorities or Impossible Choices?

Did the intelligence system fail to make counterrorism a high enough priority before September 11? Yes and no, but mainly no. Relative to other foreign policy issues, the emphasis on counterterrorism went up significantly after the Cold War. More and better measures could have been taken to interdict or defend against the attacks, but reasons to bear all of the costs—both the absolute expense and the opportunity costs—are clearer in hindsight than they could have been before the fact.

A superpower will always have more than one major potential threat to its interests, and it will seldom have clear grounds for concentrating single-mindedly on any one of them. Lack of focus or diffusion of effort account for some failures, in hindsight, but before the fact too much focus on one priority increases vulnerability to threats that are second or third on the list. Resources are always limited, and when there are numerous claims, even those with high priority get less than they might profitably use. Maximizing protection against a potential threat—that is, doing *everything possible* to prevent or defend against it—will seem prohibitively expensive as long as the threat is potential rather than both certain and immediate. If Hurricane Katrina had been assumed to be certain, for example, the costs of a stronger levee system around New Orleans would have been borne. If the political system decides not to undertake costly defensive measures in response to ample but imperfect warning, the failure is at least as much one of policy as of intelligence.

The Silberman-Robb WMD Commission concluded that the problem before September 11 was "dispersal of effort on too many priorities," and the joint congressional investigation concluded that "for much of the intelligence community everything became a priority since its customers in the U.S. government wanted to know everything about everything all the time." For example, NSA had fifteen hundred formal requirements covering "virtually every situation and target."[14] This could hardly be surprising at the turn of the century, however, when post–Cold War foreign policy engaged the United States actively in most of the problems of the world, from the Balkans to the Arab-Israeli conflict, rogue states, humanitarian crises in Africa, reform in Russia and China, and so on.

Nevertheless, terrorism was near the top of the government's list. In 1995, Presidential Decision Directive 35, the guidance on priorities for the intelligence community, included terrorism among the top few. Between the end of the Cold War and September 11, the aggregate intelligence budget fell but funding for counterterrorism grew—in most agencies it doubled.[15] These trends do not suggest that insufficient concern with terrorism caused the failure.

In December 1998 DCI George Tenet issued a directive saying, "We are at war. I want no resources or people spared in this effort, either inside CIA or the Community." The directive had little effect, however, in mobilizing new efforts in agencies beyond CIA.[16] The system took the first step in identifying the priority of counterterrorism in principle. It took part of the second step: giving that priority a larger share of available intelligence resources during the 1990s. It did not succeed in the third step: inducing policymakers to respond fully and make costly choices to hedge against a potential threat of the sort that exploded on September 11. For example, Tenet's December 1998 directive was not addressed to agencies beyond CIA and the deputy director for community management.[17] The faltering in the third step is especially reflected in reactions to recommendations to tighten airline security procedures.

In 1995 the NIE on terrorism "highlighted civil aviation as a vulnerable and attractive target." But when the Federal Aviation Administration arranged a briefing for senior figures in its industry by the chief analyst at the Counterterrorism Center and his FBI counterpart, the warning failed to persuade them to pay the price of expensive new security measures.[18] In 1996, in response to the mysterious crash of TWA flight 800, Vice President Al Gore led a commission on aviation security. The commission concentrated on the danger of bombs placed aboard aircraft and criticized the laxness of existing procedures for screening passengers. In the next few years various threat reports noted possible uses of aircraft loaded with explosives. Still, no move was made to overhaul the airline security system. The FAA's intelligence unit considered the possibility of suicide hijacking but wrote it off because it would not serve what they thought would be the aim of hijackers—to get hostages in order to negotiate the release of imprisoned Islamic radicals.[19]

Inaction is not an unusual response to warnings of dire threats that are plausible yet uncertain. Before September 11 the Federal Emergency Management Agency identified the three most probable disasters: a terrorist attack in New York, a San Francisco earthquake, and an extreme hurricane in New Orleans. By 2005 two of the three had come to pass. In none of the three cases was there a maximum effort by government or any major organization to prevent or to prepare to mitigate the consequences. Had Louisiana and the federal government undertaken every project recommended to cope with the vulnerability of New Orleans, the price tag could have been an estimated $14 billion.[20] While the future costs of doing less than the maximum possible to deal with these potential threats were uncertain, the immediate costs to other interests of doing everything possible were not.[21]

Collection and Connection

The main failure before September 11 was the insufficient collection of unambiguous information. Dots must be collected before they can be connected. The more dots, the more likely that two or three will show directly when, where, or how an assault might come. As Roberta Wohlstetter has made so tragically clear, however, more information can create noise that obscures the most meaningful data.[22] Most ambiguous warnings turn out to be erroneous, and paying full attention to every one produced by a system that excels in collection could bring the system to a halt. For example, it has been reported that "by September 2001 the F.A.A. was receiving some 200 pieces a day of intelligence from other agencies about possible threats, and it had opened more than 1,200 files to track possible threats."[23]

Few observers want to admit to the trade-off between maximizing collection and losing focus. The Silberman-Robb commission, for example, complained that "channels conveying terrorism intelligence are clogged with trivia," in part because bureaucrats pass all information on to avoid "later accusations that data was not taken seriously. As one official complained, this behavior is . . . 'preparing for the next 9/11 commission instead of preparing for the next 9/11.'"[24] But can we have it both ways? Can the handling of information be streamlined for manageability without risking a failure to expose the two critical dots that analysts or policymakers might connect?

Maximizing collection can cause catastrophic side effects. Paradoxically, the purpose of intelligence is to protect against disaster, but the lust for it can cause disaster. Risky collection ventures can produce provocations or accidents with major diplomatic and military reverberations. This has happened numerous times. In 1960 the Soviet downing of the U-2 spy plane flown by Gary Powers led to the cancellation of a summit meeting between Eisenhower and Khrushchev. In 1967 the USS *Liberty* was destroyed and dozens of its crew killed by Israeli aircraft while the ship was collecting signals intelligence during the Six Day War. The next year the USS *Pueblo*, on a similar mission, was captured by North Korea and its crew was imprisoned for a year. In 1969 an EC-121 collecting electronic intelligence was shot down off the coast of North Korea. In 2001 an American EP-3 aircraft was knocked down by a Chinese pilot, leading to a tense and prolonged international incident between Washington and Beijing. Exploitation of human sources poses similar trade-offs. If a spy is directed to take risks to get all information possible rather than lying low and waiting for a high-priority task, she may be caught, and the source lost and made unavailable when it was needed most. In short, maximizing collection cannot be automatically assumed to be a benefit; when things go wrong, it can cause far more damage to national security than it averts.

If more dots had been collected before September 11, the odds are better that they might have been connected in a manner that provided usable warning. Yet, the more dots there are, the more ways they can be connected—and which way is correct may become evident only when it is too late, when disaster clarifies which indicators were salient. Analysis failed before September 11 perhaps for the reason cited by the 9/11 commission—by ignoring certain methods that had been developed to facilitate warning.[25] One need not make excuses for various failures, however, to believe that lay observers may come to expect too much of intelligence—"like expecting the FBI to stop bank robberies before they occur."[26] A different reading of the record led Richard Posner to conclude, in opposition to the 9/11 commission, that the answer is "something different, banal, and deeply disturbing: that it is almost impossible to take effective action to prevent something that hasn't occurred previously."[27]

The special difficulty of tactical warning makes it especially important for policymakers to consider what they should do with strategic warning. If a tactical warning that will prevent attacks from being launched cannot be expected, the premium on measures to blunt their impact goes up. This means translating the warning of potential threats into programs for coping with them when they burst forth. But is there reason for confidence that the lesson of September 11 will improve the odds that this will happen? A number of severe potential threats were clearly identified in recent years, ones for which a number of defensive measures have been available. As with aviation security before September 11, however, the costs or negative side effects of some of these defensive options led authorities to decide against them and to wait for development of measures that would pose fewer costs. As long as the threats do not eventuate in disaster, these choices to do less than the maximum possible as soon as possible will seem prudent. The day after one of them does yield disaster, however, few in the public will forgive authorities for not having made the hard choice to pay the costs and accept the negative side effects.

There is the potential, for example, for terrorists to mount coordinated strikes on civilian airliners with shoulder-fired antiaircraft missiles. This risk has been understood at least since the mid-1990s. Precautions of various sorts have been heightened, but the main defensive option—installation of flare or laser systems on airliners to deflect or destroy missiles in flight—was not adopted immediately. The cost would have been many billions of dollars, and there was the risk as well that false alarms would cause dangerous side effects, such as fires started by flares, or lasers blinding people on the ground. So the government decided to wait for safer and more economical defense systems. By the time these words are read, new and better defensive countermeasures may have been put in place. But that will mean only that the gamble to leave this vulnerability incompletely covered for a decade or more has paid off, not that the risk in the interim was insignificant. Another example is the efficient dissemination of aerosolized anthrax over several cities. Timely public health response might minimize fatalities through the distribution of antibiotics, but deficiencies in stockpiles or procedures for treating millions of exposed people in untested situations might still kill thousands. Yet, the government has not mounted a crash program to overcome the obstacles to mass vaccination against anthrax for many good reasons, such as problems in the production of vaccine, limitations on its efficacy over time, or a risk to the health of some fraction of those vaccinated. For however long there are no effective anthrax attacks, the choice not to promote mass vaccination seems wise, but if the scenario of a successful attack plays out, the choice will seem as mistaken as the failure to beef up airline security before September 11.[28] The list of hard choices about which strategic warnings warrant action is long.

Seeing the failure to go far enough in exploring the potential for the kamikaze hijacking tactic ultimately used on September 11 and the failure of intelligence organizations to connect the dots more creatively, the 9/11 commission concluded that it is "crucial to find a way of routinizing, even bureaucratizing, the exercise of imagination."[29] This is an oxymoronic notion but it is on the mark. It can be tried in various ways, such as by instituting "Red Teams," devil's advocates, analytical kibitzers, or other mechanisms for thinking outside the box. Multiplying the number of scenarios given serious rather than cursory attention, however, runs up against the need for a focus on priorities and probable threats. Chapters 2 and 6 show that such innovations prove hard to sustain and rarely provide the remedies anticipated, though their periodic revival at least focuses attention on challenging assumptions.

WRONG FOR THE RIGHT REASON? WMD IN IRAQ

Having failed to connect the dots before September 11, American intelligence made the opposite mistake on Iraq—it connected the dots too well, seeing connections where they did not exist. The mistaken estimate that Iraq maintained stocks of chemical and biological weapons and an active program to acquire nuclear weapons was the worst intelligence failure since the founding of the modern intelligence community in two ways. The less damaging of the two effects was the spillover that tarnished the credibility of U.S. intelligence in general. When U.S.

armed forces invaded Iraq but did not find of the weapons so confidently attributed to Saddam Hussein by U.S. intelligence,[30] the shock struck many in the public as evidence of fundamental incompetence or chicanery in the intelligence system.

That failure distracted attention completely from the creditable performance of the intelligence community on other issues, including Iraq. For example, a postmortem led by Richard Kerr, retired head of CIA's Directorate of Intelligence, concluded that prewar intelligence concerning Iraq was quite accurate, for example, on predictions about "how the war would develop and how Iraqi forces would or would not fight," on the connections between Iraq and Al Qaeda, "the impact of the war on oil markets," and on the "reactions of the ethnic and tribal factions in Iraq." Most relevant was the anticipation of an awful aftermath to the war: "Assessments on post-Saddam issues were particularly insightful." Ironically, policymakers heeded technical intelligence about weaponry, which was wrong, "but apparently paid little attention to intelligence on cultural and political issues (post–Saddam Iraq), where the analysis was right."[31] In fact, the administration "went to war without requesting . . . any strategic-level intelligence assessments on any aspect of Iraq."[32]

The second and worst effect of the mistaken estimate was that it provided the warrant for war against Iraq, a war that was unnecessary and that cost far more blood and treasure than the September 11 attacks. If we are to believe President Bush, mistaken intelligence did not cause his decision for war because he had other reasons for wanting to destroy the Saddam Hussein regime. Bush later claimed that he would have launched the war even if he had known that Iraq did not have WMD. The presumed existence of such weapons, however, was the only reason the administration was able to secure enough public support to make the war politically feasible. Had Bush presented the case for war in 2002 as he did a few years later, denying that neutralizing WMD was a necessary condition, no one but fanatics would have lined up behind him. To this extent the intelligence failure bears responsibility for the war.

At the same time, it is fair to say that the intelligence failure, though tragic, was not egregious. It was a failure both in collection and analysis. Although the bottom-line analytic conclusion was wrong, in the absence of adequate collection *it was the proper estimate to make from the evidence then available.* No responsible analyst could have concluded in

2002 that Iraq did *not* have stocks of chemical and biological weapons concealed. The principal mistakes were in the confident presentation of the analysis and in the failure to make clear how weak the direct evidence was for reaching any conclusion and how much the conclusion depended on logic and deduction from behavior. In effect, available intelligence might have served to convict Saddam Hussein of holding WMD if the standard of civil law that bases a decision on the preponderance of evidence were applied, but not under the standard of criminal law, which requires proof beyond a reasonable doubt.

Roots of Error

When questioned at a White House meeting about how solid the intelligence was indicating that Iraq had WMD, DCI Tenet reportedly said, "Don't worry, it's a slam dunk!"[33] How could the intelligence community have been so confident about a conclusion that turned out to be so wrong, especially when it had hardly any direct evidence of the existence of the weapons? The essential reason is that the conclusion was deduced from Iraqi behavior and the motives assumed to be consistent with that behavior. To people paying attention to the issue, the conclusion seemed *utterly obvious* from the accumulated observations and experience of the preceding decade. Indeed, "apparently all intelligence services in all countries and most private analysts came to roughly the same conclusions."[34] This nearly universal consensus was rooted in experience following the first Persian Gulf War in 1991.

After that war the United Nations Special Commission (UNSCOM) uncovered a huge infrastructure of facilities and programs in Iraq for producing nuclear, chemical, and biological weapons that had been hidden from prewar Western intelligence. Forced by the surrender agreement at the end of the war to allow continuing intrusion by UNSCOM, and caught short when early inspections revealed prohibited activities, the Iraqis fought back. An Iraqi government committee gave instructions to conceal WMD activities from inspectors. This was revealed by a document the inspectors obtained. Another document retrieved from a nuclear installation showed how this order was carried out. "According to UNSCOM's final report, 'The facility was instructed to remove evidence of the true activities at the facility, evacuate documents to hide sites, make physical alterations to the site to hide its true purpose, develop cover stories, and conduct mock inspections to prepare for UN inspectors.'"[35]

From 1992 to 1998, when Saddam finally compelled UNSCOM to leave the country, the commission was regularly frustrated in its inspections by a game of cat and mouse, consisting of Iraqi delays and obstructions that seemed consistent only with attempts to conceal activities they did not want discovered.[36] While admitting to having stocks of chemical and biological weapons at the end of the war and claiming to have destroyed them later, the Iraqis never provided a credible accounting or any evidence of such destruction. Since it *seemed* obvious that it was in Saddam's interest to demonstrate compliance with legal obligations if it were possible to do so, this failure to account seemed necessarily to indicate that the stocks had been retained and hidden. UNSCOM also obtained figures on imports of equipment appropriate for WMD programs but could not get an accounting from the Iraqis of what happened to such materials. This, too, appeared to confirm that they must be up to no good.[37] As the Silberman-Robb commission concluded, "When someone acts like he is hiding something, it is hard to entertain the conclusion that he really has nothing to hide."[38] Moreover, the shock of discovering how much had been successfully concealed before the 1991 war convinced Western intelligence that the Iraqis were masters of deception, so the absence of evidence of WMD or any negative indications in later years were explained away as the result of denial and deception. Assumptions that Iraq had ambitious WMD projects and a major program of denial and deception "were tied together into a self-reinforcing premise that explained away the lack of strong evidence of either."[39]

The assessment process reflected errors in method, but these are common among analysts of any sort. It is well known from cognitive psychology that people tend to look for information that confirms what they already believe and discount information that is inconsistent with those predispositions. Instructions to collectors compounded this tendency. They were told to "seek information about Iraq's progress toward obtaining WMD" rather than about *whether* Iraq was doing so. This may have led agents to "ignore reports of lack of activity." Similarly, one major contradictory report from an important source was downplayed. Saddam Hussein's son-in-law, Hussein Kamel, defected and told his debriefers much about Iraq's WMD programs, but he said that they did not amount to much and that old stocks had been destroyed.[40] The apparent lack of interest in this aspect of the defector's testimony may be the most damning example of how negative evidence was ignored.

One of the principal disputes about evidence concerned Iraq's illegal importation of aluminum tubes. CIA, DIA, NSA, and the National Geo-Spatial Intelligence Agency concluded that the tubes were to be used in centrifuges to produce enriched uranium for nuclear weapons. The Department of Energy disagreed. Ironically, CIA and DIA would not have firmly asserted that the nuclear program was being reconstituted had they lacked the apparent evidence of the tubes, and Energy agreed with the reconstitution idea, despite writing off the tubes.[41]

In this context of seemingly obvious guilt, "analysts shifted the burden of proof, requiring evidence that Iraq did *not* have WMD" and in effect "erected a theory that almost could not be disproved."[42] The October 2002 NIE was rushed to completion in an extraordinarily short time because it had been requested by the Senate Select Committee on Intelligence in the period that appeared to be the countdown toward war. Because of the time pressure, the National Intelligence Council (NIC) did not circulate the draft for peer review or for comment by outsiders. This did not seem to be a risky omission, however, because as the vice-chair of the NIC said, "I think all you could have called in is an amen chorus on this thing, because there was nobody out there with different views."[43]

However obvious the answer seemed, the fact remained that the intelligence community had almost no hard evidence that Iraq was retaining the chemical and biological weapons it had at the time of the 1991 Persian Gulf War, or had manufactured new ones, or was reassembling its nuclear weapons program. Intellligence collection failed in two crucial ways. First, it failed to uncover much new information after UNSCOM inspectors left Iraq in 1998. Second, much of the information it did get came from defector reports that turned out to be fabricated or unreliable. The procedure for protecting sources also misled analysts into thinking that the number of human sources was greater than it was because clandestine reporting often identified the same source in different ways.[44]

American intelligence "did not have a single HUMINT [human intelligence] source collecting against Iraq's weapons of mass destruction programs in Iraq after 1998" (although there were sources on other subjects, such as political developments).[45] There were a few HUMINT reports from sources controlled by allied intelligence services, but many of them proved false. Technical intelligence collection existed, but errors resulted from "over-reliance on dubious imagery, . . . breakdowns in communication between collectors and analysts," and inadequate signals intelligence.[46] Until late 2002, shortly before the war was launched, North Korean and Iranian weapon programs had a higher priority than Iraq's; what technical collection there was in Iraq focused on the air defense system because of U.S. air operations over the southern part of the country.[47]

The biggest mistakes were the reliance on unreliable human intelligence, and the failure to correct disseminated reports when they were found to be dubious. On chemical weapons, none of the reports from human sources "was considered 'highly reliable' . . . and only six were deemed 'moderately reliable.'"[48] Most notorious was "Curveball," the code name for a chemical engineer from Baghdad who had emigrated to Germany and whose reports on biological weapons were funneled through the German intelligence service. In May 2004, a full year after the invasion of Iraq, CIA determined that Curveball's reporting was fabricated. A CIA officer claims to have raised questions about Curveball before the war, but DCI Tenet and Deputy DCI John McLaughlin say they did not know this until they read about it in the WMD commission report.[49] When the NIE was being done, Curveball's allegations about biological weapons programs appeared to be corroborated by three other sources. One of them later recanted, however, and another had already been branded a fabricator by the Defense Intelligence Agency in May 2002. Nevertheless, owing to bureaucratic miscommunication, allegations about biological weapon programs from that source still found their way into the October 2002 NIE and Secretary of State Powell's speech before the UN Security Council in February 2003.[50]

These mistakes in validating collection were egregious but apparently not the fault of the analysts who produced the NIE. Given how little direct, even erroneous evidence there was, judgments remained driven by the circumstantial evidence of Iraqi behavior and logical deductions from it. Only when no WMD turned up after the invasion did hindsight make it easy to see other explanations for Iraqi deception. For example, Iraq tried frequently to import dual-use materials (items that could be applied either to innocent or to forbidden uses) through illicit channels such as front companies. Analysts assumed this meant the materials were going to WMD programs, since there appeared to be no other reason to hide the transactions. Iraq did this as standard operating procedure even for some legitimate imports, however, precisely because the UN sanctions monitors sometimes denied permission for innocent items because the materials could be used for WMD. The UN bureaucracy for approving imports was also ponderous and required more time and effort to use than illegal channels, and working through front companies facilitated the corrupt skimming of profits.[51]

Hindsight also made it easier to entertain rationales for Saddam's encouraging his opponents to believe in the nonexistent weapons. His strategy appeared to be an attempt to have his cake and eat it too—to claim the high ground in the court of world opinion by asserting compliance, while exercising deterrence against the United States and Iran by abetting the inference that he still had the forbidden weapons. FBI interrogations of Saddam after his capture suggested that he had this rationale and was particularly worried that inspections would "expose Iraq's vulnerability in comparison with Iran." Saddam even deceived his own government, suggesting to high officials that Iraq had WMD.[52]

The most fundamental obstacle to success in the estimate was that *"it is particularly difficult for analysts to get it right when the truth is implausible."*[53] Hindsight always reminds us not to assume that what appears irrational to observers does not have a rationale. When estimating, however, which analyst will ever predict that a subject will act stupidly rather than sensibly? In 1962 the NIE was wrong about missiles in Cuba because analysts did not believe that Khrushchev would shoot himself in the foot.[54] Forty years later, the NIE on Iraq made the same mistake about Saddam Hussein. Attributing to Saddam the strategy of pretending to have WMD would have seemed too clever by half for him in October 2002, since it was assumed that he would see his survival more threatened by noncompliance with legal obligations. The correct, but counterintuitive, rationale for Saddam's behavior might have been included in a prewar estimate, but only as an alternative interpretation to the consensus judgment. Before the fact it would inevitably have seemed to be an imaginative stretch made by a devil's advocate fulfilling the requirement to think out of the box—and it would have been dismissed.

What the 2002 NIE Did, Should Have Done, and Could Have Done

The full text of the October 2002 national intelligence estimate included caveats about the limits of the evidence on which it was based as well as extensive discussion of the reasons that the State Department's Bureau of Intelligence and Research (INR) disagreed with the conclusion. (INR's dissent is sometimes wrongly characterized as a judgment that Saddam did not harbor WMD. INR simply remained agnostic, neither endorsing nor opposing that conclusion.) The tone of the NIE, however, was confident, and the key judgments section—the summary of conclusions which is all that many consumers read—did not convey the limitations with sufficient force. Apart from directing readers to the two long paragraphs summarizing INR's alternative view at the end and stating that "we lack specific information on many key aspects of Iraq's WMD programs," the key judgments mainly enumerated estimated Iraqi programs and capabilities, leaving the impression that the estimates derived from observed activities as much as deduction from behavior and assumed intentions.[55] Again, as Sherman Kent recalled, the same thing happened in the Cuban crisis estimate: "How could we have misjudged? The short answer is that, lacking the direct evidence, we went to the next best thing, namely information which might *indicate* the true course of developments."[56]

With the benefit of hindsight one might argue that the strictly correct estimate in 2002 should have been that the intelligence community simply did not know whether Iraq retained WMD in being or programs to obtain them. That would have been intellectually valid but would have abdicated the responsibility to provide the best support possible to the policy process. As Kent reminisced about Cuba in 1962, when dealing with something that cannot be known for sure, "there is a strong temptation to make no estimate at all. In the absence of directly guiding evidence, why not say the Soviets might do this, they might do that, or yet again they might do the other—and leave it at that?" Fore-swearing any educated guess "has the attractions of judicious caution and an exposed neck, but it can scarcely be of use to the policy man and planner who must prepare for future contingencies."[57]

Ironically, it was because they were conscious of their responsibility to contribute to decision that managers of the analytic process did not err on the side of caution. They wanted to avoid equivocation to keep the estimate from sounding useless. They believed that good analysis needed "to go beyond certain knowledge" even if this meant occasion-ally being wrong. As Mark Lowenthal, former assistant director of cen-tral intelligence, put it, "willingness to take such risks is undermined by fears of 'failure.' No one wants intelligence that is brash and wrong; pusillanimous intelligence is not any better."[58]

If estimators were to act realistically and earn their pay, yet remain accurate given what was known and knowable at the time, they should have posed three key judgments in the October 2002 NIE:

• Iraq is probably hiding stocks of chemical and biological weapons and active programs to develop and produce chemical, biological, and nuclear weapons;
• That conclusion is deduced primarily from its obstruction of UN-SCOM, the failure to account for destruction of stocks known to exist in 1991, and some other circumstantial evidence;
• There is very little direct evidence, and no highly reliable direct evi-dence, to back up the deduction.

This would have averted the irresponsibility of offering no judgment and could have fit within the one-page president's summary.[59] It would also have been unwelcome to policymakers looking for the warrant for war but would have been accurate given what was known and know-able at the time. In terms of what is reasonable to expect when estimat-ing, these revisions would have been the proper course to take, even though the conclusion would still have been wrong. To most observers looking back after the invasion and the missing WMD, however, the difference between these and the actual key judgments would appear to be a matter of nuance rather than an acceptable analysis. Hindsight inevitably makes most people assume that the only acceptable analysis is one that gives the right answer.

Was this failure a symptom of the system's core weakness? The context in which the October 2002 NIE is seen determines how terrible it looks. If measured by its relation to the justification for invading Iraq, it looks epochally terrible. If measured as an entry within the set of assessments related to counterproliferation in general, however, it looks different. This is what the British postmortem on London's intelligence failure before the war did. The Butler report investigated all proliferation-related intelligence projects, including Libya, Iran, North Korea, and the A. Q. Khan network in Pakistan, as well as Iraq. These other intelligence projects were more or less successful, which made the Iraq case "one failure against four successes. Hence, it was viewed as a failure due to Iraq-specific factors that somehow tripped up an otherwise effective system," not as evidence of a thorough breakdown. The Silberman-Robb commission also gave the U.S. system some credit for success on other proliferation cases. The Senate Intelligence Committee report came out first in the United States, however, was unremitting in criticism, and set the tone for public understanding of the Iraq failure.[60]

Being factually wrong is not in itself evidence of mistakes that could have been avoided or that show dereliction. The Senate Intelligence Committee postmortem tended to make this common conflation, and most lay critics did as well.[61] But so what? It is good news to find "that the system was not horribly broken, but bad news in that there are few fixes that will produce more than marginal (but still significant) improvements."[62] Being wrong for the right reasons means little to citizens who must live with the result, but it does provide a caution against drawing too many lessons from a single failure.

As the dust from the collapsed Twin Towers was still settling, the charges began to fly. CIA was asleep at the switch! The intelligence system is broken! Reorganize top to bottom! The new conventional wisdom was typified in the *New York Times*: "What will the nation's intelligence services have to change to fight this war? The short answer is: almost everything."[1] Less than two years later, the mistaken estimate that Saddam Hussein's Iraq possessed stocks of chemical and biological weapons reinforced that public consensus about the U.S. intelligence system: drastic change must be overdue.

The failures not only made clear that a lot should be done to shore up intelligence, they gave political impetus to the movement for change. Reforms that should have been made earlier became live options. New ideas got more attention and were less easily sidetracked than in normal times when inertia prevails. Finally, the Intelligence Reform and Terrorism Prevention Act of 2004 charted a major reorganization of the intelligence community, the most far-reaching since its establishment in the National Security Act.

Early in the twenty-first century there has been no shortage of proposals and initiatives to shake the system up, but there has been a shortage of perspective. Reacting to the failures with business as usual would have been unthinkable, but the only thing worse would be to proceed from naive assumptions about what reform will accomplish. There is a chasm between the universal cry to *"Do something!"* and the confused collection of ideas about what that should be.

How should the system do two things that do not always easily go together? The first of these is better collection and analysis to reduce the odds of missing particular warning indicators. The second is to coordinate the complexity of the system more effectively to avoid squandering the gains from having accomplished the first. This chapter begins by surveying the main issues since 2001 and some of the less problematic ideas for innovation to achieve the first aim. Then it surveys the political context, the deepening politicization, and the political trade-offs that have constrained more ambitious schemes for change. Finally, it looks in detail at the costs, benefits, and dilemmas of reorganization solutions that have been legislated or proposed.

It is the inherent enemies of intelligence that threaten progress most. Outside enemies have virtually no leverage on the initiatives government takes to adapt itself to the challenge that they pose to national security. The roles which innocent enemies do or do not perform, in turn, are entirely in the eye of the beholder; that is, which officials or interest groups are blamed for blocking proper innovations or undertaking misbegotten ones depends on the political judgments of their opponents in the domestic debate. No matter what the wisdom behind them, however, the adjustments that are ultimately made will be inevitably beset by many of the managerial and intellectual dilemmas discussed earlier.

STRAIGHTFORWARD SOLUTIONS

Paradoxically, the news is worse than the angriest critics have thought because the intelligence community has worked better than they think. The network of U.S. agencies, in liaison with foreign intelligence services, has often performed quite well. Successes in thwarting previous terrorist attacks were too easily forgotten in the shock of a single catastrophe or the embarrassment of a big misjudgment. Examples of such successes were the foiling of plots to bomb the Lincoln and Holland tunnels in 1993, to bring down a dozen American airliners in Asia in 1995, to mount attacks around the millennium in Jordan and on the U.S. West Coast, and to strike U.S. forces in the Middle East in mid-2001.

The awful truth is that the best of intelligence systems will have big failures. The terrorists that intelligence must uncover and track are not inert objects, but live, conniving strategists. They also fail frequently and are caught in time, but they will not always fail to find ways to work around even a proficient intelligence system. Counterterrorism is a competitive game. Even minor-league pitchers can sometimes strike out a major leaguer who bats .350. In counterterrorism, however, a strikeout means that people die. That makes a .350 average in that business (or a .900 average for that matter) look far worse than it does in baseball—but the fact that the consequences are far worse does not mean that a far higher average is easier to achieve than in baseball.

Throw Money at the Problem

There are many ways to try to improve intelligence. There are very few, however, that involve cheap fixes that have never been tried, or changes that guarantee a payoff for a specific, targeted investment. Some improvements come from the rising tide that lifts all boats, an overall increase in the level of effort. This means throwing money at the problem, which in turn means that the price will be much waste, a price more easily paid in wartime. It is easier to add resources and functions than to reorient priorities or change existing norms. Criticism of FBI after September 11, for example, led the bureau to make progress toward becoming a real intelligence organization as well as a police institution. Hundreds of analysts were added to the rolls, and barriers to sharing information were scaled down. Nevertheless, criticism persisted on the grounds that the bureau still had not changed the culture that overemphasized law enforcement and prosecution or the training curriculum, which added only token amounts of time for intelligence instruction.

Additional effort also needs to be properly apportioned so that intelligence gained in one phase of the cycle is not lost in another. For example, Congress funded additional signals intelligence collection systems for NSA but failed to fund the personnel necessary to keep processing, analysis, and reporting up to speed with them. As a result, much of what was collected went unexploited.[2] Moreover, additional efforts can occasionally be not just wasteful but counterproductive, by generating unforeseen side effects.[3] On average, though, extra effort will produce more positive than negative results.

There have been plenty of misallocations of effort in the past, but no silver bullets have gone unused before the twenty-first century. Nor is there any crucial area of intelligence that has been neglected altogether and which could be cured by a few well-targeted investments. There is no evidence that more spending on any particular program would have averted the September 11 attacks. The group that carried them off had formidable operational security, and the most critical deficiencies making their success possible were in airport security, legal limitations on domestic surveillance, and breakdowns in coordination within and between agencies. In many areas of intelligence, however, there was ample room for improvement, as efforts were extensive but spread thin or slowed down.

It takes large investments to reduce the chance of disaster even marginally because most intelligence work leads nowhere. Reliable information is hard to get when it is concealed, and it is often found only after many trips down blind alleys. Marginal improvements, however, can spell the difference between success and failure in some cases. If effective intelligence collection increases by only 5 percent for the year, but the critical warning indicator of an attack turns up in that 5 percent, spending a lot for a little more information gains a lot of protection. Streamlining for efficiency is unobjectionable in principle, but risky unless it is clear what is not needed. When threats are numerous and complex, it is easier to know what additional capabilities would be nice to have than to know what can safely be cut.

After the Cold War, intelligence resources decreased as requirements increased. A new set of high priority issues and regions replaced the old Soviet threat, the coverage of which had been thoroughly institutionalized. At the end of the 1990s there was an uptick in the intelligence budget, but the system was still spread thinner over its targets than when it was focused on the Soviet Union. Three weeks before September 11, Director of Central Intelligence Tenet gave an interview that seems tragically prescient. He agonized about the prospect of a catastrophic intelligence failure. "Then the country will want to know," Tenet warned, "why we didn't make those investments; why we didn't pay the price; why we didn't develop the capability."[4]

The sluice gates for intelligence spending opened after September 11, the budget increasing by almost half in the next several years. (The U.S.

intelligence budget is classified, but the total was widely reported to be around $30 billion in 2001. In 2005 an official accidentally revealed that the total was then $44 billion.) The main problem has been not to buy some essential element of capability that was ignored before but to help the system do more of everything better, and to do so without creating destructive complexity and confusion. Doing more of everything increases the odds that bits and pieces of critical information will be acquired and noticed, but nothing can guarantee that the right innovations will be chosen or the bad ones avoided.

Collection

What can be improved easily helps marginally, while what can help more than marginally cannot be improved easily. The National Security Agency (NSA), National Geo-Spatial Intelligence Agency (NGA), and associated organizations can increase technical collection—primarily satellite and aerial reconnaissance and signals intelligence—by buying more platforms, devices, and personnel to use them. Yet, increasing useful human intelligence, which all agree is the most critical ingredient for rooting out secretive terrorist groups, cannot easily be done by quick infusions of money.

Technical collection is invaluable and has undoubtedly figured in counterterrorist successes in ways not publicized. But obtaining this kind of information got harder after the Cold War. For one thing, so much has been revealed over the years about U.S. technical collection capabilities that the targets came to understand better what they have to evade. States may know satellite overflight schedules and time their observable activities accordingly. They can utilize more fiber optic communication systems, which are much harder to tap than transmissions over the airwaves. Competent terrorists learned long ago not to use cell phones for sensitive messages, and even small groups now have access to impressive encryption technologies.

Human intelligence is the key because the essence of the terrorist threat is the capacity to conspire. The best way to intercept attacks is to penetrate the organizations, learn their plans, and identify perpetrators so they can be taken out of action. Better human intelligence means bolstering the National Clandestine Service, the new name given in 2006 to CIA's Directorate of Operations (in the early Cold War, the Directorate of Plans). It is the primary, traditional espionage organization of the U.S. government. The service was troubled and periodically disrupted after the crack-up of the Cold War consensus in the late stage of the Vietnam War, which provoked more oversight and criticism than is congenial to spies. Personnel turnover, tattered esprit, and a culture of risk aversion spawned by controversies over the legality of some operations constrained the service's effectiveness at the turn of the century.

Some of the constraint was a reasonable price to pay to prevent excesses when such organizations are subject to little scrutiny and, in a post–Cold War world, where covert operators were working for national interests that are less important than direct defense and survival. Worries about excess receded after the collapse of the World Trade Center, and measures were taken to make it easier for the clandestine service to move. One simple reform, for example, was to implement a recommendation made by the National Commission on Terrorism fifteen months before September 11—to roll back the additional layer of cumbersome procedures instituted in 1995 for approving the employment of agents with unsavory records, procedures that had a chilling effect on recruitment of the thugs appropriate for penetrating terrorist units.[5]

Building up human intelligence networks worldwide is a long-term project. It also spawns concern about waste (many such networks never produce anything useful), deception (human sources are widely distrusted), and complicity with murderous characters (such as the Guatemalan officer who prompted the 1995 guidelines on agent recruitment). These are prices that can be borne politically in the atmosphere of crisis that persisted after September 11. When a sense of crisis abates, however, commitment to long-term projects can falter.

More and better spies help, but no one should expect breakthroughs if they are deployed. It is close to impossible to penetrate small, disciplined, alien organizations like Al Qaeda—and especially hard to find reliable U.S. citizens who have even a remote chance of trying. U.S. intelligence generally has to rely on foreign agents of uncertain reliability, and even the American case officers who handle them may not be equipped to understand the full context of what they are told. Despite our huge and educated population, the base of Americans on which to draw for the right combination of skills is small. There are simply few genuinely bilingual, bicultural, well-educated Americans capable of operating like natives in exotic reaches of the Middle East, Central and South Asia, or elsewhere that shelter the Osama bin Ladens of the world. True, the immigrant population is a source of recruits, but one limited by problems in granting security clearances to those with relatives in the countries most of interest. Immigrants without such complicating ties are likely to be more removed from those countries. A former CIA station chief gave examples of Arab and Latino Americans whose accents and dialects gave them away when they were dispatched to the Middle East or Cuba.[6]

For similar reasons there have been limitations on the capacity to digest and use information that does get collected. Years after September 11, despite putting a higher priority on translating intercepted communications, documents, and other items, the FBI still had massive backlogs of untranslated material. The bureau failed to meet hiring targets for translators in more than half of fifty-two languages checked in a report by the Justice Department inspector general.[7] Contrary to the parochial assumption made by Americans, the role of English as the international language is growing at best among business elites, not middle- or working-class populations from whom revolutionary foot soldiers are drawn. As two NSA officials have noted, "The use of native languages in international communication is growing both on and off the Internet."[8] Intelligence needs not just people who have studied Arabic, Pashto, Urdu, or Farsi, but those who are really fluent in those languages and fluent in obscure dialects. Beyond that, the need is for people who are also sufficiently literate, energetic, and scrupulous to translate with reliable accuracy. Some languages, for example, have constructions that cannot be rendered directly in English but that determine understanding of crucial elements in a message—such as exactly which members of a group are going to blow up an embassy! A cursory translation can lose the point completely, with the reader having no clue that anything might be missing.[9]

Should U.S. intelligence trust recent, poorly educated immigrants for these jobs if they involve highly sensitive intercepts? How much will it matter if there are errors in translation, or willful mistranslations, that cannot be caught because there are no resources to cross-check the translators? Money can certainly help here, by paying translators more and, over the long term, promoting educational programs to broaden the base of competent recruits. For certain critical regions of the world, however, there are not enough potential recruits waiting in the wings to respond to a crash program.

The biggest challenge is to develop a pool of people fluent in the languages of crucial regions who are not just translators but substantive operators and analysts in political, economic, and military issues. It is harder to put confidence in judgments made about situations in alien cultural settings on the basis of information translated into English than it is to rely on the judgment of someone who is genuinely bicultural and more or less at home in that setting. Would we consider an Iranian who does not speak English but relies on translations into Farsi a reliable analyst of developments in the United States? To increase the small pool of public servants with dual expertise in substance and language would require a more ambitious set of incentives in the educational system than has been envisioned. Scholarship or loan forgiveness programs would have to be tailored to induce students not just to major in an exotic language, but to gain fluency—real fluency, not shaky reading knowledge—as a sideline to a major in economics, history, anthropology, or political science.

Disasters prompt demands for quick fixes. To overcome problems like the shortages of human capital, however, the fixes must be long term, and to politicians long-term solutions sound vague and uncertain. Proposals that invoke grandiose needs for systemic change in education and occupational norms also seem to reek of the lamp. But if the United States is going to have markedly better intelligence in parts of the world where few Americans have lived, studied, or where they understand local mores and aspirations better than Mohamed Atta and his colleagues understood ours, it is going to have to overcome a cultural disease. This is the disease of thinking that American primacy makes it unnecessary for American education to foster broad and deep expertise on foreign, especially non-Western, societies. The United States is perhaps the only major country in the world where one can be considered well educated yet speak only the native language. In American secondary schools and universities, requirements for the study of foreign languages did not increase as overall investment in education grew, but instead declined in the late twentieth century. The need to reverse this trend has been recognized, and the government is developing programs to promote language study.[10] But the distance still to go is vast.

The disease of complacent ethnocentrism has even infected the academic world, which should know better. American political science drove area studies out of fashion in the last decades of the twentieth century. Some putatively good departments have not a single Middle East specialist on their rosters, and hardly any have a specialist on South Asia—a region of over a billion people, two nuclear-armed countries with a history of war and unresolved conflict, and swarms of terrorists—yet the same departments can afford a plethora of professors who conjure up models meant to apply globally.

Reforms that can be undertaken easily and quickly will make the intelligence community a little better. To make it much better, however, ultimately requires revising educational norms and restoring the prestige of public service. Both are lofty goals and tall orders, requiring general changes in society and professions outside government. Even if achieved, such fundamental reform will not bear fruit until far in the future.

Analysis

Intelligence faces important gaps in its capacity to gather and use certain types of information. Nevertheless, it has vast information with which to work, often more than the system can use effectively. Money can buy additional competent people to analyze collected information more readily than it can buy spies who can pass for members of Al Qaeda. The cost of a substantial number of additional analysts is also modest in the context of the total intelligence budget, most of which goes to expensive technical collection systems. Pumping up the ranks of analysts is one measure that can make a difference within the relatively short span of a few years.

The U.S. intelligence community has hordes of analysts and hordes of countries and issues to cover. Between the end of the Cold War and the proclamation of the global war on terror, the coverage on many apparently low-priority subjects was only one analyst deep—and when that one went on vacation or quit, the account might be handled out of the back pocket of a specialist on something else. The system rarely guesses in advance which of a number of low-priority accounts might turn into the highest priority overnight (for example, Korea in June 1950, Afghanistan in December 1979, or Al Qaeda with the East Africa embassy bombings in 1998).

Hiring more analysts can be an efficient use of resources in the context of the intelligence budget as a whole, but the payoff for much of what they do may still be low. A half-dozen analysts for some small country might be a good thing if that country suddenly becomes central to U.S. foreign policy, but those analysts need to be in place before they are known to be needed if they are to hit the ground running when the need bursts forth. In most cases there will never be such a burst, and those analysts will serve their whole careers without producing anything the U.S. government really needs. Good analysts, however, will not want to be buried in obscure accounts no one is interested in.

One solution is to make better use of an intelligence analyst reserve corps. This idea has been broached in the past but never developed to full potential. There have been experiments, but without enough satisfaction or confidence in information security to institutionalize an ambitious program. Official initiatives have focused on arrangements for the reemployment of former intelligence professionals, use of military reservists, or keeping civilians in other professions on retainer to do unclassified work.[11] These stop short of a full reserve system comparable to that of the armed services. In the more ambitious model, civilians with other jobs would have regular security clearances and spend weeks or months on active duty for training if they are not former intelligence professionals. Thereafter, they would come in for a weekend or so each month to maintain currency by reading reports from the field and other accumulated intelligence on their accounts. They would also be available for mobilization on a full-time basis if a crisis erupts.[12] Hesitancy to go this far has been due in part to worries about providing access to classified information to too many part-time personnel. The vast number of cleared consultants in other foreign affairs agencies, the new imperative to emphasize information sharing over information security, and the norm that the reserve corps focus primarily on low-priority issues all are grounds for taking the risk involved.

A standard recommendation for reform of the analytic system—one made regularly by people discovering the problems for the first time—is to encourage "out of the box" analyses that challenge conventional wisdom and consider scenarios that appear low in probability but high in consequence. In principle this is the sort of intellectual shake-up that might have led the intelligence system, rather than Tom Clancy, to anticipate the kamikaze hijacking tactic of September 11.[13] All well and good. The problem lies in figuring out what to do with the work this exercise produces. There are always several dozen equally plausible dangers that are improbable but possible—as most strategic surprises seem before they happen. How should policymakers be convinced to focus on any of these hypothetical warnings or to pay the costs of taking preventive action against them? One answer is to use such analysis to identify high-danger scenarios for which low-cost fixes are available. If President Clinton had gotten a paper two years before September 11 that outlined the scenario for what ultimately happened, he probably would not have considered its probability high enough to warrant an effort to revolutionize air travel security, given all the obstacles of opposition from business and the irritation of the traveling public. He might, however, have pushed for measures to check the rosters of flight schools systematically and to investigate students who seemed uninterested in takeoffs and landings.

The intelligence failures of 2001–2002 spurred strong efforts to improve methods of analysis and to find mechanisms and practices for overcoming psychological sources of faulty assessment. The intelligence community in the past few years has undertaken a breathtaking array of training programs, conferences, and experiments aimed at making analysts confront unconscious biases and unscientific habits of mind. These have included exercises that bring together experts from diverse disciplines traditionally unconnected to intelligence, such as anthropology, business, medicine, and philosophy. It will take some years to get a sense of how much these efforts succeed in beating down permanent enemies of intelligence. In any event, while there are many obstacles blocking perfection in analysis, the good faith of the managers responsible for the process is not one of them.

Approaches to change discussed so far do not evoke universal support. When compared with many other proposed solutions, however, the controversies they pose seem modest. Deeper constraints on reform come from the political context in which solutions are offered.

THE NEW POLITICS OF INTELLIGENCE

Disasters and scandals have generated impulses to reform intelligence at several points over decades. Public dismay focuses on apparent incompetence or illegitimate activity. As blame is being assigned, partisan incentives to exploit controversies or to conceal blunders draw the intelligence profession into the political maelstrom. But political points are scored by painting issues in broad swaths of black and white while the real choices are to be found among shades of gray. Political heat risks provoking changes that respond more to partisan conflict than to the needs of intelligence itself. At the same time, the urge to prevent corruption of intelligence by politics encourages reforms that could remove management so far from the political arena that intelligence ceases to be effective in informing policy.

Professionals and Politicians

When strategic intelligence was a national political issue in the past, partisan alignments kept the controversies within bounds. After Pearl Harbor, executive commissions and congressional investigation revealed mistakes and charges of cover-up that critics tried to use against Franklin Roosevelt in the 1944 election. But by the time the full story was out, FDR was dead, the war was won, and the country had moved on.[14] Conspiracy theories about dereliction regarding Pearl Harbor roiled Republican and isolationist opponents but gained no traction in the broader public.

In the 1960 presidential campaign, John Kennedy attacked the Eisenhower administration for allowing a "missile gap" favoring the Soviet Union. He did so, despite administration denials, on the basis of alleged intelligence that turned out to be wrong. (There was indeed a gap, but in favor of the United States.) Once in power, Kennedy had nothing to gain from calling attention to the error of his earlier charge, and the

Republican opposition no longer had to defend the Eisenhower record. The issue died.

In the mid-1970s, investigations by the Rockefeller commission, the Church committee in the Senate, and the Pike committee in the House led to CIA, FBI, and NSA misdeeds being splashed across national headlines. The main controversies concerned covert operations and abuses of civil liberties rather than the accuracy of information and analysis about America's enemies. Moreover, the lurid revelations tarred several administrations of both parties. To fuel his anti-Washington campaign for the presidency, for example, Jimmy Carter combined the sins of intelligence and policy in a three-word mantra of indictment of a decade of mistakes and misdeeds: Vietnam-Watergate-CIA. The legacy of the controversies of the 1970s was the suppressing of legal or moral abuses more than boosting the functional effectiveness of intelligence.

The one-two punch of terrorist attacks and the war in Iraq put the focus squarely back on effectiveness, spawned a gaggle of official investigations, and increased partisan tensions in the oversight process. On the September 11 disaster, the two congressional intelligence oversight committees reported jointly on their investigation at the end of 2002. After that the national 9/11 commission was established under Thomas Kean and Lee Hamilton. Its work was delayed by the slow pace of executive compliance with its requests for evidence. The commission's application to extend its original May 2004 deadline so that it could complete interviews and review documents became a political football. On Iraq, Democrats and Republicans on the Senate Intelligence Committee wrestled with whether their investigation should be limited to the mistakes of agencies in producing intelligence or should also consider the handling of intelligence by political leaders in the Bush administration before they finally demanded documents the White House wanted withheld. To contain the gathering storm over invisible Iraqi WMD, President Bush was finally pushed into appointing a blue-ribbon commission under Judge Laurence Silberman and Senator Charles Robb to investigate intelligence performance, with its report coming after the 2004 presidential election.

Previous investigations reined in overzealous activism by intelligence agencies. The focus of overlapping inquiries in the early twenty-first century, in contrast, was on how to get the agencies to do more, how to optimize intelligence collection and assessment, how to use information correctly, and to whom responsibility should be assigned for failing in these tasks before September 11, 2001, and the 2003 invasion of Iraq. Better production and better use, however, are distinct issues. Those who wanted to score political points against the Bush administration naturally emphasized misuse of intelligence by the president and his political lieutenants, while those who wanted to get the administration off the hook for the disasters on its watch naturally blamed the intelligence bureaucracy for failing to provide good information. This situation put intelligence professionals in the middle, threatening their perceived nonpartisanship, an image vital to their effectiveness over time.

If intelligence personnel back up White House claims that presidential actions were correct, they are seen by the opposition party as administration toadies who will need to be put in their place when power changes hands. If top policymakers are backed into a corner and have to defend an initiative that events have made suspect—such as the mission to rid Iraq of WMD—subordinate intelligence bureaucrats can be blamed for misinforming them. If the professionals defend themselves by showing that they produced the right information but it was ignored or misrepresented by the administration, they alienate the people for whom they work, which can only cripple their ability to function effectively. When intelligence failures become matters of partisan feuding, intelligence professionals cannot avoid being buffeted in the search for accountability.

Failure to intercept the September 11 hijackers fixed attention on whether warnings were or were not provided by the intelligence community. One revelation that threatened to become politically potent was that in August 2001 the president's daily brief (PDB)—the supersensitive digest of current intelligence presented to him each morning—warned that Al Qaeda might mount an attack using hijacked aircraft. The existence of this report did not justify indicting the president. Many inconclusive warnings of potential dangers are usually sprinkled in with the flood of information going to high officials in times of tension, without any indication of which are more likely or any evidence about which are worth the diversion of scarce resources to counter. This warning, which appeared much clearer in hindsight, could have been embarrassing, depending on how explicit it was. Controversy flared over the White House's refusal to release the PDBs to the 9/11 commission and its insistence on restricting access to limited portions of the documents for a few of the members. While the White House claimed executive privilege for the documents, critics pointed out that PDBs in previous administrations had often been shared with numerous people, apart from the president.[15]

The longer-lasting imbroglio was over the quality of intelligence behind the administration's unequivocal claim that Saddam Hussein possessed stocks of chemical and biological WMD (see chapter 5). The extent of the blame for the mistaken October 2002 NIE that should be levied on the professionals or on the politicians depends on matters that are too arcane to be politically salient, viz., the nature and extent of the caveats and warnings about the limitations of the evidence that were and were not included in the estimate. These subtleties and nuances could not be fully judged in public, since only part of the NIE was declassified, and they are not the stuff of hardball politics anyway.

Rectitude or Responsiveness?

Intensified politicization dramatized the question of how close the chief of national intelligence should be to the president. Some argued for legislation to give the director of national intelligence a fixed term of office like the director of FBI or the chairman and members of the Joint Chiefs of Staff. This would ostensibly reduce the odds that the DNI could be co-opted by the administration to support its agenda. If the alternative to this statutory protection is a weak-willed intelligence chief truckling to a manipulative president, the idea makes sense, though it would come at a cost—a drag on the potential contribution of the intelligence system to high-level decision making. The typical problem in whirlwind policymaking at the top of government is less often the misuse of intelligence than the failure to use it. Having all of the most objective information in the world will not matter if the president and his inner circle operate without giving serious attention to it, and they will not pay much attention unless they interact frequently and have rapport with the intelligence leadership. Critics who saw politicization by the political leadership as a problem cited the role of the special Policy Counterterrorism Evaluation Group set up in Rumsfeld's Pentagon to search for connections between Al Qaeda and Saddam Hussein. If misrepresentation of intelligence at high levels is a danger, it can be countered only by a chief of intelligence as close to the president as the secretary of defense is.

The ten-year term of the FBI director is not a promising model, since it has not proved clearly preferable to standard political appointment. The main charge against the bureau after September 11 was not that it was politically compromised but that it was too insulated and unresponsive to demands from outside that it match its ingrained orientation to law enforcement and criminal prosecution with equal concern for intelligence gathering to support counterterrorism. The era of J. Edgar Hoover is also a caution against institutionalizing longevity in office. Hoover's practical independence from a series of presidents did more harm than good to the objective of ensuring the legality and political propriety of FBI activities.

Nor are the Joint Chiefs of Staff a good model. Although they have four-year terms, they work under the secretary of defense, a prime political appointee. The secretary can bridge the communication gap between the politicians and the professionals, ensuring that military expertise and concerns get through to the top even when the president does not know or trust the generals. The DNI is not a secretary of intelligence, however. If the public expects a shake-up of hidebound intelligence organizations, it will take presidential muscle, applied unrelentingly through a trusted manager of the intelligence system, to make it happen. The role of intelligence agencies in executing covert policy operations abroad also makes keeping careful political control of the clandestine service imperative, rather than fostering its independence, buffered by a director of CIA and DNI distant from the president.

Close connection between the president and director of intelligence does pose risks, but without the personal confidence of the president no manager will be able to ensure proper consideration of intelligence in decision making. After the revelation of mistakes over Iraqi WMD, a common criticism of DCI Tenet was that he became too close to the inner circle, was "one of the boys." If the criticism is valid, it is not clear how much worse that problem was than its opposite. The intelligence-policy connection did not work obviously better when Clinton's DCI, James Woolsey, could not even get an appointment with the commander in chief. (Woolsey later declared that he did not have a bad relationship with Clinton—just no relationship at all.)[16] The most common problem of DCIs in doing their jobs was not that presidents corrupted them, but that they rarely cared enough about intelligence to include them in the inner circle of top advisers.

There is a solution to this dilemma in theory, but not in legislation. It requires a president and intelligence director with particular personality traits. The best chief of intelligence is one who has the personal confidence and trust of the president but who delights in telling those in the inner circle what they do not want to hear. This is more easily proposed than instituted, since such a relationship can work only if presidents, in effect, want to hear what they don't want to hear. Intellectuals enjoy challenges to their thinking, in no small part because they are not responsible for achieving results. But politicians succeed by being active and decisive more than by wringing their hands over uncertainties and complexities. Most presidents will not consciously want to be told what accords with their predispositions, but they will appreciate hearing what simplifies their problems. As a practical matter, that will be hard to distinguish from what they want to hear. There is no formula that resolves this tension between the need for a scrupulous DNI who resists co-optation (which increases the risk that intelligence will have less impact in the councils of decision) and the need for a DNI who has the confidence of the political leadership (which increases the risk of succumbing to pressures to get with the administration program).

Political heat from intelligence problems after the invasion of Iraq was stoked by parallel publicity over scandals in America's closest ally. In Britain the controversy over misleading prewar claims about Iraqi WMD was more intense than in the United States. Developments there shook that country's traditionally tight-lipped consensus on keeping intelligence within the shadows of *raison d'état*. The most dramatic example of the British crack-up came with former cabinet minister Clare Short's stunning revelation that the UN secretary-general had been bugged. This apparent breach of the Official Secrets Act followed by a day the government's decision not to prosecute a linguist in British intelligence for revealing other such collection operations. The reform of the intelligence system in the United States was unaffected by this degree of political division over how far the government should go to gather information, but only because the shock of September 11 had not yet dissipated. In an atmosphere of less crisis, a counterattack to buttress civil liberties against the demands of counterterrorism can gather steam. At that point, debate can shift from how to produce greater forward-leaning activism by intelligence agencies back toward how to cut them down to size. In the politics of intelligence there is a long-standing silent battle, periodically public, about how to keep the perceived requirements of competence and integrity from diverging.

After 2003 American politics pitted intelligence producers and consumers against each other in the search for blame. Both inside and outside the Washington Beltway, however, politics demanded reform of the system no matter who was to blame. Although the consensus for reform was more intense than in other periods of scandal and investigation in the decades after Pearl Harbor, it was a consensus without content. Until the 9/11 commission settled on a set of proposals, there was scant agreement about which concrete changes were mandated by the failures of the previous years.

Where do periodic urges for reform lead? Nowhere, unless they are translated into changes of structure and process. While politicians and the public demand change, the solutions on offer from experts push in conflicting directions. In most cases these conflicts stalemate choices, as valid conservative concerns, together with parochial vested interests, underscore the risks in each of various proposals. The result is usually stalled reform. After the Rockefeller commission and Pike and Church committee investigations in the mid-1970s, for example, hardly any legislation resulted, apart from the establishment of permanent oversight committees. In contrast, the failures of 1941 and of 2001–3 revealed such unambiguous threats to security that the risks of continuity seemed too great. Change became politically imperative, but the kind of change needed remained contentious. The result of this gap was that reform legislation at the end of 2004 included significant structural adjustment but left fundamental issues unresolved.

RED TAPE, REORGANIZATION, AND RESISTANCE

Reform in a bureaucracy means reorganization, reorganization means changing relationships of authority, and that means altering checks and balances and the balance of power within government institutions. Radical reform not only alters checks and balances, it washes many of them away to clear obstacles blocking the path to action. Disaster makes radicalism respectable; indeed, expected. Five days after September 11, DCI Tenet issued a directive that was leaked to the press. In it he proclaimed the wartime imperative to end business as usual, to cut through red tape, and "give people the authority to do things they might not ordinarily be allowed to do. . . . If there is some bureaucratic hurdle, leap it. . . . We don't have time to have meetings about how to fix problems, just fix them."[17] Such refreshing activist rhetoric was the appropriate spirit for the time, but it was not a solution that could be institutionalized.

Sweeping away obstacles is risky because they block bad action as well as good. As Herbert Kaufman reveals in his classic essay, *Red Tape*, most administrative obstacles to efficiency do not come from mindless obstructionism.[18] The sluggish procedures that frustrate one set of purposes have usually been instituted to safeguard other valid purposes. Red tape is the natural offspring of checks and balances. More muscular management to speed up action will help some objectives and hurt others. Sometimes, bureaucratic and political resistance to change comes from pure blindness or narrow self-interest, but at least as often from a proper concern to avoid damage.

In what follows there are four main points. First, proposals for major reorganization of the intelligence community are not at all novel, but they never got far until 2004. The reasons for this failure to follow through with recommendations for radical change have something to tell us about the prospects for progress from the 2004 legislation. Second, reorganizations sometimes produce benefits, but they always have costs. The risk of reorganization is hard to justify unless the anticipated benefits are substantial and likely. Third, the new main issues for reorganization are variations of the question in the last epochal reorganization in the 1940s: Should the system be centralized and streamlined or should it be pluralistic and redundant? Crises like Pearl Harbor and

September 11 promote arguments for centralization, but day-to-day concerns about various government functions work in the other direction. Fourth, the reform process tends to be dialectical. Changes usually create new problems and highlight the importance of old values that had been slighted by the reform. This recognition eventually pushes the pendulum back toward earlier priorities. If a reform is to find a reasonable synthesis, it needs to take account not only of what it will make function better but of how it will cope with negative side effects. Synthesis or balance is defined concretely in changes in organization and procedure.

Lay readers may be put off by the acronyms peppering the prose below. The political and administrative dilemmas of organizing intelligence functions, however, can be truly grasped only by grappling with the nuts and bolts of alternate institutional arrangements. Speaking a modicum of bureaucratese is the unavoidable price of entry to meaningful debate about intelligence reform.

What's Wrong with Reorganization?

The crying need for intelligence reorganization is a perennial lament, amplified every time intelligence stumbles. Some proposals are adopted, usually with mixed results. Many go nowhere, sometimes because of unwarranted parochial resistance, but sometimes because their benefits do not promise to outweigh their costs.

Inventories of major recommendations for reorganization after the establishment of the intelligence community in 1947 reveal between fifteen and twenty sets of official proposals (depending on which are counted as important) by high-level commissions, congressional committees, and elder statesmen engaged as consultants.[19] Some of these were implemented in part, and numerous internally generated reorganizations, major and minor, occurred in the community's first fifty-odd years.[20] No one ever stayed satisfied with reorganization, however, because it never seemed to do the trick, if the trick is to prevent intelligence failure. To some this pattern of episodic reorganization must reflect a lack of imagination in diagnosis or incompetence in implementation.

Most proposals are not even attempted. For example, Amy Zegart reports that between the end of the Cold War and September 11 there were "six bipartisan blue-ribbon commissions, three major unclassified governmental initiatives, and three think-tank task forces," in which "the common theme was the need for major change." Barely 10 percent of the 340 recommendations in these efforts were adopted successfully, and almost four-fifths "resulted in no action at all."[21] In the view of many outside critics, this frequent lack of response to recommendations just reflects political irresponsibility or bureaucratic constipation.

Incompetence and lack of imagination have plagued attempts to find the right organization for intelligence, but these are not the most important reasons for inaction. Reorganizations privilege some concerns over others. When this rights a badly mistaken set of priorities, the net result is a good thing, but there is still a loss to some objective that must count in the balance. Most reorganizations amount to two steps forward and one step back in terms of a unit's effectiveness across its range of missions. When the transaction costs of change are added to the mix, the net result can sometimes come closer to a wash.

If a reorganization is significant, its transaction costs are likely to be significant. Disrupted work reduces output as offices move, records get lost, new procedures are confused, lines of authority become tangled, unanticipated complications thrust new responsibilities onto unprepared subunits, and staff spend chunks of their workdays figuring out where the bathrooms are. If the net benefits of reorganization are significant, the start-up costs can be accepted as the price of improvement; if the benefits are modest but long lasting, the costs diminish as they are amortized over time. But if the reorganization does not clearly move more steps forward than back, its benefits are dubious. For example, when William Casey became Ronald Reagan's DCI, he was frustrated by the organization of CIA's analytical directorate under functional rubrics because he wanted one office to which he could go for everything on the Soviet Union. Rather than deal with offices of economic, political, and strategic research, each with regional subunits, he shifted the structure to one of regional units with functional subunits. Perhaps this helped on balance. It is unclear, however, whether evidence shows that the change produced consistent improvement in analytical products. And in any case, even a proponent of the change admitted that "the rate of output of products slowed in early 1982 as managers and analysts tried to come to grips with the new ground rules for formats and new approach to programming."[22]

In other cases, reorganization experiments may prove obviously inadequate, giving rise to another reorganization not long after. Then the effect of the change is clearly negative. Rufus Miles, one of the most astute observers of government structure and process, captured the issue in a compelling comparison:

Traumatic reorganizations may be analogized to surgical operations. It is important that their purposes be carefully assessed and a thoughtful judgment reached that the wielding of the surgical knife is going to achieve a purpose that, after a period of recuperation, will be worth the trauma inflicted. And the surgical knife should not be wielded again and again before the healing process from earlier incisions has been completed. Yet this is what sometimes happens in government reorganizations. . . . Repetitive reorganization without proper initial diagnosis is like repetitive surgery without proper diagnosis.[23]

One form of change avoids shuffling boxes back and forth on the organizational wiring diagram; that is, the simple elimination of whole units or procedures judged to be unnecessary. Many professionals suffocating under the inertia of the sprawling intelligence bureaucracy, and bearing daily witness to waste, sloth, and gridlock, frequently recommend streamlining the system. For example, writing shortly before the 2004 reform legislation, Richard Russell noted that analysts at the working level had "about eight bureaucratic rungs" between them and the DCI and that the review process was an unwieldy "inverted pyramid."[24] Better to cut away layers and fences to make collection and analysis quicker and sharper, to catch up with the networked nature of the twenty-first century information system and leave behind the sluggish hierarchies of the twentieth.

The problem with this urge is in weighing the benefits of leanness against the losses of coverage and the cautionary checks on fast-and-loose action. If lots of chaff is tossed out, some wheat is bound to go with it. Thinning out the ranks or the paperwork will usually open up new risks. The message of popular anger over September 11 was the need to maximize coverage of problems, to prevent information on dots that might be connected from being overlooked. The message of dismay over mistaken estimates of Iraqi WMD was that analysis must be more careful and avoid jumping to conclusions. Responding to these messages systematically would multiply activities and checks and balances—thus, personnel and organizational complexity—rather than trim them.

In truth, bureaucratization is both the great weakness *and* the great strength of the U.S. intelligence community. The weaknesses are obvious, as in any large bureaucracy: various forms of sclerosis, inertia, pettiness, and paralysis, which drive out many vibrant people and deaden the spirits of many who remain. The strength, however, is taken for granted: a coverage of issues that is impressively broad and often deep. Bureaucratization makes it hard to extract the right information efficiently from the mass of it tucked in various nooks and crannies of the system, but in a leaner and meaner system much less will be available to be found. If the priority is taking action no matter what, a streamlined system is better. If the priority is taking action only after the best efforts to be sure that it is the right action, the price is red tape.

Centralization vs. Pluralism

The 2004 reform legislation pushed the intelligence community toward centralization. This was not a novel departure, only the latest move in a long struggle. Since World War II, management of the modern U.S. intelligence system has been pulled in opposite directions by attempts to integrate intelligence functions under one coordinator and by the insistence of government departments—especially Defense—that they maintain control of their own intelligence units.

Demands for centralization to remedy the fragmentation that contributed to Pearl Harbor led to the creation in 1946 of the position of director of central intelligence, to coordinate activities of the various departmental intelligence agencies, and the Central Intelligence Group (CIG), to staff this function. President Truman's directive gave the DCI "the right to inspect the operations of the intelligence services of the departments," but only with the approval of those departments.[25] Four years later the in-house history of CIA recorded that "the thought that the director might invade the precincts of the departments was revolutionary. The provision was for the future. It still is."[26] One might reasonably say that it still was more than a half century later.

Because CIG's coordination function was hobbled by military resistance to sharing data and by State Department insistence on providing its own analyses directly to the president, CIG became a producer of intelligence itself. Having been created to reduce duplication, CIG came to increase it.[27] With the National Security Act of 1947, CIG became CIA, which grew into the premier national intelligence organization, while the departmental intelligence agencies continued as they had, and multiplied. Ever since the founding, tension remained between the responsibility of DCIs to coordinate and integrate and their authority to control resources and assignments for agencies beyond CIA. As the Aspin-Brown commission reported a half century after the National Security Act, "Today intelligence remains the only area of highly complex government activity where overall management across department and agency lines is seriously attempted."[28]

As with Pearl Harbor, the failure to connect the dots before September 11 reignited demands for centralization. The 9/11 commission's diagnosis was that "the agencies are like a set of specialists in a hospital, each ordering tests, looking for symptoms, and prescribing medications. What is missing is the attending physician who makes sure they work as a team."[29] The 2004 legislation that replaced the DCI with a new DNI responded to the renewed push for centralization. The DNI's document presenting the first official national intelligence strategy declared that "transformation of the Intelligence Community will be driven by the doctrinal principle of integration."[30] In both cases of major moves toward centralization—the National Security Act of 1947 and the Intelligence Reform and Terrorism Prevention Act of 2004—assignments of greater responsibility to the DCI, and later to the DNI, were not matched by grants of command authority over all intelligence agencies (which as of 2006 numbered fifteen in addition to CIA). In between, the DCI incrementally gained greater budgetary authority over the community as a whole, and centralization progressed fitfully.

In the run-up to the 2004 legislation, some promoted the Goldwater-Nichols Act, which reorganized the Defense Department in 1986 and strengthened the role of the chairman of the Joint Chiefs of Staff in relation to the military services, as a model for imposing coherence on the intelligence community. This was not an apt analogy, however, because all of the military organizations that became more integrated under Goldwater-Nichols were in the same department, in the hierarchy under the secretary of defense. Unless intelligence reform created a secretary of intelligence, and transferred the intelligence arms of the other cabinet departments to a new Department of Intelligence, the Goldwater-Nichols model would not hold. A single intelligence department would be unworkable because line departments—especially the military—need in-house intelligence capacity to support their planning and operations. No political will has ever been demonstrated for forcing the armed forces to rely on external civilian agencies for what they consider core functions.

When it comes time to implement mandates for centralization, the drawbacks become more noticeable. Centralization improves efficiency by reducing redundancy and waywardness among organizations, but it is just those inefficient qualities that foster diverse views and challenges to any single orthodoxy. Pluralism fosters disorder, but centralization suppresses diversity and innovation.[31] Some resist centralization on principle. Lt. Gen. William Odom, a former director of the National Security Agency, recommended reform that would beef up the National Intelligence Council but get rid of much of CIA's Directorate of Intelligence. On balance this would boost the influence of departmental intelligence.[32]

If decentralization spawns inefficiency and duplication, that is not all bad. Overlapping responsibilities reduce the odds of gaps in coverage and generate contention that is sometimes productive. National intelligence estimates that must reflect the judgments of numerous agencies with different perspectives are less likely to overlook or dismiss alternative interpretations of evidence. (For example, recall the October 2002 NIE on Iraq's WMD, which would have had even fewer challenges to its bottom line had it not included dissenting interpretations on some points from the departments of State and Energy.) Disputes among agencies also force issues to the surface for attention by higher authorities who would otherwise remain unaware of important uncertainties. Pluralism makes intelligence production more like a marketplace of ideas, while centralization is more conducive to narrowing interpretations toward a single party line.[33] Richard Posner criticized the recommendations of the 9/11 commission on intelligence reform for focusing too much on preventing "a more or less exact replay of 9/11" and argued that "since the tendency of a national intelligence director would be to focus on the intelligence problem du jour, in this case Islamist terrorism, centralization . . . could well lead to overconcentration on a single risk."[34]

With definite advantages of different sorts in both centralization and decentralization, the natural urge is to have it both ways. Less than a hundred pages after making the case for a single strong coordinator, the report of the 9/11 commission tilted in the other direction, endorsing "a decentralized network model, the concept behind much of the information revolution."[35] Analysts of organization understand the need for both qualities in complex systems of this sort. As Rovner and Long suggest, "In order to deal with complexity and the unforeseen, the system should be decentralized to give operators or analysts latitude in thinking and problem solving. At the same time, the tight coupling requires centralization to ensure prompt and coordinated response." But because it is necessary to exploit both forms does not mean that it is possible to do so. "These demands are incompatible, so no optimal organizational solution exists. Charles Perrow relates the frustration . . . [of] officials from the nuclear industry: 'We could recognize the need for both; we could not find a way to have both.'"[36]

To those committed to having both, better mechanisms for coordination are seen as the solution. Indeed, the role of the old DCI, and of the new DNI, has always been defined as being the coordinator of the intelligence community. Intuitively, coordination is the middle ground between centralized command and decentralized anarchy. But because coordination is not command, it cannot resolve real conflicts of interest or mission, and a coordinator's preferences can be resisted. The main obstacles to integration of intelligence are not simple bureaucratic self-aggrandizement but differences in statutory responsibilities. The Defense Department has the primary mission of planning and fighting wars, and it seeks to optimize intelligence assets for those purposes; the FBI's primary mission is law enforcement, which traditionally required segregating certain types of evidence; and so on. "Where conflicts result from clashes in statutory missions or differences in legislative mandates, they cannot be reconciled through the magic of coordination," observes Harold Seidman. "Too often organic disease is mistakenly diagnosed as a simple case of inadequate coordination." Moreover, "Coordination is rarely neutral. . . . Inevitably it advances some interests at the expense of others." To seek relief from the tradeoff between decentralization and pluralism through coordination is "the search for the philosopher's stone."[37] This uncomfortable reality made the reform legislation of 2004 problematic from the start.

Shaking Down the New Structure

The main change in the 2004 reform legislation was the replacement of the old director of central intelligence by the new director of national intelligence. For those skeptical about the reorganization the main questions were whether the new office would amount to more than an added layer of bureaucracy and whether the DNI would be stronger or weaker than the DCI had been. Answers to these questions depend largely on development of the DNI's relationships with the Pentagon and the CIA. The intent of the legislation was to strengthen the top intelligence official's influence over the first and to weaken it over the second. If the latter were to happen while the former did not, the net result would be a step backward, since CIA has been the main counterweight to military intelligence.

One reason that skeptics saw creation of the DNI position as less revolutionary than advertised is that few people outside the intelligence community, or even within the wider national security community, understood what the old DCI was. From the beginning the position had been legally designated as responsible for coordinating the activities of all government intelligence agencies, *in addition to* being the director of the Central Intelligence Agency. As the intelligence community burgeoned over the years, adding huge organizations like the National Security Agency (NSA), Defense Intelligence Agency (DIA), National Reconnaissance Office (NRO), and others, the DCI remained the official responsible for knitting their functions together. His ability to do so was always limited, but it increased periodically. For example, President Ford extended the DCI's authority over resource allocation and beefed up the intelligence community staff, and Carter extended the budget authority further and created additional deputies to the DCI, as well as a national intelligence tasking center. Similar incremental changes and organizational experiments occurred over the years. Yet hardly anyone but professionals within the intelligence community fully understood that there *was* a DCI distinct from CIA. Indeed, not just the press but even presidents and government officials uniformly used to refer to the DCI not by that title, but as director of CIA, as if he were simply an agency head, forgetting the importance of the larger coordinating responsibility. And few who pushed creation of a DNI (an idea that long preceded the 2004 legislation)[38] reflected on the fact that the old DCIs could have had about as much centralizing authority as a DNI if presidents had wanted to buck the policy departments and give it to them.

What always held the DCI's authority short of what it could have been, and incommensurate by some measure with the office's responsibility, was the Pentagon. About four-fifths of the functions and resources of the intelligence establishment have always been within the Department of Defense, where primary lines of authority and loyalty run to the armed services and the secretary of defense. There is nothing surprising about this. In all major states it has always been assumed that the primary function of intelligence is to support the military's readiness for war and its capacity to wage it effectively. Indeed, in most countries, foreign intelligence is the exclusive preserve of military organizations. U.S. intelligence evolved to a broader purview during the Cold War, but the first priority never changed even after the Cold War. In the 1990s even increased priority was given to the mission of support for military operations (SMO) for the whole intelligence establishment, civilian agencies included. This was odd, given that military threats to the United States after the Cold War were lower than at any other time in the existence of the modern intelligence community, while a raft of new foreign policy involvements in various parts of the world were coming to the fore. But the SMO priority was the legacy of the 1991 Persian Gulf war and the problems in intelligence support felt by military commanders, combined with the Clinton administration's unwillingness to override military preferences.

The test for the significance of the DNI's new authority lies in how much he or she controls the activities of NSA, DIA, NRO, or other defense intelligence agencies. In the period before and after the 2004 legislation, Secretary of Defense Rumsfeld was not preparing to cede any authority in this realm. Instead, the Pentagon was expanding the activities of the military in collecting human intelligence and conducting covert operations, traditionally core functions of CIA, and was increasing the secretary's own control of the military intelligence establishment.[39] This was reflected organizationally in the creation of an undersecretary of defense for intelligence, bureaucratically a much higher position than usual for coordination of these functions within the department. (For one brief period in the Ford administration there had been an even higher official charged with overseeing intelligence: a second deputy secretary, Robert Ellsworth.)

The most decisive change of management would be to take several of the agencies out of Defense and place them directly under the DNI. A review by the President's Foreign Intelligence Advisory Board under Brent Scowcroft reportedly recommended this early in the administration of Bush the Younger. Implementing a proposal this revolutionary would leave Capitol Hill and Pennsylvania Avenue awash in blood. Moreover, while moving control of the Pentagon's intelligence units would strengthen the DNI, it would not produce efficiency. It would almost certainly end in expensive cloning. The military services will never accept dependence on other departments for performance of their core functions, which include tactical intelligence collection, and politicians will not override military protests that their combat effectiveness was being put at risk. The least implausible political compromise would split up the several agencies in question, giving some of their elements to the DNI and leaving some in Defense. Then, without fail, the lost units would reappear within the Pentagon under other names and programs.

Consider what happened in the 1960s when the secretary of defense tried to rationalize and consolidate military intelligence, by transferring duplicative activities of the three separate army, navy, and air force intelligence agencies to the newly created Defense Intelligence Agency. The result was more redundancy. The services soon regenerated most of what they had lost so that one could barely tell the difference between their agencies before and after creation of DIA. This was not necessarily all bad; the standard defense of organizational overlap is that "a lap . . . is better than a gap."[40] This time around, however, redundancy in high-technology collection systems would present a radically bigger price tag than duplication of human collection and analysis functions—in a period when the exploding budget deficit puts brakes on the big defense spending increases that sailed through in the wake of September 11.

Without dramatically increased control over Defense Department intelligence, the DNI's loss of direct control of the CIA would make the office weaker, not stronger, than the old DCI. This point was lost on those who campaigned for splitting the two jobs. A common criticism was that one person could not do both jobs well, since the incumbent tended to get swallowed by the job of running CIA. Another was that the overall coordinator of intelligence should not be partial to one particular agency above others in the community, and directing CIA would bias the DCI in its favor. CIA's assets, however, were the main source of institutional support for the DCI, the only troops at his own command. For example, when George Tenet attempted to build up the Counterterrorism Center (CTC) in the 1990s, he was criticized for staffing it disproportionately with CIA personnel. After September 11 CTC was criticized for lacking sufficient resources to integrate intelligence across the community. Tenet drew on CIA, however, because he met resistance from the various outside departments to his requests that they assign their own personnel to the center. If he had not been able to draw on CIA at will, the CTC would have been even weaker.

CIA's Directorate of Intelligence has also been the only large corps of analysts independent of the departments with line-operating responsibilities, and it is therefore free of pressure to support the policy preferences of parent departments. It is natural for the top manager of the intelligence community to rely disproportionately on such independent analysis. (Even Secretary of Defense McNamara chose to rely more on CIA's Office of Strategic Research than on his own departmental intelligence units because he considered CIA analysis more objective.) This autonomy from departmental missions should have secured CIA's position as the *central* agency, at least the first among equals, but many politicians as well as other members of the intelligence community have regarded the agency simply as one among many producers, with no legitimate claim to superior status.

In the new framework, the only analytical assets initially placed under the DNI's direct supervision were the National Intelligence Council (NIC), which was primarily responsible for developing national intelligence estimates, and the new National Counterterrorism Center (NCTC) and National Counterproliferation Center. The DNI can maintain as much leverage over analysis as the old DCI had by only three means: siphoning staff from CIA to expand the NIC, creating more centers like NCTC for other issues, or treating the director of CIA (who under the 2004 law reports to the DNI) as a deputy, and exerting as much day-to-day control of the agency as the old DCI did. The latter approach would vitiate the intent of the reform law. Creating more centers, in turn, risks excessive focus on old problems and opening up larger gaps in coverage of less obvious potential problems. This had already happened to some degree under the old system, when the DCI built up centers like CTC. One official postmortem on the failure of intelligence regarding Iraqi WMD attributed uneven performance in significant part to "the community's tendency to establish single-issue centers and crisis-response task forces. By stripping expertise from regional offices, they diminish the overall ability to provide perspective and context."[41]

Delicate Balance or Pendulum Swing?

Reforms respond to the latest mistake. Conservatives who resist, on grounds that change will hurt more than help, are usually seen as the problem. The interests the conservatives worry about, however, usually have some merit. The problem is that in intelligence, like other difficult tasks, all good things do not go together. An optimal solution must somehow synthesize competing concerns or produce a delicate balance between them. Sometimes this is not recognized, and a reform grabs only one horn of the dilemma. Or when a reform tries to strike the proper delicate balance, circumstances make it hard to hard to maintain the balance. As a result, priorities and patterns of error tend to shift back and forth as addressing one problem aggravates another. Consider a few examples.

In the late 1950s, intelligence assessments overestimated the size and rate of growth of Soviet long-range striking capability in the illusory "bomber gap." A few years later, claims of a missile gap emerged, and these, too, were soon shown to be wrong. By the 1960s, intelligence estimators had been burned twice, caught in what appeared to be false alarmism. This undoubtedly had something to do with how the community then handled uncertainty in predicting the rate of Soviet intercontinental missile deployment. Throughout the 1960s, NIEs consistently *under*estimated the rate. Even air force intelligence, typically the most alarmist, predicted numbers below what turned out to be real.[42] More recently, the chastening experience of the mistaken judgments on Iraq's WMD led estimators to require higher standards of evidence and greater caution in reaching conclusions about threats posed by Iran. This in turn led conservative critics to charge complacency. Where liberals had chided intelligence for exaggerating Iraq's threat, former Speaker of the House Newt Gingrich complained, "The intelligence community is dedicated to predicting the least dangerous world possible."[43]

Over the past several decades, the most politically sensitive changes have related to covert activities, primarily political intervention, but including clandestine collection. In the first half of the Cold War, a period of ample consensus for an activist U.S. foreign policy, CIA's covert activities became extensive and energetic. Domestic intelligence collection by the FBI and even by military intelligence was substantial. The scandals of the 1970s highlighted abuses in both types of action and put the brakes on them. Public and congressional skepticism about covert activities peaked soon afterward, however, and with the Cold War revivified in the Reagan administration restraints on clandestine activities were loosened again. Then in 1995 a scandal broke involving a Guatemalan officer who had been a paid informant for CIA and was involved in covering up the murder of an American citizen. This triggered the imposition of additional standards and review processes for recruiting informants and led to purging the rolls of CIA sources with problematic criminal activities on their résumés. Concern with improving intelligence for counterterrorism, however, pushed back against the new limitations, and after September 11 the new restraints were limited and then rolled back.[44] Which way the pendulum moves is likely to depend on which shocks dominate public consciousness: another scandal about unsavory associations or another successful terrorist attack.

William Casey's desire to focus intelligence organization on regions rather than functions has been noted here. After September 11, however, critics complained that the community was too regionally oriented and should organize more in terms of functional issues. Establishment of new high-powered centers on counterterrorism and nonproliferation under the DNI reflect this shift. Whenever transnational terrorism slips from the most urgent priority, and conflict grows with another major country such as China, however, an urge to reemphasize organizing in terms of regions is likely.

The failures of 2001 and 2003 elicited a chorus of complaint that analysts had become completely absorbed in current intelligence, leaving no time for research projects that look beyond the horizon. Writing for the president's daily brief had become the overwhelming priority, but such a focus shortchanges the understanding that would come from fleshing out the context that makes current intelligence more informative. As Paul Pillar, one of the top experts on terrorism in the intelligence community, has argued, "Because terrorism is an epiphenomenon of broader political and social developments, to forecast terrorism requires the forecasting of many of those developments."[45] One of the Iraq WMD postmortems charged that the quality of analysis had been damaged by the priority that had been placed on short-range support to policy: "This shift seems to have had the result of weakening elements of the analytic discipline and rigor that characterized Intelligence Community products through the Cold War."[46] With the 2004 reform, priorities were officially adjusted, as the new DNI made "long-term and strategic analysis a part of every analyst's assigned responsibilities."[47]

It was not the first time the pendulum had swung on this issue either, as noted in chapter 4. In the earliest days of CIA, incentives to publish in the president's daily summary and weekly publications were so high that long-range analysis was squeezed out.[48] In subsequent years this overemphasis was rectified, and the imperative to focus on the present was contained by creating an Office of Current Intelligence (OCI) in CIA which enabled other offices to do deeper, long-range analysis. Over the years the offices of political, economic, and strategic research turned out numerous in-depth assessments on a wide range of topics.

Consumers, however, often resist research papers and demand more current intelligence. By the 1970s, much of the analysis produced by the intelligence community was criticized by policymakers as academic and irrelevant to their needs. (One high-ranking veteran of both military intelligence and the National Security Council staff once quipped to me in the 1980s that CIA's analysis was "a bunch of verbose answers to questions nobody asked.") Their skepticism is understandable because the comparative advantage of the intelligence community, when matched against analysts outside government, lies in bringing together secret information with open sources. The more farseeing a project, the less likely secret information is to play a role in the assessment. No one can match analysts from CIA, DIA, or NSA for estimating what Al Qaeda might do in the next month. But what is their advantage over Middle East experts in think tanks or universities for estimating worldwide trends in radical Islamist movements over the next decade? By the 1990s, in any case, management was pushing to make intelligence production "customer driven." Current intelligence had again been elevated to the overwhelming first priority, OCI had been abolished, and current intelligence was considered the responsibility of all organizational units.

In the response to the mistaken national intelligence estimate on Iraq's WMD, the pendulum swung back. DCI Porter Goss told John Kringen, the head of CIA's Directorate of Intelligence, that the priority of current intelligence had become excessive.[49] As longer-range strategic analysis becomes the established imperative again and its profile grows anew, issues of politicization will come to the fore because no trenchant interpretations of high-priority problems can escape political coloration and suspicion of bias. Critics will weigh in either way—because analysis has done too much uncontroversial, CNN-style, up-to-the-minute reporting or has become embroiled in partisan assessments of high policy.

In response to consumers' chronic complaints that NIEs were equivocal mush, intelligence producers sometimes try to make them sharper. Ironically, this was done explicitly in the October 2002 estimate on Iraq. The acting chairman of the National Intelligence Council wanted to avoid using mealy-mouthed qualifiers such as the words *maybe* or *probably* in the key judgments to keep the estimate from seeming to be useless "pablum."[50] After the disaster of that estimate, caution, admission of uncertainty, and communication of disagreements among analysts, rather than emphasis on consensus, became the watchwords. The heads of the reorganized intelligence community, DNI John Negroponte and his deputy, Michael Hayden, encouraged "a higher tolerance for ambiguity" than had been the norm as well as stricter procedures for establishing levels of confidence in conclusions.[51] This will make estimates more ponderous and equivocal again. Analysts trying to avoid the October 2002 sort of mistake will become risk averse, like doctors worried about being sued for malpractice who order extra medical tests of dubious necessity in order to cover themselves. It will be no surprise if, within a decade, consumers will again be complaining about the mushiness of intelligence products, and producers will be moving to make them punchier.

Surveying the shifts back and forth of the past fifty years, it would be foolish to bet that the 2004 reform legislation found the right balance for good. Professionals are ahead of politicians in recognizing the need for balances between conflicting aims, but there is no consensus on what mechanisms or mandates will strike the right balance and keep it. If delicate balances are impossible to maintain, we are condemned to cyclical pendulum swings, as events come to reveal the costs of tilting in either direction. This is not necessarily bad if we have a modest standard for what to expect from intelligence, but it will periodically frustrate those who believe that lasting solutions to mistakes in intelligence can be found.

Reorganization may still be a proper response to failure, if only because the masters of intelligence do not know how else to improve performance. The greatest underlying causes of mistakes in performance, however, lie not in the structure and process of the intelligence system. They are inherent in the issues and targets with which intelligence has to cope—the crafty opponents who strategize against it, and the alien and opaque cultures which are not second nature to American minds.

7 / WHOSE KNOWLEDGE OF WHOM?

The Conflict of Secrets

Secrecy is the enemy of knowledge. That does not make it bad, since knowledge is not always good. Whether it is good or bad depends on who has it. It is good if we know things that others are trying to hide and bad if they know things we want to hide. In popular political debate we usually think of lines being drawn between those who favor secrecy and those who oppose it, but this dichotomy obscures the depth of the problem. Everyone favors secrecy and everyone opposes it, depending on whose secrets are at issue.

In the politics of intelligence secrecy is usually debated in terms of the government's interest in concealing information versus the public's right to know. Edward Shils argues that liberal democracy rests on promoting privacy for individuals but rejecting it for government. He also recognizes that *"raison d'état* as a barrier to publicity and a generator of secrecy attained its maximum power in the domain of foreign policy and, above all, of military policy." He considers this a problem.[1]

Interests in concealing information cannot be neatly pigeonholed. Although the government guards secrets to keep adversaries in the dark, it has an interest in reducing secrecy when it interferes with the effective correlation and exploitation of information. In the wake of September 11, the imperative of breaking down walls of classification and compartmentation became the watchword of intelligence reform. Journalists fight against official secrecy on the grounds that the public has a right to know what the government is doing, but they fight tenaciously to protect their own secrets when their right to conceal the identity of their informants is challenged. Citizens, in turn, question government secrecy when it appears to conceal official misconduct or incompetence, but they value secrecy greatly when it keeps their personal lives free from scrutiny. The right to privacy means the right to personal secrecy, which limits the government's right to know. Privacy is traditionally popular with both the liberal Left and the libertarian Right.

My characterization of privacy as secrecy will not make sense to some because secrecy has a pejorative connotation. It is useful, however, to focus on the question of standards for limiting access to information—standards for keeping government secrets or personal secrets. In what follows, the term *privacy* refers to the limitation of the government's means of acquiring knowledge of individuals' associations, communications, and activities. This usage is not fully consistent with the legal concept of privacy, which involves more complex rights of personal autonomy, which in turn are linked to rights of due process of law. In this chapter I argue for de-linking rights to privacy from those guaranteeing due process. Readers are forewarned that throughout this chapter my arguments are meant to make sense in terms of political and strategic logic and may sometimes conflict with accepted legal ideas.

The analysis here does not pretend to determine what is or is not permitted by existing statutes or the Constitution. The courts and Congress sort these questions out. Some of my arguments may require stretching traditional legal interpretation if they are ever to be implemented, and that may prove impossible in practice. A political and strategic argument separate from consideration of the practical and legal obstacles is relevant nonetheless. When the political and moral context of legislation and judicial interpretation changes in dramatic ways, even established precedents can be overturned. The Constitution is sufficiently ambiguous or silent on some aspects of these problems that if the pressures on adjudication change, the political imperatives of the day could impose the reading of it that would be necessary to justify whatever statutes might be needed to undertake actions deemed strategically necessary.

The balance of risks that politics and policy establish among conflicting legal and strategic concerns shifts back and forth over time. In principle, how should the balance between conflicting rights to secrecy be struck for the long haul? What safeguards in practice should prevent the pendulum from swinging too far in any direction? Combining liberty and security involves a large array of questions about classification of information, oversight within government, constitutional checks and balances, rights of citizens, responsibilities of the state, and abuses of authority. This chapter reflects on only a few aspects of these issues that bear on the adequacy of intelligence for national defense. How should intelligence for national security be combined with civil liberties and personal security? How should policy and law adapt to each other? How can restraints on sharing intelligence information be loosened to improve analysis and warning, without making sensitive information available to adversaries?

INTELLIGENCE COLLECTION AND CIVIL LIBERTIES

There is a world of difference between the problems of collecting intelligence abroad and at home. All U.S. intelligence operations must conform to U.S. law, but that law leaves operations outside U.S. territory relatively unconstrained. When doing their jobs abroad, American agents may break the laws of the countries in which their operations are undertaken. They may give money to political parties, plant bugs in defense ministries, bribe legislators, tap the phones of diplomats, and do all sorts of things to gather information that the FBI could not normally do within the United States, at least without a court order. More intrusive collection inside the United States would have done the most to boost the chances of averting the September 11 attacks. Great changes in that direction may make Americans fear that the costs exceed the benefits—indeed, that if civil liberties are compromised, the terrorists will have won.

The unique responsibility of intelligence collectors is to penetrate enemy secrecy, to uncover information that adversaries try to conceal. Since spies or terrorists pose as innocents, *maximizing* collection of *potentially* useful information means that intelligence collection becomes a fishing expedition, and that most suspects made subject to surveillance and searches are innocent. To minimize intrusion against innocents, as well as to target intelligence resources efficiently, collection is not maximized, at least in situations short of immediate threats to national survival. Normally, only those who present some substantial cause for suspicion have been subjected to surveillance. How substantial that reason must be—or whether large numbers of innocent people should be observed to determine which among them are suspects to be scrutinized—are matters of regular political and legal debate.

Critics of aggressive government intrusion often cite a famous warning by Benjamin Franklin. In congressional debate on the USA Patriot Act, for example, Senator Patrick Leahy cited the gist of what Franklin said as "If we surrender our liberty in the name of security, we shall have neither." As Michael J. Woods points out, however, "Franklin's actual words are more nuanced. . . . 'Those who give up *essential* Liberty, to purchase a *little* temporary safety, deserve neither Liberty nor Safety.'"[2] Whatever Franklin meant, security and liberty can go together, but only if each is compromised *to some extent* to protect the other.

Priorities Among Liberties

There are two big mistakes one can make when confronted by the trade-off between national security and individual liberty. One is to deny that there is such a trade-off. The other is to embrace it without qualifying which specific aspect of liberty is at issue, instead lumping all liberties together. The first mistake, common only among the most fervent supporters of individual rights, denies the trade-off because it is psychologically unacceptable to admit that good things do not all go together. If forced to admit the trade-off, some zealots insist categorically that civil liberties must always take precedence over security, that if any liberty is sacrificed for the sake of combating terrorists, the terrorists will have won, or that any contraction of liberty is the camel's nose in the tent that portends the collapse of the Constitution. This sort of thinking is a recipe for dangerous constraints on the government's ability to gather intelligence, especially the type that offers the best hope of foiling terrorist plots.

The second mistake is more common: the assumption that the trade-off is between collective national defense and individual civil liberties, period. Thinking in terms of a dichotomy makes it much harder to strike a balance. Civil liberties should not and need not all suffer for the sake of security, because liberties are not all of a piece. The most legitimate trade-off is not between security and liberty in general, but between security and privacy, the one aspect of liberty that inhibits the government's acquisition of information. Limiting the government's knowledge of one's life and activities is an important freedom, but not the most important one. There is no need to compromise the more important elements of civil liberties having to do with freedom of speech, political organization, religion, or especially the right to due process of law—the freedom from arbitrary arrest and incarceration without the chance to contest one's guilt. Having one's phone tapped without proper cause is not as damaging as being imprisoned for years without trial. I argue that it is more vital to keep within strict interpretations of the limits for the First and Fifth amendments in the Bill of Rights than for the Fourth Amendment. This argument is another that does not have support in the jurisprudence of the Constitution, which recognizes no hierarchy of rights; it is asserted as a practical matter of common sense, not as accepted law.

Zealots at both ends of the spectrum are allied against compromisers. (Consider one set of strange bedfellows: the American Civil Liberties Union has "entered into an alliance, called Patriots to Restore Checks and Balances, with conservative groups such as Grover Norquist's Americans for Tax Reform, Phyllis Schlafly's Eagle Forum and the Citizens Committee for the Right to Keep and Bear Arms.")[3] Libertarian absolutists mimic the National Rifle Association. Like ardent proponents of the right to bear arms, they see even a limited concession as the first step in the unraveling of all privacy rights. Supporters of highly intrusive intelligence collection, on the other hand, too often rest their case on such a breathtaking assertion of presidential powers that any significant improvement in the public's sense of security, or a change of administration, is bound to produce an antiauthoritarian backlash. The compromise argument in this chapter tilts toward liberty on the issue of due process and away from it on the issue of privacy. The latter part of the argument relates to intelligence: It is reasonable to invade the privacy of some citizens in order to gain information that might help to protect the lives of all citizens.

This compromise of one aspect of liberty ultimately serves to protect liberty and the rule of law in general. In the Constitution, life comes before liberty. Life without liberty is possible, but liberty without life is not. Without security, few Americans would be grateful for liberty. This is not readily apparent at most times—and the proposition strikes some as authoritarian alarmism—because Americans have habitually taken basic security for granted. They rarely give even a fleeting thought to the tremendous protection afforded the United States by its geography, the two huge ocean moats to the east and west and weak neighbors to the north and south. Indeed, it was the assumption of basic security by most Americans that made the Al Qaeda attacks such a shock to them, even though they caused damage no greater than many counterterrorism specialists had been warning about for a long time.

If those on either side of the debate insist on lumping all civil liberties together in a trade-off with national security, liberty comes out on top in the competition only as long as Americans are spared more attacks on the scale of September 11. Even then, some compromises of liberty remain, as represented by the USA Patriot Act and by congressional acquiescence to warrantless surveillance programs by the National Security Agency (NSA). If September 11 fades into history and terrorists manage only occasional, small provocations, political tides may roll back some of those constraints on freedom. Experience of more dramatic attacks, however, especially ones involving chemical, biological, or radiological weapons, would sweep away most concern for civil liberties in a panic. It is important to differentiate types and priorities of liberties so that they do not get thrown out wholesale in an emergency. It follows that it is also important to do so in order to facilitate intelligence collection that would raise the odds of preventing just the sort of emergency that could produce the panic. In short, reducing a bit of liberty today buttresses a lot of it tomorrow.

Does this exaggerate the risk that vital freedoms could be jettisoned when much greater insecurity puts them under pressure? Not at all. Consider how big a dent was put in privacy and due process just by September 11. The strikes against the World Trade Center and Pentagon were a milder shock than biological weapons attacks that might kill tens or hundreds of thousands would be. If such attacks were attributed to an alienated group of Muslims living in this country, demands for preventive detention of Muslim Americans would hardly remain unthinkable. Recall the internment of Japanese Americans during World War II. Although this event came to be seen, decades after the defeat of Japan, as an aberrant miscarriage of justice rooted in a racist past, it was practically uncontroversial during wartime. More to the point, the Supreme Court decision in the *Korematsu* case upholding the action has never been overturned. In 1983 Korematsu's individual conviction was reversed because of false information in the government's case. The factual basis was overturned in a *coram nobis,* "error before us," decision, but the legal point was not readdressed, so the Supreme Court decision technically stands. Before September 11 this was probably among the cases that, although never officially overruled, are universally recognized to be without continuing validity. Yet, if desperate circumstances were to create political demands strong enough, its technical standing could become effective as a precedent, allowing jurists to accede to a repetition.[4] If the Supreme Court decision upholding internment of Japanese Americans can remain standing, it should not be impossible to put the arguments here for less drastic measures to compile information about Americans into law if they are deemed necessary.

One might believe that all this is a moot point, since after September 11 the American system tilted clearly toward the compromises of privacy endorsed here. But the tilt in favor of permissive rules for surveillance and searches is vulnerable to reversal because the Bush administration based its actions in implementing some of them on the overriding of an existing statute, the Foreign Intelligence Surveillance Act (FISA). Stretching the interpretation of legal authority to an extreme is not a solution, irrespective of its damaging effect in subverting the basis of constitutional government. If policy is pursued extralegally because of panic, it is likely to be rejected when alarm subsides. Standards that are to survive for the long haul must be found between the libertarian absolutists and the champions of unlimited presidential authority in wartime.

Although the system tilted against civil liberties in the trade-off with security after September 11 (as it did in several wars), some of that tilt was the wrong kind—depriving American citizens of due process of law. Abuse of this sort threatens to discredit desirable compromises of privacy rights when times get better. As the war on terror developed, however, public debate reflected the wrong priorities. Aspects of the Patriot Act allowing the scrutiny of library records, for example, generated as much protest as did the imprisonment of American citizens without trial.

The Wrong Tilt

Immediately after September 11, hundreds of aliens were detained and questioned in the United States, and many were deported. These round-ups and the conditions of confinement were controversial for critics on the left, but the arrests were temporary and deportations were based on immigration violations. The imprisonments were terminated within months. In the years that followed, dozens of people, many of them U.S. citizens, were held without trial as material witnesses, sometimes for two months or more. Other American citizens who claimed to be businessmen mistakenly suspected of anti-U.S. activity were arrested in Iraq and held in military prisons for long periods.[5] If these were abuses, their duration was limited. The most troubling cases, however, were those of U.S. citizens or legal residents imprisoned as unlawful combatants, without recourse to the courts, for prolonged periods. The most prominent case involved José Padilla, arrested in 2002 on U.S. soil not for committing a violent act but for allegedly having a plan to build and detonate a radiological weapon in a city. Padilla was held for three years without trial, without a chance to contest his guilt in court. (Facing the prospect of a judicial ruling against Padilla's imprisonment without trial, the government eventually changed the accusations, charged him, and put his case into the courts.)[6]

The national security rationale for denying normal rights of due process to citizens in these cases was weak. Attorneys for the executive branch did convince the Fourth Circuit Court of Appeals that giving Padilla the right to contest the accusations against him could materially aid Al Qaeda, but the only reasonable grounds were that a trial could damage intelligence sources. In cases of this sort, the courts may not ultimately rule in favor of the basic right of a defendant to see and contest evidence, but the intelligence problem should not be used as an excuse to imprison a suspect indefinitely. Procedures should be adopted so that secrets can be protected in a legal proceeding that compels the government to prove the suspect's guilt. This is not easily done in any manner that does not compromise the traditional constitutional rights of the accused, but compromised rights to due process are better than none at all. The defense could be allowed to confront secret evidence using procedures similar to those in deportation cases that provide for defense counsels with security clearances to see and challenge evidence.[7] Denying the right of the defendant to see the evidence would have to be conditioned on proving that doing so would reveal a specific and important intelligence source or method that would be lost as a result—not simply that the defendant would learn something classified. Constitutional issues and legal differences between immigration and criminal cases might keep such solutions in the realm of theory. But either the legal impediments must be overcome or some risk has to be taken with the demonstration of the evidence to strike a reasonable balance in the trade-off between security and liberty.

Experience, as well as principle, precludes justifying a tilt against due process by assuming that the executive's prerogative to imprison suspects indefinitely without charge will not lead to gross injustice. One need look no further than the case of Capt. James Yee, the hapless Muslim army chaplain at Guantanamo who was arrested on suspicion of espionage in 2003. Because Yee was not denied access to judicial procedures, his lawyers were able to probe the evidence and demolish the case against him (although the government did not concede his innocence, even after removing punishment as mild as a reprimand from his record).[8] He was tried not on the original charge of concern to national security, but for adultery. Had authorities been able to hold Yee without trial, he could have been locked away as long as Padilla.

The strongest version of the argument here applies to U.S. citizens but might concern others as well. Philip Heymann notes that the Bush administration consistently maintained "that the location at which a non-citizen is held, the battlefield conditions under which he was seized, the absence of uniform, or a threat to willingly cause civilian deaths will preclude any significant form of judicial review for almost anyone whom the administration suspects of involvement with terrorists." Yet even Israel when facing the intifada had a supreme court that exerted some judicial review over actions against Palestinians. Heymann says that "though our danger is far less than the danger Israel faces, our willingness to abandon the most fundamental judicial protections of personal security has been far greater."[9] (The most difficult issues in this regard were posed by the indefinite imprisonment of suspected enemy combatants at Guantanamo and their trial by military tribunals, but this important set of problems is not considered here.)

Not all customs of due process should be sacrosanct. For example, the demolition of the so-called wall between criminal law enforcement investigations and intelligence collection missions after September 11, allowing the FBI to pass information from the former to the latter in ways not previously permitted, was a good change in policy. But the main point is that the most fundamental right of being presumed innocent until proven guilty need not be abandoned. Protecting American security does not require putting suspects in dungeons and throwing away the keys. Without secure rights to due process in the face of accusations that one is an unlawful combatant, all Americans are vulnerable to the whim of any overzealous president.

Threats to Privacy vs. Threats from Privacy

It is not so vitally important to risk security for the sake of all other civil liberties. The main argument here is in the other direction, in favor of compromising privacy rights for the sake of national security. Personal secrecy is valuable and should be respected when it does not endanger American lives, but it is not as vital as the right to freedom from imprisonment without trial. The government's discovery of embarrassing details about one's personal life may be undesirable, but it does not deprive one of the more essential freedoms.

Unlimited rights to privacy would threaten the ability of the government to gather intelligence that could be important in detecting and blocking enemy plots. Terrorists in particular have one basic advantage: the capacity to conspire—to mobilize, coordinate, and plan destructive activities under the cover of secrecy. Privacy provides some of the necessary secrecy. If terrorists were able to lower the odds of having communications intercepted by police and intelligence services, and if they were safer from police searches of their property, they could conspire more effectively and the odds that they could successfully execute attacks would improve.

Minimizing limits on intelligence collection would not assuredly prevent disaster, nor can it be proved that reduced intelligence collection would produce more attacks. The easier it is to get information from people who are trying to hide it, however, the better the odds that authorities will get some useful information about plots in time to break them up. If terrorists know that the government has the authority for it, surveillance also provides some deterrent effect and complicates and retards the coordination of plots by inhibiting prompt and efficient communication among plotters. If aggressive invasions of individual privacy for the sake of intelligence collection were to save, say, ten lives in a decade, would that limitation of civil liberties be legitimate? If not, would saving one hundred lives justify such a shift? One life? How many saved lives would warrant major compromises of privacy? The problem, of course, is that it is impossible to know how many lives, if any, will be saved by intrusive intelligence collection. Given that uncertainty, however, it is preferable to err in the direction of saving lives than of maximizing privacy.

Consider the case of Zacarias Moussaoui, who was ultimately convicted and sentenced to life in prison for his involvement in the September 11 plot. The joint congressional investigation concluded that because the FBI had problems applying for FISA warrants during the summer of 2001, there was "a diminished level of coverage of suspected al-Qa'ida operatives in the United States." Some surveillance operations against Al Qaeda suspects stopped because authorizations expired and the FBI did not want to apply for renewal because of uncertainty about the accuracy of their case. "Most of the FISA orders targeting al-Qa'ida that expired after March 2001 were not renewed before September 11," according to the joint congressional investigation. The complications in the FISA process at the time, the "thicket of procedures" and "the wall between intelligence gathering and law enforcement," effectively reduced the chance of interdicting the plot.[10] The FBI did not seek a warrant to target Moussaoui, despite the facts that he was enrolled in flight school and that French intelligence had warned that he was a radical. As a result, his computer was not searched until after September 11. It is by no means certain that intense surveillance of Moussaoui before that day would have revealed the plot—that possibility was cited by the prosecution in his trial as grounds for requesting the death penalty—but at the very least it would have connected a few dots and increased the chances of following clues back to the nineteen hijackers.[11]

The hesitation to mount aggressive surveillance and searches in this case was not absolutely required by law. It developed naturally alongside the highly developed set of legal safeguards rooted in the traditional American reverence for privacy and the additional restraints inspired by abuses of domestic intelligence gathering in the first half of the Cold War. Hindsight makes clear that this constraint should have been loosened. (The National Commission on Terrorism realized this more than a year before September 11 when it recommended that the Office of Intelligence Policy and Review stop applying standards more stringent than those required by the FISA statute when approving applications for electronic surveillance.[12] Like the other good recommendations by the commission, it was not adopted before September 11.) If the argument that the restraint of surveillance should have been loosened before September 11 is persuasive, it should remain loosened as long as outside enemies of consequence remain at large. High standards for protecting privacy are like strictures against risking collateral damage in combat. They take precedence more easily when the security interests at stake are not the survival of one's own people but become harder to justify when they are.

Erring on the side of security rather than privacy makes fishing expeditions attractive, although there are legal barriers to promiscuous surveillance. Effective counterterrorism, however, requires fishing. Judge Richard Posner criticized demands for court warrants for eavesdropping on the grounds that they require, in effect, that the government know in advance who the terrorists are. "The challenge is not to track down known terrorists," he said. "It's to find out who the terrorists are."[13] Standards for deciding who is a legitimate target should be based on a combination of indices that are empirically correlated with service to a foreign power or support of terror tactics. To some this raises the specter of "racial profiling." It is profiling, make no mistake, but not racial profiling. It does not mean targeting anyone solely on the basis of ethnicity—for example, Arab Americans. Instead, proper profiling should rely on a combination of indicators correlated with past cases of espionage or involvement with terrorism. Nationality or religious practice might be included in a set of several actuarially relevant indicators but would not in themselves suffice to trigger investigation.

Any permissive standards for surveillance will worry civil libertarians fearful of the slippery slope toward abuse. For example, controversies developed over reports that the Census Bureau disclosed demographic data on Arab Americans to the Department of Homeland Security and that the FBI and Department of Energy were conducting radiation monitoring of mosques and Muslim businesses to detect possible radiological weapons. The FBI claimed that its actions were based on intelligence leads and patterns associated with Al Qaeda activities, not with Muslims per se.[14] This is where the delicacy of balance is hard to manage, but the answer to the problem is to work on the delicacy, not to abandon either concern.

Until the mid-1970s, effective legal constraints on domestic intelligence collection were weak. Congressional investigation revealed abuses in targeting activists in the civil rights and anti–Vietnam War movements, or other questionable targeting of individuals under programs such as the Huston Plan, COINTELPRO, Operation Chaos, and others.[15] Constraints were tightened, most notably in the Foreign Intelligence Surveillance Act of 1978, which institutionalized the special process for obtaining warrants for surveillance within the United States.[16] There were also so-called attorney general procedures governing legally sensitive aspects of intelligence collection, including "minimization procedures" for handling personal information acquired as a byproduct of legitimate collection. After September 11 the tide moved back in the other direction, diminishing privacy, as recommended here. More intrusive information gathering is controversial, but if it helps avert future attacks it will also avert more severe blows against civil liberties. Americans should remember as well that many solid and humane democracies that have had more permissive rules for collecting information on people than Americans have had seem to live with them without great unease. After the shift toward more intrusion after 2001, the problems became how to keep policy and law in conformity and how to institutionalize safeguards to prevent abuses of power as the government acquired domestic information more freely.

POLICY AND LAW

The policy pendulum swung away from privacy after September 11 and can swing back. If there is hope for establishing some enduring balance between liberty and security, rather than periodic overcorrections, it is vital to have policy and law in alignment, lest disrespect for legal constraint come to undermine intelligence collection once again, as it did in the 1970s. The Clinton administration was timid about pushing policy up to the limits of the law on matters of intelligence operations. The Bush administration was careless about keeping operations within the limits of law. These are the tendencies between which the norm for balance should be found.

The New Permissiveness

When regulation of counterintelligence activities was tightened after the revelation of abuses in the 1960s and '70s, concern arose that FISA warrants for surveillance not be used to get around protections in criminal law. This concern led to establishing the wall between counterintelligence and criminal investigations. An unintended consequence was that counterintelligence officers were deprived of certain kinds of information. With September 11 came the recognition that the wall was not actually required by law and that the constraints on sharing information between criminal investigators and intelligence were a policy choice encouraged by cautious attorneys. In 2002 a special federal appeals court ruled that the USA Patriot Act had eliminated the wall, and that it had never been necessary.[17]

The rules for maintaining the wall were developed in the 1980s but codified in the Clinton administration. On other aspects of intelligence, particularly the authorization to kill Osama bin Laden, the Clinton administration was particularly hesitant about pushing to the limit of legal constraints.[18] Relevant legal changes loosening limitations nevertheless did occur in the 1990s—the Antiterrorism and Effective Death Penalty Act of 1996 was one—but many more constraints were put aside after 2001.[19] Conventional wisdom became, as Gen. Michael Hayden said when nominated to be deputy director of national intelligence, that "intelligence agencies needed to push 'right up to that line' established under privacy laws in using eavesdropping."[20] Debate continued over where the legal line was and should be.

When national security letters originated in the 1970s, they were for examining commercial records in investigations related to espionage and terrorism, but they were used "as narrow exceptions in consumer privacy law." By 2005, however, the FBI was issuing "more than 30,000 national security letters a year."[21] These permit scrutiny and compilation of data from telephone calls, banking transactions, credit reports, and so on. Among the most controversial initiatives was the provision of the Patriot Act authorizing the government to examine library records. (The provision was not used in the years after passage of the law, but the same purpose was accomplished with the use of national security letters.) Investigation of library records had long been allowed in criminal cases, but on the basis of the probable discovery of evidence of a crime. Section 215 of the Patriot Act relaxed that constraint by changing the standard of "'specific and articulable facts giving reason to believe' that the target is an agent of a foreign power to a standard of 'relevance to an authorized investigation to protect against international terrorism or clandestine intelligence activities.'"[22] This exemplifies the shift away from requiring probable cause and toward encouraging fishing expeditions that is the essence of my argument.

In the years immediately following the act, government agencies sparked protests about privacy rights when they developed plans to amass data on university students and to track mail going to and from people who were the subjects of intelligence investigations. The former initiative moved toward the pre–September 11 recommendation of the National Commission on Terrorism to establish a system for monitoring the status of foreign students.[23] The intelligence rationale was, in effect, that if an Iranian student admitted to an American university to study English literature switches her major to nuclear physics, the U.S. government should know. The second initiative had a counterterrorism rationale but dredged up memories of CIA's illegal program of opening mail to the Soviet Union, which spurred the congressional investigations of the intelligence community in 1975.

What is most novel about the new initiatives against privacy is the emphasis on data mining, the systematic collection and correlation of large amounts of information on economic transactions and common means of communication, with the aim of finding patterns that highlight certain individuals as potential suspects. Such intelligence does not reveal the content of the communications or the substance of the transactions, but it may provide clues as to who has an interest in threatening activities. "Transactional" information is potentially valuable because "terrorists can limit their exposure to the interception of the content of communications by using counter-surveillance techniques" but cannot as easily cover their tracks in telephone company call records, bank wire transfers, credit card purchases, and so on.[24] Computer technology made such searches more feasible in recent times, but they had been inhibited by privacy norms.[25] This approach to collection is in effect a systematic fishing expedition. Mining records to find patterns of association or action is a preliminary step to deciding who to target as a suspect for closer investigation. The rationale is that in selecting the indices for correlation in a pattern it is better to find too many potential suspects than too few. "Although the number of false positives in pursuing terrorism could be reduced to a very small number by increasing the number of items in the pattern until the pattern suggested nothing other than terrorism, the price of doing this would be to increase the false negatives (the 'missed' terrorists) greatly," according to Heymann and Kayyem.[26]

If the imperative suggested by September 11 is centralization of intelligence to connect the dots, data mining is a natural tool. It remained controversial because of images of Big Brother intrusions against privacy. Most controversial was the Bush administration's program allowing NSA to intercept communications without a warrant even when one of the parties was in the United States—a clear contradiction of the FISA statute. As of 2007 the full rationale for the administration's refusal to seek the warrants stipulated under FISA is impossible to evaluate, since details of the program remain classified. Justifications for the administration position included the argument that "FISA, written in 1978, is technologically antediluvian" because the legislation's drafters "had no concept of how terrorists could communicate in the 21st century or the technology that would be invented to intercept those communications." The FISA statute's loophole for emergency wiretaps without authorization, to be followed by applications for retroactive warrants within seventy-two hours, was cited by opponents of the NSA program as obviating the need to dispense with warrants but dismissed by supporters of the program as impossible to implement.[27]

The Bush administration advanced two arguments for the legality of overriding the FISA statute. One was that it was superseded after September 11 by the Authorization to Use Force that was passed by Congress because signals intelligence is assumed to be an element of waging war. The other was that the president had inherent constitutional authority as commander in chief to use such means.[28] Critics countered the first point with the argument that the FISA statute was the more specific law and thus the controlling one. The second argument, they said, implied a breathtaking lack of any limits to the president's prerogative to violate any law if he deemed it necessary as commander in chief in wartime.[29] Holding in abeyance the question of which of the contending legal arguments is valid, the proper solution would have been for the administration to seek legislation amending FISA to allow the warrantless NSA program. Attorney General Alberto Gonzalez said that the administration did not attempt to avert controversy in this way because it doubted that Congress would provide the dispensation.[30] This admission that the program was thwarting legislative will was inconsistent with the argument that the Authorization to Use Force legislation amounted to congressional permission to override the FISA statute. In any case, the argument was hardly a solid basis on which to build a legal regime. But the hesitancy to seek positive authorization was also dubious. The fact that only a single senator (Russell Feingold) voted against the Patriot Act indicates the receptivity of Congress to major reversals of previous constraints on intelligence.

In the political climate of 2006, these controversies were not a major problem for initiatives to reduce privacy. Despite protests in Congress and the media, the administration's position carried without much difficulty. Gen. Hayden, who had initiated the warrantless surveillance program when he was director of NSA, was nominated to direct CIA after the program was revealed. In confirming his nomination with only brief hearings and constrained critical questioning, Congress gave up the opportunity to signal rejection of the administration claim of legality. The administration's success in quashing further legal challenge was confirmed when it refused personnel from the Justice Department's Office of Professional Responsibility the security clearances necessary to pursue investigation of the conduct of the lawyers at NSA who had approved the program.[31]

Within half a decade after September 11, it seemed clear that civil libertarians' emphasis on privacy rights had been trumped by national security concerns. The government's right to know citizens' secrets was under the least constraint in thirty years. In terms of strategic interests in intelligence collection, this development comports with the argument earlier in this chapter. The risk that the pendulum will swing back and reimpose significant constraints on government surveillance will increase, however, if the threat of terrorism recedes, if instances of abuse occur and are publicized, and if power shifts in Congress lead to reaction against the sweeping claims of presidential power on which the Bush administration's legal position rested. The durability of permissive standards for intelligence collection is likely to depend on the credibility of safeguards intended to prevent abuse of the enhanced authority.

Safeguards

The main reasons for restraining government invasion of privacy are to prevent the misuse of information that is unrelated to counterintelligence or to the evidence of a crime, and to prevent overzealous agencies from confusing political protest with threats to national security and from interfering with legitimate political activity. Civil libertarians usually maintain that the way to prevent such abuses is to enjoin the government from undertaking surveillance without probable cause to suspect a connection to a crime. Preventing abuses without giving up the benefits of increased intelligence collection requires establishing effective norms, incentives, and mechanisms for ensuring bureaucratic compliance with legal limitations and for disciplining government abuses. This is not easy to do without vitiating a mandate for enhanced collection, but it is the only way to sustain such a mandate when the dangers of war and terrorism appear to be in remission.

Concerns about abuse have merit. Before the congressional investigations of 1975–76, and again after September 11, intelligence agencies have often targeted groups of Americans engaged in normal political protest and violated regulations for purging personal information irrelevant to security from databases. Many of the recent instances appear to be innocent mistakes owing to new agents' unfamiliarity with details of restrictions, but some were apparently caused by the naïveté of military officials who viewed peace protesters as subversives.[32] As Heymann points out, "Unless there are substantial efforts to be clear, the lines separating mere opposition or permissible dissent in politics from a real internal danger are likely to be crossed by whoever controls intelligence capacities."[33]

One way to contain anxieties about using irrelevant information acquired incidentally is to promulgate strict standards against disseminating such information or using it for purposes other than counterintelligence or counterterrorism operations. Another is to establish severe disincentives for breaking the rules. For example, police or FBI personnel could face firing, heavy fines, or jail terms if they leak information about a suspect's sexual habits or other irrelevant information uncovered incidentally in the course of national security surveillance. A third step is to fortify internal oversight of the bureaucracies that do the domestic collection. The 2004 reform legislation sought to do so by establishing a civil liberties protection officer reporting to the director of national intelligence and a Privacy and Civil Liberties Oversight Board in the White House.[34]

The main point is that *the focus of concern should shift from limiting government acquisition of private information to measures for strictly limiting its use of that information.* Of course, the wall was designed to prevent misuse, but primarily for a purpose other than protecting privacy. The strict limitations endorsed here should concern the revelation of personal information that does not bear on the purpose of intelligence collection. Striking the right balance in rules is hard for interested organizations, but necessary to avoid pendulum swings. This makes the role of oversight organs important, not just pro forma.

Oversight mechanisms do not guarantee strong discipline. Some, such as the Intelligence Oversight Board established in the Ford administration, have occasionally been weak or inactive.[35] If the new organs are to be meaningful, they will have to strike down the behavior of bureaucracies once in a while. Oversight, or sanctions that are effective against violation of rules by intelligence agencies, inevitably increases friction. Bureaucratizing safeguards will exert some inhibiting effects on intelligence collection. That is a fair price to pay if the formal, legal constraints on surveillance and searches can be kept relaxed.

INTELLIGENCE SECRECY VS. INTELLIGENCE ANALYSIS

Intelligence is generally understood as a highly secretive business. We do not want outside enemies to know what we know, and spies or informants must be assured that they will not be exposed. Limiting the distribution of particular secrets to those working on the problem to which they are relevant (what is called compartmentation) is a standard practice to maintain the security of sensitive information. But secrecy has two edges for security. While it protects against the revelation of information, it limits the knowledge of producers and consumers of intelligence. This is the problem that jumped to first place in the conventional wisdom after 2001.

Need to Share

After September 11, intelligence agencies were berated for failing to share information with each other. Because the FBI and CIA kept some bits of information to themselves, terrorists were allowed to slip away from observation, as responsibility for their tracking was handed off from one organization to the other. Analysts lacking full access to data collected outside their own agencies could not efficiently connect dots because there were dots they did not know about. Analysts who did not know who the human sources were could not judge the credibility of the reports they were given and could not make optimal use of the information in them. The compartmentation of information seemed especially retrograde to younger personnel who are accustomed to the Internet as a model of communication and are shocked when entering the intelligence community to find that they have "left a world that was totally wired."[36]

The September 11 experience produced a clamor to make sharing of intelligence the norm. Section 892 of the Homeland Security Act of 2002 directed the president to put in place procedures for information sharing among federal agencies and state and local law enforcement and crisis response organizations. The 9/11 commission recommended that "information be shared horizontally, across new networks that transcend individual agencies."[37] The Silberman-Robb commission charged that CIA compartmentation of sensitive HUMINT reporting remained excessive. It argued that the agency should provide more operational detail about the nature of sources to analysts, and even to policymakers.[38] Six pages of the 2004 reform legislation (Section 1016) were devoted to endorsing improved information sharing and including a program manager to develop a formal information-sharing environment and an information-sharing council to assist the president. The first strategy statement of the new director of national intelligence showcased the intent to "remove impediments to information sharing within the community, and establish policies that reflect need-to-share (versus need-to-know) for all data, removing the 'ownership' by agency of intelligence information."[39] The head of CIA's Directorate of Intelligence announced new emphasis on information sharing between the directorate and the clandestine service and on giving policymakers more detailed information about sources.[40]

The need to share was not discovered for the first time after September 11. Other events have periodically exposed the downside of information security. In the preparation for the 1961 Bay of Pigs operation, for example, both the U.S. military and the analytical branch of CIA were for the most part denied knowledge of the invasion plan to minimize the chance of leaks. As a result, standard military staff work to assess the feasibility of the plan was not done, analysts did not have the chance to challenge the assessment that a popular uprising in Cuba was likely after the invasion, and insulated planning allowed illusions about prospects for the operation to carry the day.[41] The 1966 Cunningham report noted the adverse effects of compartmentation on cooperation across disciplines, and a decade later the Church committee discovered that CIA analysts were kept ignorant of American research and development programs, hurting their ability to assess countermeasures that emerged in the development of Soviet nuclear forces.[42] Pike committee hearings revealed that before the intelligence community was surprised by the October 1973 War in the Middle East, some vital intelligence had not gone to the watch committee because not all members of that warning unit had the necessary clearances.[43] And the staff of the permanent Senate Intelligence Committee blamed compartmentation indirectly for failure to predict the 1973–74 Arab oil embargo and price rise because analysts who were unable to verify the credibility of clandestine sources of information from CIA's Directorate of Operations had relied instead on embassy reporting.[44]

Compartmentation for the sake of information security is a means toward the end of national security. Yet, if the means can conflict with the end so often, why is it not abandoned? Why was adoption of the new directives to increase information sharing so slow that the Government Accountability Office issued a 72-page report concluding that "more than 4 years after September 11, the nation still lacks the governmentwide policies and processes that Congress called for to provide a framework for guiding and integrating . . . efforts to improve the sharing of terrorism-related information"?[45] Part of the reason is normal bureaucratic sluggishness in coordinating complex organizations, but part of it is that information sharing is not the unalloyed good that the latest pendulum swing implied it is.

Need to Know

The more secret information is shared widely by government personnel, the more probable it is that it will become available to adversaries via espionage or leaks to the press. When a revelation includes the sources and methods by which secrets were obtained, new information is lost, as the targets react and stop using the communication systems that were compromised. The benefit of sharing information is thus reduced if the price is having less of it for anyone. In the glare of disasters that followed insufficient sharing, the problem of information security appeared exaggerated. It is not a rare problem, however, as the United States suffers frequent losses of major intelligence.

In the 1980s and '90s the pendulum swung in the other direction in an alarmed reaction to a spate of espionage cases. The Walker family, Aldrich Ames, Robert Hanssen, Ana Belen Montes, Jonathan Pollard, Edward Howard, Ronald Pelton, Larry Wu-Tai Chin, and Felix Bloch were only the most well known. More than thirty Americans who spied for the Soviet Union, Russia, Cuba, China, East Germany, Israel, South Africa, and other countries have been identified since the final years of the Cold War.[46] The frequency of espionage was obscured for some time because in the late 1960s and 1970s the Justice Department stopped prosecuting spies for the most part. Instead, effort went into covering up their apprehension and turning them into double agents. Public awareness also lagged because spies in the military were prosecuted in courts martial with little of the publicity attendant to the civilian judicial system. The Carter and Reagan administrations reversed this trend. By 1985 a dozen individuals were awaiting trial for various acts of espionage. When even more espionage disasters occurred, demands rose in the 1990s for tighter control of information.[47] In sharp contrast to the conventional wisdom after September 11, the report on the Aldrich Ames case by the Senate Select Committee on Intelligence presented two strong recommendations to restrict access to information, including a review of "practices and procedures for compartmenting information relating to clandestine operations to ensure that only those officers who absolutely need access can obtain such information."[48]

Leaks to journalists are usually rationalized as serving the public's right to know, and justified by the journalist's judgment that classification of the leaked information was unnecessary. But nothing ordains that the judgment of either a leaker or a journalist is better than that of the bureaucracy that classified something. Leaks have the same effect as espionage in making secret information available to adversaries. Often the result is harmless, but not always. The best example of a bad mistake was a set of articles in the *Washington Times* in 1998 according to which the United States was intercepting Osama bin Laden's satellite phone calls. Bin Laden and Al Qaeda senior leadership immediately stopped using this means of communication.[49] Another notorious example was the report by Jack Anderson in 1971 exposing U.S. interception of radio-telephone conversations among Soviet Politburo members (including Leonid Brezhnev), which cut off a unique source of highest level intelligence. Even *Washington Post* publisher Katherine Graham once called attention to the cutoff of intelligence from Syrian and Iranian plotters that followed the disclosure that the United States had intercepted their communications in 1983—and to the bombing of the barracks in Beirut that followed five months later and killed 241 Marines. [50]

For reasons cited in the postmortems of September 11 and other intelligence failures, the recent swing in favor of sharing information more widely is more good than bad. The question is where to strike the balance, how far compartmentation should be reduced. In an era of networked computer databases, a traitor can potentially do much greater damage: "In the past, a hostile mole could steal the papers on his desk; now he can steal his own work and everyone else's . . . to which he has access."[51] If cuts in compartmentation are precipitous, whenever another spy scandal on the scale of the one involving Aldrich Ames occurs, there will be an eruption of demands to know why whatever information that was sold to Al Qaeda, Iran, or North Korea had been so easily available to so many, and why damage had not been better contained by need-to-know norms.

In principle the main answers to how to strike the balance are: first, eliminate proprietary control of data; second, limit access to information according to how much its revelation would endanger sources. An agency must not deny analysts of another agency access to the information it holds simply on the grounds that it owns what it has gathered itself. This principle may be hard to turn into practice because of tradition and inertia, but it can be observed if the focus is kept on the second issue.

That is easier said than done. The WMD commission recommended that analysts "become security gate-keepers, revealing enough about the sources for policymakers to evaluate their reporting and conclusions, but not enough to disclose tightly-held, source-identifying details."[52] This is unrealistic because it is too big a responsibility for analysts, especially junior ones. Overcoming the obstacles to change is far more difficult than most reformers realize because the natural default option when risks are uncertain is to overclassify. When it is hard to be sure that a source would not be endangered by the revelation of an item of intelligence, it will always seem safer to limit the odds of disclosure, which means limiting distribution of the item. Only an organ positioned at a high level and held responsible for failures to disseminate widely can overcome that default. The information-sharing council established by the 2004 legislation is the logical unit to promulgate new standards for compartmentation and to make them stick. Whether it succeeds in changing the default option, or whether it atrophies, depends on which new jolts to the system—disasters from revelation of information or from insufficient sharing—get political traction.

Pessimism about how much to expect from intelligence is widespread among those who have studied the history of strategic surprise. Dismal expectations, however, are not accepted by most political leaders, strategists, or normal citizens who demand better. This is as it should be, lest pessimism abet lethargy in efforts to improve performance. After September 11, 2001, change in the intelligence system became politically imperative, although there was no consensus about what the content of the change should be. The dominant sentiment was for more integration to ensure coordination of effort, since coordination had faltered at some crucial points before Al Qaeda's attacks. In the eyes of some critics, the fact that tight coordination was not consistently institutionalized when the intelligence community was formed in the middle of the twentieth century accounts for much of what went wrong ever after.[1]

Confidence in that diagnosis undervalues the adaptive qualities and the checks and balances that are by-products of dispersion and inefficiency. As Robert Jervis says, "A well-integrated system can neither take advantage of unforeseen opportunities nor cope with unexpected difficulties. . . . When unforeseen interactions appear, several alterations are likely to be necessary. The tighter the design of the system, the greater the ramifications of these disruptions."[2] Presidents and legislators have always backed away from maximizing centralization in reorganizations, not just because they were bowing to bureaucratic vested interests, but because they sensed the risks in a complete integration of intelligence. Nevertheless, the principal change in the Intelligence Reform and Terrorism Prevention Act of 2004—the replacement of the director of central intelligence with the new director of national intelligence—embodied the demand for firmer centralization. Yet it still did so with limitations, avoiding unambiguous settlement of longstanding jurisdictional tensions with the Defense Department. For all the sentiment in favor of revolution, Congress proved unwilling to go all the way.

Those informed insiders who propose a revolution in intelligence tend to become ambivalent when they consider the risks. Barger, for example, endorses concurrent revolution and evolution, "parallel processes" and "competing streams of change activity" that combine bold experimentation and gradualism.[3] This is theoretically possible, just as an emphasis on the high-technology forces and strategies of the revolution in military affairs should be able to coexist with old-fashioned, low-tech counterinsurgency in the Defense Department. But such a combination is very hard to manage. It is difficult to turn a system upside down and tweak it at the same time.

The conservative argument in this book derives from the tragic view of intelligence failure, but it definitely does not imply that the problems are hopeless. Conservatism is quite compatible with a search for limited but meaningful improvements. It suggests that the enemies of intelligence cannot be driven from the field, though they may be contained or pushed back. This argument aims to preempt disillusionment, backlash, and a drop in public support for intelligence activity that could result from dashed hopes if more boldly ambitious reform initiatives founder. To be useful, the conservative argument must cope with two main problems. First, critics tend to overlook its qualifications and to see its pessimism as exaggerated and its implications as defeatist. Second, if politicians accept the pessimism of the argument, they may conclude that intelligence efforts should be reduced because they do not provide value worth their cost.

DO BENEFITS BALANCE COSTS?

Some who study "predictable surprises" have a less forgiving view. But they, too, attribute the critical errors more to a lack of response to warning than to a failure to warn. In this view, not only was September 11 a predictable surprise, given the work five years before by the Gore commission (the White House Commission on Aviation Safety and Security), but if major airline security measures had been undertaken, the hijackings might not have succeeded. The failure was in bowing to business pressures to keep expenses down.[4] In hindsight the indictment is incontestable. Before the fact, however, the choices were not so simple.

The problem with predictable surprises is that there are too many of them—too many plausible threats of great consequence whose probability is neither high nor negligible. Undertaking maximum precautions against all of them would court bankruptcy. For example, if Louisiana and the federal government had undertaken every project recommended to cope with the vulnerability of New Orleans before Hurricane Katrina, the estimated cost would have been $14 billion.[5] If all the potential national security threats of low probability but high consequence were listed, the cumulative costs of doing everything possible to prevent or blunt them would be astronomical. And because few of those threats would eventuate in catastrophe, most of the expense would come to appear as waste resulting from alarmism.[6] As soon as one of those threats does become real, however, failure to have invested in all possible preventive measures will be judged as irresponsible. Intelligence services will be judged to have failed if they do not provide actionable tactical warning of the events, even if they provide ample strategic warning of their rising probability.

Other critics charge that an emphasis on the inevitability of surprise is a counsel of despair, that it ignores evidence that justifies more optimism, or that it lets intelligence professionals off the hook with a "no-fault" view of failure.[7] This misunderstands the conservative argument. Asserting that failures are inevitable does not mean that intelligence will *always* fail or that failures will be *complete*. If that were true there could be no reason to maintain intelligence services, since they would provide no benefit to justify their cost. The fatalistic view means simply that a high incidence of some degree of failure is inevitable even if success is also frequent. Nor does belief in the inevitability of surprise necessarily exonerate intelligence officers. No baseball fan who recognizes that batters will often strike out would be said to have a no-fault view of hitting. A batter who strikes out is certainly at fault for failing to be smarter or quicker than the pitcher. Whether the batter should be judged incompetent depends on how often he strikes out against what quality of pitching. A batter with a .300 average should easily be forgiven for striking out occasionally, while one who hits .150 should be sent back to the minors. Nor should pessimism's prediction of severe limits on the improvement of intelligence performance be misread as promising no improvement. A batter may improve his average by changing his stance or swing, and such changes are worth making even if the improvement is small. Raising a few players' averages from .275 to .290 is an incremental improvement, but it could turn out to make the difference in whether the team finishes the season in second place or in first.

Pessimism is not the same as defeatism, but it is naturally a basis for skepticism about the value of an expensive national intelligence apparatus. A budget running at nearly one-tenth of defense expenditures is huge. Within a few years after September 11, it would have taken the liquidation of the entire endowments of Harvard, Yale, and Princeton to pay for little more than a single year of U.S. intelligence activities.[8] If failure dominates the image of the system's performance, public support for high levels of effort in intelligence may falter.

How should the net value of the intelligence system be judged? If the blood and treasure saved because setbacks were averted by good intelligence exceed the blood and treasure spent to get the intelligence, the system pays for itself. But how can one estimate the value of disasters that do not happen? We can speculate about dogs that didn't bark and vulnerabilities that were not exploited by outside enemies because the functioning of intelligence deterred them from striking. To the extent that intelligence is a deterrent, its expense can be justified in the same way that the peacetime cost of maintaining the military is justified. U.S. defense budgets totaled close to $18 trillion (in 2005 dollars) during the Cold War, and the vast majority of the forces generated were never deployed in combat. If there was never any real danger of Soviet aggression, most of that amount could be deemed wasted or counterproductive. If deterrence prevented World War III, however, it was a bargain. In any case, attention usually focuses most on notable intelligence failures. While it is important to understand why frequent failures are inevitable, it is also important to place pessimism in perspective and to judge the record in terms of the ratio of successes to failures.

APPRECIATING SUCCESS

A batting average is an appropriate metaphor for intelligence performance in theory. It is quite impossible, however, to compute an intelligence batting average in reality. Unlike baseball, competition in national security is irregular and the scoring rules are murky.

First of all, what defines success? An assessment that leads directly to blocking a threat or to exploiting an opportunity, such as a warning that would have pinpointed the identity of the September 11 hijackers and the date of their planned attack? Does indirect or incomplete action in that direction count for anything, such as the ample strategic warnings before September 11 that a major attack was imminent? Does the simple transmission of a warning or an accurate assessment fill the bill, or must it be unambiguous and transmitted in a manner to compel action by consumers to rate as effective? Depending on the answers to these questions, a given case could be counted as either a failure or a success.

Second, how should predictions be measured? Secrecy hides success more often than failure. A self-negating prophecy cannot be judged accurate unless the records of the adversary's decision making are bared. If the attack does not occur after the potential victim's intelligence agency issues a warning, is it because the warning caused a cancellation, or because the attack had not been planned and the warning was wrong? For example, U.S. intelligence reportedly warned in detail in 2003 of a bomb plot against a passenger plane, citing the specific company, airport, and date.[9] Nothing happened. Perfect warning or false alarm? A general problem in scoring performance is that any effective intelligence assessment causes leaders to do something, which changes the situation and the facts associated with the prediction. This is a political instance of the Heisenberg observer effect: measuring the phenomenon changes it.[10] Unlike canceled attacks, an attack that occurs after failure to warn admits of only one answer. Failures can be tabulated more reliably than successes, so the record of failure is much more definite and more evident. Successes are also much less publicized, with reports usually buried at the bottom of newspapers' inside pages, often without a byline.[11]

Third, what constitutes a case, or a time at bat, as it were? International conflicts have numerous aspects and phases. Intelligence figures all along the way and may do well in one respect and badly in another. It may do superbly in collection and abysmally in analysis or perfectly in uncovering the crucial evidence on aspects one and two of an issue, while falling down on aspect three. Indeed, the scorecard on most cases of any complexity is likely to be quite mixed.

Inability to compute a systematic average means that judgment about the success-to-failure ratio can only be subjective and utterly unreliable by the standards of a statistician. This does not relieve the umpires of intelligence performance of the need to seek at least some ballpark sense of whether success is frequent enough to make up for the clearer list of failures. One thing that intelligence managers should do to help develop this sense is to keep a rough inventory of cases that appear to demonstrate success in collection, assessment, and dissemination. This has not been done as a matter of course. For example, the product review division (PRD) of the intelligence community staff in the mid-1970s prepared numerous postmortems of intelligence failures in that period, but only one paper on a success. "It was the only such paper ever prepared in PRD and the only one ever asked for."[12] Long ago, Frank Stech paid attention to what constituted the ingredients of success in estimating intentions, but few open-source studies have focused on success.[13] In recent years high-level staff in the intelligence community have taken up the call for more attention to successes, but a half-dozen years into the twenty-first century no coherent rendering of that record has reached the public. One problem is that no thorough compilation can be done in open literature, since some successes inevitably are not reported outside classified government channels. But for a rough sense, at least, that successes are substantial, even if we cannot tabulate their ratio to failures, consider an unsystematic but illustrative list.

In the war on terror, President Bush cited ten terrorist plots that had been foiled in the first four years after September 11, including a plan to destroy the U.S. Bank Tower in Los Angeles, the tallest building in the western United States.[14] By one accounting, in the nine months after September 11, seven terrorist attacks were executed and six were nipped in the bud—a batting average of .462, as it were.[15] Before September 11, plots to bomb the Lincoln Tunnel and other points in New York and to destroy a dozen airliners over the Pacific were also exposed. At the time of the millennium alert, several plots in Jordan, including plans to bomb the Radisson Hotel and religious sites, and a plan by Ahmad Ressam to attack Los Angeles International Airport, were disrupted. "Afterward, the CIA and friendly intelligence services conducted another major dragnet . . . to roll up terrorist cells abroad," according to Daniel Benjamin and Steven Simon. "The results were spectacular: it was the most successful operation against jihadists to date, with cells broken up in more than a dozen countries."[16]

The mistaken estimate of Iraq's WMD before the U.S. invasion was a major failure of intelligence related to nuclear proliferation, but intelligence did much better on other related issues. With a few quibbles about particular deficiencies, the Silberman-Robb commission credited the system with success for uncovering Libya's WMD program and the network for selling nuclear technologies that had been spawned by A. Q. Khan, the leading manager of Pakistan's nuclear weapons program.[17]

Numerous examples of performance are widely recognized as on the mark with regard to big events. A random set of examples includes forecasting the launch of Sputnik, the Sino-Soviet split, China's detonation of a nuclear weapon, the 1967 Six Day War, the India-Pakistan War of 1971, the Chinese invasion of Vietnam in 1979, and Iraq's invasion of Kuwait.[18]

On other issues, success and failure were more mixed.

- The intelligence community monitored the deployment of Soviet military forces with reasonable precision throughout most of the Cold War and provided excellent backstopping for the Strategic Arms Limitation Talks with the USSR in the 1970s, but it fell down in forecasting the rates of deployment of Soviet intercontinental nuclear forces.
- In the biggest crisis of the Cold War, over Soviet missiles in Cuba, the relevant national intelligence estimate was proved completely wrong. However, intelligence collection functioned well in detecting the missiles while they were under construction and in time to allow the U.S. government to deliberate and take effective action to force them out before they could become a fait accompli. On the other hand, again, intelligence collection failed to detect facts that might have yielded catastrophic results if Moscow had not backed down immediately. U.S. intelligence did not know that Moscow "had not only sent 60 nuclear warheads to Cuba for the medium and intermediate-range missile force,

but also 100 tactical nuclear weapons," that an IL-28 bomber squadron "was configured for delivery of tactical nuclear bombs against an invasion force," or that four Soviet diesel attack submarines carried nuclear torpedoes. Nor did American intelligence detect "the extent of Soviet military alert, in particular of Soviet strategic forces."[19] These were facts that would have been crucial matters for the deliberations and risk calculations made by American leaders had they known about them.

• Before the end of the Cold War, intelligence did not give advance warning that the Soviet Union would collapse, though it did provide ample analysis indicating the intractable challenges facing the Soviet economy and the inevitability of major change if Moscow were to avert major decline.[20]

We do not have a comprehensive scorecard, but the point is simply that the fact of frequent failure should not obscure the fact of frequent success. Intelligence often does its job quite well. Although we cannot calibrate a specific return or loss for a given level of intelligence investment, and thus cannot estimate the economic efficiency of the enterprise very well, we can see that some degree of improvement in effectiveness is possible.

KNOWLEDGE, POLICY, AND POWER

These illustrations assume that in most cases we know an intelligence success when we see one. A path to progress, however, should rest on conscious standards for what constitutes good intelligence. This brings us back to the relations among information, understanding, and government action. Worthwhile intelligence must be both true and useful. If it is not true it is irrelevant at best and destructive at worst. If it is true but not useful, it is a waste of taxpayers' money and policymakers' time.

The first step in providing real knowledge is the acquisition and reporting of accurate data. Facts do not speak for themselves, but the communication of facts, more than their interpretation, is the essential function when the context of a question and assumptions about it are not problematic. When the purpose of reporting is to educate generalists about technical points or to provide an update in an unfolding situation where policy has already been determined, reporting alone can be useful. Monitoring the pace of construction of missile sites during the 1962 Cuban crisis, briefing drug enforcement agents on detection of co- caine shipments from Colombia, or pinpointing the location of Osama bin Laden would count as successful performance in themselves.

Combining truth and utility becomes a tricky task when the implica- tions of data are at issue, so analysis is the more controversial part of the intelligence cycle. Truth is more problematic because the specter of politicization haunts all analyses on controversial issues. Utility falters when policymakers believe that finished intelligence papers tell them little more than they already know. On some matters the two problems are related, since attempts to minimize political controversy in the pro- duction process can yield watered-down conclusions without depth or nuance.

Progress against both problems may come from abandoning the tra- dition of seeking to transmit a single consensus estimate to consumers. After the 2004 reform legislation, intelligence leaders endorsed more highlighting of disagreements in reports to consumers, but there is a very deep tradition of seeking consensus, in no small part because con- sumers often want it. The norm should be to convey *both* the single best judgment of the analyst (or, for collective products like national intelligence estimates, the conclusions endorsed by a majority of the intelligence community), *and* the best case for differing views. The ex- ecutive summary or key judgments sections of products should (1) give the majority view of the intelligence community, (2) have a section labeled key disagreements to flag matters where the consumers them- selves will have to judge which case is more convincing, and (3) give cross-references to direct the reader to the pages in the full text that en- gage disagreements about logic or evidence on particular conclusions. Consumers who dislike such belaboring of analysis can choose to skip the portions beyond the majority judgment if they wish, but all con- sumers will have less reason to complain that the products they receive suffer from bland, naïve, or uninformative analysis.

It is not as bad to be uninformative as it is to be misleading, but being uninformative will discredit the analytical enterprise in general if it is seen to be typical. This common complaint from policymakers, how- ever, is not entirely justified. True, the problem arises easily in situations where the policymaker is a senior expert with long experience and the analyst is a neophyte. Ample experimental research has shown, however, that consumers tend consistently to overestimate what they knew all along and to undervalue what they learn from intelligence products.[21] It does not matter if analysis is sometimes a thankless task as long as the product continues to be read. To keep readers, analysts must avoid sending up papers that state only the obvious.

The importance of successful intelligence ultimately varies with the policies it has to support. Confidence in intelligence about the outside world is more important for countries that are very weak or very strong than for those in between. A vulnerable state seeking just to survive against powerful enemies needs all the knowledge of those enemies, and of potential allies, that it can get. At the other extreme, a secure country with broad interests, ambitious goals, and wide-ranging impulses to activism needs more and better intelligence than does one with policies that are restrained, selective, and defensive. The more a government aims to shape foreign societies and induce foreigners to bend to its will, the more it needs to be sure that it understands with whom it is dealing, what levers are likely to be effective, and what countermeasures should be anticipated. The more we try to control, the better intelligence needs to be.

After September 11 many Americans felt highly vulnerable and threatened. Others recognized that this country's power and geographical position give it more inherent security than almost any other, but they wished to use these advantages to create a congenial world order and discipline bad actors elsewhere. Fear on one hand and confidence on the other provide a warrant for big investments in intelligence and strong efforts to improve it. But a historically conscious view of the performance of both producers and consumers of strategic intelligence provides caution against expecting that Americans will get intelligence good enough to underwrite their most ambitious attempts to shape the world to their liking. There are just too many enemies. The inherent enemies of intelligence—the dilemmas, trade-offs, and paradoxes that can never be fully resolved—compound the threats posed by outside enemies of American policy and the innocent enemies inside who may fall down on the job.

The thinly veiled argument here is that there is some logical relation between pessimism about how well knowledge can be summoned by national security policy and the aggressive ambition with which that policy should try to control the course of events everywhere in the world. Smuggling this notion by insinuation into the end of this book would represent politicization of my analysis in the worst sense of the term. Making the point forthrightly, however, represents politicization in the best sense—bringing intelligence into the realm of politics, which is where national security policy is thrashed out. Having a modest view of how well the intelligence system will ever work is only one reason to favor military policies more restrained than those the United States pursued after the Cold War. It is not sufficient in itself, however, to discredit more ambitious interventionism. Either choice—cautious restraint or confident activism—is a policy decision, the responsibility of politicians and officials above intelligence officers.

Whichever thrust in policy makes sense when all the larger political, economic, social, and military questions are considered, keeping U.S. policymakers informed will remain an unchallenged priority. Recognizing that success in this enterprise will be inconsistent simply underlines the need to have it both ways: to invest heavily in bumping up the intelligence batting average and to incorporate hedging elements in policy to protect against the inevitable, occasional failure of intelligence.

NOTES

1. TWENTY-FIRST-CENTURY INTELLIGENCE: NEW ENEMIES AND OLD

1. Normally classified, this information was exposed by accident. Scott Shane, "Official Reveals Budget for U.S. Intelligence," *New York Times*, November 8, 2005.

2. Amy B. Zegart, *Flawed by Design: The Evolution of the CIA, JCS, and NSC* (Stanford: Stanford University Press, 1999), chaps. 6–7.

3. "Harman Calls for Real Action on 9–11 Commission Recommendations," press release, August 4, 2004.

4. For example, Jennifer E. Sims and Burton Gerber, eds., *Transforming U.S. Intelligence* (Washington, DC: Georgetown University Press, 2005).

5. Deborah G. Barger, *Toward a Revolution in Intelligence Affairs* (Santa Monica, CA: RAND, 2005).

6. Ibid., 123, 56.

7. Carmen A. Medina, "The Coming Revolution in Intelligence Analysis: What to Do When Traditional Models Fail," *Studies in Intelligence* (unclassified edition) 46, no. 3 (2002): 24–26.

8. Jack Davis, *Sherman Kent and the Profession of Intelligence Analysis*, Kent Center Occasional Papers, vol. 1, no. 5 (November 2002), 3.

9. Scott Shane, "Intelligence Center is Created for Unclassified Information," *New York Times*, November 9, 2005.

10. Gregory F. Treverton, *Reshaping National Intelligence for an Age of Information* (New York: Cambridge University Press, 2001), 10.

11. Senate Select Committee to Study Governmental Operations with Respect to Intelligence Activities, *Final Report*, bk. I, *Foreign and Military Intelligence*, 94th Cong., 2nd sess., April 1976, 347–48.

12. "Technical collection lends itself to monitoring large-scale, widespread targets, a condition not met in the Iraqi case." Richard Kerr, Thomas Wolfe, Rebecca Donegan, and Aris Pappas, "Collection and Analysis on Iraq: Issues for the US Intelligence Community," *Studies in Intelligence* (unclassified edition) 49, no. 3, (2005): 50.

13. Thom Shanker and Scott Shane, "Elite Troops Get Expanded Role on Intelligence," *New York Times*, March 8, 2006.

14. Max H. Bazerman and Michael D. Watkins, *Predictable Surprises: The Disasters You Should Have Seen Coming and How to Prevent Them* (Boston: Harvard Business School Press, 2004), 1 (emphasis added).

15. Stanley Hoffmann, *Gulliver's Troubles, Or the Setting of American Foreign Policy* (New York: McGraw-Hill, 1968), 146–51.

16. Dianne Vaughan, *The Challenger Launch Decision: Risky Technology, Culture, and Deviance at NASA* (Chicago: University of Chicago Press, 1996); John Schwartz and Christopher Drew, "Louisiana's Levee Inquiry Faults Army Corps," *New York Times*, December 1, 2005; Eric Lipton, "White House Knew of Levee's Failure on Night of Storm," *New York Times*, February 10, 2006; Charles Perrow, *Normal Accidents: Living with High-Risk Technologies* (New York: Basic Books, 1984).

17. Robert Jervis, *System Effects: Complexity in Political and Social Life* (Princeton: Princeton University Press, 1997), 61.

18. "Kriegspiel," http://www.chessvariants.com/incinf.dir/kriegspiel.html.

19. Hoffmann, *Gulliver's Troubles*, 149.

20. Richards J. Heuer, *Psychology of Intelligence Analysis* (n.p.: Central Intelligence Agency, Center for the Study of Intelligence, 1999), especially chaps. 1–3, 9–13.

21. *Webster's Third New International Dictionary* (Springfield, MA: Merriam-Webster, 1986), 633.

22. The Commission on the Intelligence Capabilities of the United States regarding Weapons of Mass Destruction, *Report to the President of the United States* (Washington, DC, March 31, 2005) 312, 328, 390.

23. Ibid., 422.

24. Arthur S. Hulnick, "The Intelligence Producer-Policy Consumer Linkage: A Theoretical Approach," *Intelligence and National Security* 1, no. 2 (May 1986): 217–18, 220–23.

25. House Permanent Select Committee on Intelligence, Subcommittee on Evaluation, *Staff Report: Iran: Evaluation of U.S. Intelligence Performance prior to November 1978* (Washington, DC: Government Printing Office, January 1979), 3.

26. Cord Meyer, "The U.S. Stake in Turkish Bases," *Washington Star*, March 31, 1979); Henry Bradsher, "Monitoring Sites in Turkey Feared Run Down," *Washington Star*, April 4, 1979; John Lawton, "Turkey Demands More U.S. Aid for Use of Bases," *Washington Post*, May 9, 1979.

27. Scott Shane, "C.I.A. Role in Visit of Sudan Intelligence Chief Causes Dispute within Administration," *New York Times*, June 18, 2005.

28. Ashton B. Carter, "A Failure of Policy, Not Spying," *Washington Post*, April 3, 2006.

29. For example, Mark M. Lowenthal, *Intelligence: From Secrets to Policy*, 2nd ed. (Washington, DC: CQ Press, 2003); Jeffrey T. Richelson, *The U.S. Intelligence Community*, 4th ed. (Boulder, CO: Westview, 1999); Michael Herman, *Intelligence*

Power in Peace and War (Cambridge, UK: Cambridge University Press, 1996); Loch K. Johnson, *America's Secret Power: The CIA in a Democratic Society* (New York: Oxford University Press, 1989); Abram N. Shulsky with Gary Schmitt, *Silent Warfare: Understanding the World of Intelligence*, 3rd ed. (Washington, DC: Potomac Books, 2002); Walter Laqueur, *A World of Secrets: The Uses and Limits of Intelligence* (New York: Basic Books, 1985); Bruce D. Berkowitz and Allan A. Goodman, *Best Truth: Intelligence in the Information Age* (New Haven: Yale University Press, 2000); Gregory Treverton, *Covert Action: The Limits of Intervention in the Postwar World* (New York: Basic Books, 1987); John Ranelagh, *The Agency: The Rise and Decline of the CIA from Wild Bill Donovan to William Casey* (New York: Simon & Schuster, 1986); Loch K. Johnson and James J. Wirtz, eds., *Strategic Intelligence: Windows into a Secret World* (Los Angeles: Roxbury, 2004); Roger Z. George and Robert D. Kline, eds., *Intelligence and the National Security Strategist: Enduring Issues and Challenges* (Washington, DC: National Defense University Press, 2004); Harold P. Ford, *Estimative Intelligence: The Purposes and Problems of National Intelligence Estimating* (Lanham, MD: University Press of America, 1993); Tyrus G. Fain et al., eds., *The Intelligence Community: History, Organization, and Issues* (New York: R.R. Bowker, 1977).

2. PERMANENT ENEMIES: WHY INTELLIGENCE FAILURES ARE INEVITABLE

1. In addition to the few examples mentioned in this chapter, evidence for the argument is elaborated in Richard K. Betts, *Surprise Attack* (Washington, DC: Brookings, 1982), chaps. 2–5.

2. For example, Klaus Knorr, "Failures in National Intelligence Estimates: The Case of the Cuban Missile Crisis," *World Politics* 16, no. 3 (April 1964): 455, 465–66; Harry Howe Ransom, "Strategic Intelligence and Foreign Policy," *World Politics* 27, no.1 (October 1974): 145. In the ferment after September 11, 2001, the intelligence community took a stronger interest in the theoretical principles that should govern its activities. See the proceedings of a RAND conference on the issue in Gregory F. Treverton, Seth G.. Jones, Steven Boraz, and Phillip Lipscy, *Toward a Theory of Intelligence: Workshop Report* (Santa Monica, CA: RAND National Security Research Division, 2006). See also Loch K. Johnson, "Bricks and Mortar for a Theory of Intelligence," *Comparative Strategy* 22, no. 1 (January 2003) and David Kahn, "An Historical Theory of Intelligence," *Intelligence and National Security* 16, no. 3 (September 2001).

3. Thomas L. Hughes, *The Fate of Facts in a World of Men—Foreign Policy and Intelligence-Making*, Headline Series no. 233 (New York: Foreign Policy Association, December 1976), 46.

4. Compare the prescriptions with George Carver's critique, both in Peter Szanton and Graham Allison, "Intelligence: Seizing the Opportunity," *Foreign Policy* 22 (Spring 1976).

5. Among the many studies of such cases are: Joint Committee on the Investigation of the Pearl Harbor Attack, *Hearings: Pearl Harbor Attack*, 79th Cong., 1st sess., 1945–46, (39 volumes); Roberta Wohlstetter, *Pearl Harbor: Warning and Decision* (Stanford: Stanford University Press, 1962); Barton Whaley, *Codeword Barbarossa* (Cambridge: MIT Press, 1973); Harvey De Weerd, "Strategic Surprise in the Korean War," *Orbis* 6, no. 3 (Fall 1962); Alan Whiting, *China Crosses the Yalu* (New York: Macmillan, 1960); James J. Wirtz, *The Tet Offensive: Intelligence Failure in War* (Ithaca, NY: Cornell University Press, 1991); Michael I. Handel, *Perception, Deception, and Surprise: The Case of the Yom Kippur War,* Jerusalem Paper no. 19 (Jerusalem: Leonard Davis Institute of International Relations, 1976); Avi Shlaim, "Failures in National Intelligence Estimates: The Case of the Yom Kippur War" and Abraham Ben-Zvi, "Hindsight and Foresight: A Conceptual Framework for the Analysis of Surprise Attacks," both in *World Politics* 28, no. 3 (April 1976); Uri Bar-Joseph, *The Watchman Fell Asleep: The Surprise of Yom Kippur and Its Sources* (Albany: State University of New York Press, 2005); House Select Committee on Intelligence (hereafter cited as the Pike Committee), *Hearings: U.S. Intelligence Agencies and Activities,* pt. 2, *The Performance of the Intelligence Community,* 94th Cong., 1st sess., 1975; Pike Commitee, *Draft Report,* partly reprinted in *The Village Voice,* February 16, 1976, 76–81; Douglas J. MacEachin, *Predicting the Soviet Invasion of Afghanistan: The Intelligence Community's Record* (Washington, DC: Center for the Study of Intelligence, Central Intelligence Agency, April 2002).

6. This summary draws on data in Betts, *Surprise Attack,* 87–149. See also Ephraim Kam, *Surprise Attack: The Victim's Perspective* (Cambridge: Harvard University Press, 1988).

7. David Halberstam, *The Best and the Brightest* (New York: Random House, 1972), passim; Morris Blachman, "The Stupidity of Intelligence," in *Inside the System,* ed. Charles Peters and Timothy J. Adams (New York: Praeger, 1970); Patrick J. McGarvey, "DIA: Intelligence to Please," in *Readings in American Foreign Policy: A Bureaucratic Perspective,* ed. Morton Halperin and Arnold Kanter (Boston: Little, Brown, 1973); Chester Cooper, "The CIA and Decision-Making," *Foreign Affairs* 50, no. 2 (January 1972); George W. Allen, *None So Blind: A Personal Account of the Intelligence Failure in Vietnam* (Chicago: Ivan R. Dee, 2001); Don Oberdorfer, *Tet!* (Garden City, NY: Doubleday, 1971); Richard K. Betts, *Soldiers, Statesmen, and Cold War Crises,* 2nd ed. (New York: Columbia University Press, 1991), chap 10.

8. House Committee on Armed Services, Oversight and Investigations Subcommittee, *Report: Intelligence Successes and Failures in Operations Desert Shield/ Storm,* 103rd Cong., 1st sess., August 1993, 22; Richard Russell, "CIA's Intelligence in Iraq," *Political Science Quarterly* 117, no. 2 (Summer 2002): 202–3.

9. Helms is quoted in Christopher Andrew, *For the President's Eyes Only: Secret Intelligence and the American Presidency from Washington to Bush* (New York: HarperCollins, 1995), 323. The incident is also reported, with different language,

in Henry Brandon, *The Retreat of American Power* (Garden City, NY: Doubleday, 1973), 103.

10. Betts, *Soldiers, Statesmen, and Cold War Crises,* 160–61, 192–95. On bias within CIA, see James Schlesinger's comments in Senate Select Committee to Study Governmental Operations with Respect to Intelligence Activities (hereafter cited as Church Committee), *Final Report,* bk. I, *Foreign and Military Intelligence,* 94th Cong., 2nd sess., 1976, 76–77.

11. Church Committee, *Report,* bk. IV, *Supplementary Detailed Staff Reports on Foreign and Military Intelligence,* 56–59; William T. Lee, *Understanding the Soviet Military Threat: How CIA Estimates Went Astray,* Agenda Paper no. 6 (New York: National Strategy Information Center, 1977), 24–37; Albert Wohlstetter: "Is There a Strategic Arms Race?" *Foreign Policy* no. 15 (Summer 1974); A. Wohlstetter, "Rivals, But No Race," *Foreign Policy* no. 16 (Fall 1974); A. Wohlstetter, "Optimal Ways to Confuse Ourselves," *Foreign Policy* no. 20 (Fall 1975). There are exceptions to this pattern of military and civilian bias; see Wohlstetter, "Optimal Ways," 185–88; Lt. Gen. Daniel Graham (ret.), "The Intelligence Mythology of Washington," *Strategic Review* 4 (Summer 1976), 61–62, 64; Victor Marchetti and John Marks, *The CIA and the Cult of Intelligence* (New York: Knopf, 1974), 309.

12. Before 1973 coordination for national estimates was done through the Office of National Estimates, and since then, through the National Intelligence Council. The community management staff (formerly, intelligence community staff) assists the director of national intelligence in managing allocation of resources and reviewing the agencies' performance. Since the Intelligence Reform and Terrorism Prevention Act of 2004, all elements in the Office of the Director of National Intelligence are community staffs.

13. Pike Committee, *Hearings,* pt. 2, 656–57.

14. Eliot A. Cohen and John Gooch, *Military Misfortunes: The Anatomy of Failure in War* (New York: Vintage, 1990), 41.

15. Ariel Levite, *Intelligence and Strategic Surprises* (New York: Columbia University Press, 1987).

16. Richard K. Betts, "Surprise, Scholasticism, and Strategy," *International Studies Quarterly* 33, no. 3 (September 1989): 329–43.

17. Harold Wilensky, *Organizational Intelligence: Knowledge and Policy in Government and Industry* (New York: Basic Books, 1967), 42–62, 126, 179.

18. Cooper, "The CIA and Decision-Making," 236; Wilensky, *Organizational Intelligence,* passim. The counterpoint between Cooper and McGarvey, "Intelligence to Please," is a perfect illustration, although McGarvey's discussion of DIA is something of a caricature.

19. Graham Allison and Peter Szanton, *Remaking Foreign Policy: The Organizational Connection* (New York: Basic Books, 1976), 204.

20. Quoted in Church Committee, *Report,* bk. I, 82.

21. Ibid., 267, 276; Church Committee, *Staff Report: Covert Action in Chile 1963–1973*, 94th Cong., 1st sess., 1975, 48–49.

22. Church Committee, *Report*, bk. I, 443; Pike Committee, *Draft Report* (in *Village Voice*, 78); Ben-Zvi, "Hindsight and Foresight," 386, 394; Amos Perlmutter, "Israel's Fourth War," *Orbis* 19, no. 2 (Summer 1975): 453.

23. Winston Churchill, *The Gathering Storm* (Boston: Houghton Mifflin, 1948), 587–88.

24. Wilensky, *Organizational Intelligence*, 77.

25. Quoted in Church Committee, *Report*, bk. I, 274.

26. Sherman Kent, "Estimates and Influence," *Foreign Service Journal* 46 (April 1969), 17.

27. Hughes, *Fate of Facts*, 43.

28. "The textbooks agree, of course, that we should only believe reliable intelligence, and should never cease to be suspicious, but what is the use of such feeble maxims? They belong to that wisdom which, for want of anything better, scribblers of systems and compendia resort to when they run out of ideas." Carl von Clausewitz, *On War*, ed. and trans. Michael Howard and Peter Paret (Princeton: Princeton University Press, 1976), 117.

29. Robert Jervis, *The Logic of Images in International Relations* (Princeton: Princeton University Press, 1970), 132; Jervis, *Perception and Misperception in International Politics* (Princeton: Princeton University Press, 1976), chap. 4; Floyd Allport, *Theories of Perception and the Concept of Structure*, cited in Shlaim, "Failures in Naitonal Intelligence Estimates," 358; John Steinbruner, *The Cybernetic Theory of Decision* (Princeton: Princeton University Press, 1974), 105–8.

30. See William J. McGuire, "Selective Exposure: A Summing Up," in *Theories of Cognitive Consistency,* ed. R. P. Abelson and others (Chicago: Rand McNally 1968), and Irving L. Janis and Leon Mann, *Decision Making: A Psychological Analysis of Conflict, Choice, and Commitment* (New York: Free Press, 1977), 213–14.

31. "Remarks of the Chief of the Nanking Military Academy and Other Chinese Leaders on the Situation in South Vietnam," CIA intelligence information cable, June 25, 1964, in Lyndon B. Johnson Library National Security Files, Vietnam country file (hereafter cited as LBJL/NSF-VNCF), vol. XII, item 55.

32. See, for example, Department of Defense, *The Senator Gravel Edition: The Pentagon Papers* (Boston: Beacon Press, 1971) (hereafter cited as *Pentagon Papers*), vol. II, 99; Frances Fitzgerald, *Fire in the Lake* (Boston: Atlantic-Little, Brown, 1972), 364; Special national intelligence estimate 53-64, "Chances for a Stable Government in South Vietnam," September 18, 1964, and McGeorge Bundy's covering letter to the president, in LBJL/NSF-VNCF, vol. XIII, item 48.

33. House Committee on Armed Services, *Report: Inquiry Into the U.S.S. Pueblo and EC-121 Plane Incidents*, 91st Cong., 1st sess., 1969, 1622–24, 1650–51 and *Hearings: Inquiry Into the U.S.S. Pueblo and EC-121 Plane Incidents*, 91st Cong., 1st sess., 1969, 693–94, 699–700, 703–7, 714, 722, 734, 760, 773–78, 815–16;

David Wise and Thomas B. Ross, *The U-2 Affair* (New York: Random House, 1962), 56, 176, 180; Trevor Armbrister, *A Matter of Accountability* (New York: Coward-McCann, 1970), 116–18, 141–45, 159, 187–95.

34. Patrick J. McGarvey, *CIA: The Myth and the Madness* (Baltimore: Penguin, 1974), 16.

35. Michael Schrage, "Give Us Odds on 'Slam Dunk,'" *Washington Post National Weekly Edition*, February 29–March 6, 2005, 22.

36. Church Committee, *Report*, bk. I, 61–62; Pike Committee, *Draft Report* (in *Village Voice*, 82).

37. *Intelligence Reform and Terrorism Prevention Act of 2004*, Public Law 108-458, (December 17, 2004), title I, sec. 1031.

38. McGarvey, *CIA: The Myth*, 16.

39. Eric Lipton, "U.S. Borders Vulnerable, Officials Say," *New York Times*, June 22, 2005.

40. Shlaim, "Failures in National Intelligence Estimates," 375–77. On the U.S. intelligence failure in 1973, see the Pike Committee, *Draft Report* (in *Village Voice*, 78–79).

41. Shlaim, "Failures in National Intelligence Estimates," 379; Handel, *Perception, Deception, and Surprise*, 62–63.

42. Handel, *Perception, Deception, and Surprise*, 55. "Success may be indistinguishable from failures." If analysts predict war and the attacker cancels his plans because surprise has been lost, "success of the intelligence services would have been expressed in the falsification of its predictions," which would discredit the analysis. Shlaim, "Failures in National Intelligence Estimates," 378.

43. Shlaim, 358–59; Michael I. Handel, personal communication with author, November 15, 1977.

44. H. D. S. Greenway, "Begin Formally Invites Sadat to Visit Israel," *Washington Post*, November 16, 1977.

45. William Westmoreland, *A Soldier Reports* (Garden City, NY: Doubleday, 1976), 316. See the postmortem by the President's Foreign Intelligence Advisory Board, quoted in Herbert Y. Schandler, *The Unmaking of a President* (Princeton: Princeton University Press, 1977), 70, 76, 79–80.

46. Philip Shenon, "High Alerts for Terror Get Harder to Impose," *New York Times*, September 13, 2003.

47. Wohlstetter, *Pearl Harbor*, 69.

48. Alexander L. George, "The Case for Multiple Advocacy in Making Foreign Policy," *American Political Science Review* 66, no. 3 (September 1972). My usage of the term *multiple advocacy* is looser than George's. See also Alexander L. George, *Presidential Decisionmaking in Foreign Policy: The Effective Use of Information and Advice* (Boulder, CO: Westview, 1980), chaps. 9, 11, 12.

49. Henry F. Graff, *The Tuesday Cabinet* (Englewood Cliffs, NJ: Prentice-Hall, 1970), 68–71; Leslie H. Gelb with Richard K. Betts, *The Irony of Vietnam: The System Worked* (Washington, DC: Brookings, 1979), chap. 4; Ball memorandum of

October 5, 1964, reprinted as "Top Secret: The Prophecy the President Rejected," *Atlantic Monthly* (July 1972); John McCone, memorandum of April 2, 1965, in LBJL/NSF-VNCF, troop decision folder, item 14b.

50. George P. Shultz, *Turmoil and Triumph: My Years as Secretary of State* (New York: Scribner's, 1993), chaps. 37–38; Caspar W. Weinberger, *Fighting for Peace: Seven Critical Years in the Pentagon* (New York: Warner Books, 1990), chap. 12; Bob Woodward, *Veil: The Secret Wars of the CIA, 1981–1987* (New York: Simon & Schuster, 1987), 412, 433, 489.

51. Betts, *Soldiers, Statesmen, and Cold War Crises*, 199–202; Schandler, *Unmaking of a President*, 177.

52. George, "Multiple Advocacy," 759.

53. Quoted in Steinbruner, *Cybernetic Theory of Decision*, 332.

54. Clausewitz, *On War*, 117–18; Pike Committee, *Hearings*, pt. 2, 634–36; William J. Barnds, "Intelligence and Policymaking in an Institutional Context," in U.S. Commission on the Organization of the Government for the Conduct of Foreign Policy (hereafter cited as the Murphy Commission), *Appendices* (Washington, DC: Government Printing Office, June 1975), vol. VII, 32.

55. Pike Committee, *Hearings*, pt. 2, 778.

56. Church Committee, *Report*, bk. IV, 57; Roger Hilsman, *Strategic Intelligence and National Decisions* (Glencoe, IL: Free Press, 1956), 40. During my brief service as a junior staff member of the National Security Council long ago, even I never had time to read all the intelligence analyses relevant to my work.

57. Church Committee, *Report*, bk. I, 344 and bk. IV, 95 (emphasis deleted).

58. Ray S. Cline, *Secrets, Spies, and Scholars* (Washington, DC: Acropolis, 1976), 20.

59. Gilbert W. Fitzhugh et al., *Report to the President and the Secretary of Defense on the Department of Defense by the Blue Ribbon Defense Panel* (Washington, DC: Government Printing Office, July 1970), 45–46.

60. Alexander George, "The Devil's Advocate: Uses and Limitations"; Murphy Commission, *Appendices*, vol. II, 84–85; Jervis, *Perception and Misperception*, 417.

61. Jervis, *Perception and Misperception*, 416.

62. George H. Poteat, "The Intelligence Gap: Hypotheses on the Process of Surprise," *International Studies Notes* 3, no. 3 (Fall 1976): 15.

63. Cline, *Secrets, Spies, and Scholars*, 140.

64. Church Committee, *Report*, bk. I, 352.

65. Church Committee, *Report*; Betts, *Soldiers, Statesmen, and Cold War Crises*, 196–97.

66. Church Committee, *Report*, bk. I, 82.

67. Ibid., 77–82. See also Senate Committee on Foreign Relations, *Hearing: National Security Act Amendment*, 92nd Cong., 2nd sess., 1972, 14–24. MIRV stands for Multiple Independently Targetable Re-entry Vehicles, which allowed a single intercontinental missile to strike numerous dispersed targets.

68. Quoted in Adm. Elmo R. Zumwalt Jr., *On Watch* (New York: Quadrangle, 1976), 459.

69. Wilensky, *Organizational Intelligence*, 164.

70. Jervis, *Perception and Misperception*, 181–87.

71. For fifty-eight years the director of central intelligence wore two hats, the second being director of CIA. The reform legislation of 2004 separated the jobs.

72. Knorr, "Failures in National Intelligence Estimates," 460.

73. Church Committee, *Report*, bk. I, 276 and bk. IV, 85; House Committee on Appropriations, *Hearings: Supplemental Appropriations for Fiscal Year 1977*, 95th Cong., 2nd sess., 1977, 515–621; *Washington Post*, February 15, 1977; Paul W. Blackstock, "The Intelligence Community Under the Nixon Administration," *Armed Forces and Society* 1, no. 2 (February 1975): 238.

74. Joseph C. Goulden, *Truth is the First Casualty* (Chicago: Rand McNally, 1969), 101–4; Phil G. Goulding, *Confirm or Deny* (New York: Harper & Row, 1970), 130–33, 269; House Committee on Armed Services, *Pueblo and EC-121 Hearings*, 646–47, 665–73, 743–44, 780–82, 802–3, 865–67, 875, 880, 897–99 and *Pueblo and EC-121 Report*, 1654–56, 1662–67; Armbrister, *A Matter of Accountability*, 196ff, 395; House Committee on Armed Services, *Report: Review of the Department of Defense Worldwide Communications: Phase I*, 92nd Cong., 1st sess., 1971, and *Phase II*, 2nd sess., 1972.

75. See, for example, James Blaker and Andrew Hamilton, *Assessing the NATO/Warsaw Pact Military Balance* (Washington, DC: Congressional Budget Office, December 1977).

76. Church Committee, *Report*, bk. I, 61; Thomas G. Belden, "Indications, Warning, and Crisis Operations," *International Studies Quarterly* 21, no. 1 (March 1977): 192–93.

77. *Pentagon Papers*, vol. 4, 111–12, 115–24, 217–32. On CIA critiques of bombing results begun even before the Tonkin Gulf crisis, see CIA/OCI current intelligence memorandum, "Effectiveness of T-28 Strikes in Laos," June 26, 1964; CIA/DDI intelligence memorandum, "Communist Reaction to Barrel Roll Missions," December 29, 1964. Ambivalence remained even within the CIA, which occasionally issued more sanguine evaluations, e.g., CIA memorandum for National Security Council, "The Situation in Vietnam," June 28, 1965 (which McGeorge Bundy called directly to the president's attention), and CIA/OCI intelligence memorandum, "Interdiction of Communist Infiltration Routes in Vietnam," June 24, 1965. (All memoranda are in LBJL/NSF-VNCF, vol. I, item 5; vol. III, items 28, 28a, 28b; vol. VI A, items 4, 5, 8.) See also *Pentagon Papers*, vol. 4, 71–74 and the opposing assessments of the CIA, the civilian analysts in the Pentagon, and the Joint Chiefs in NSSM-1 (the Nixon administration's initial review of Vietnam policy), reprinted in the *Congressional Record*, vol. 118, pt. 13, 92nd Cong., 2nd sess., May 10, 1972, 16749–836.

3. THEORY TRAPS: EXPERTISE AS AN ENEMY

1. The germ of this paragraph and the next comes from Richard K. Betts, *Surprise Attack: Lessons for Defense Planning* (Washington, DC: Brookings, 1982), 20. My elaboration of the notion mentioned parenthetically there benefited greatly from a discussion long ago at Cornell University with Norman Uphoff, who may not necessarily have agreed with all the ways I developed the point.

2. Sherman Kent, "A Crucial Estimate Relived," *Studies in Intelligence* (unclassified edition) 36, no. 5 (1992): 115. (A reprint of an article originally published in the Spring 1964 issue.) See also the article by a member of the Board of National Estimates at the time: Klaus Knorr, "Failures in National Intelligence Estimates: The Case of the Cuban Missiles," *World Politics* 16, no. 3 (April 1964).

3. Special national intelligence estimate 85-3-62, "The Military Buildup in Cuba, 19 September 1962," 2, partially declassified and reprinted in Mary S. McAuliffe, ed., *CIA Documents on the Cuban Missile Crisis, 1962* (Washington, DC: History Staff, Central Intelligence Agency, October 1992), 93.

4. Willis C. Armstrong, William Leonhart, William J. McCaffrey, and Herbert C. Rothenberg, "The Hazards of Single-Outcome Forecasting," in *Inside CIA's Private World: Declassified Articles from the Agency's Internal Journal, 1955–1992*, ed. H. Bradford Westerfield (New Haven: Yale University Press, 1999), 241, 243.

5. I use the term *theory* in the accepted sense, which is looser than that preferred by Kenneth Waltz in *Theory of International Politics* (Reading, MA: Addison Wesley, 1979), chap. 1. For predictive purposes, officials can sometimes rely on "laws" that establish empirical relationships between variables, rather than theories that explain causes (Aristotle, Galileo, and Newton, for example, had different theories for identical laws of motion). Reliance on laws can be useful for probabilistic prediction (Will the enemy attack in any of the next five crises?) but fatal for specific prediction (Will the enemy attack in the current crisis?). This is because, far more than in physics, political laws can never incorporate all the relevant variables and circumstances—critical data are often unavailable (such as policy discussions in the adversary's inner sanctum), and the permutations and combinations of human volition and idiosyncrasy are infinite. Factors that are peripheral or irrelevant in most cases can be essential in any particular one.

6. Kent, "A Crucial Estimate Relived," 118.

7. Douglas J. MacEachin, *Predicting the Invasion of Afghanistan: The Intelligence Community's Record* (Washington, DC: Central Intelligence Agency, Center for the Study of Intelligence, April 2002), 45–46.

8. Central Intelligence Agency, Directorate of Intelligence, Kent Center for Analytic Tradecraft, "A Tradecraft Primer: Structured Analytic Techniques for Improving Intelligence Analysis," *Tradecraft Review* 2, no. 2 (June 2005).

9. John D. Steinbruner, *The Cybernetic Theory of Decision* (Princeton: Princeton University Press, 1974), 56, 110–12.

10. Mark M. Lowenthal, "Tribal Tongues: Intelligence Consumers, Intelligence Producers," *Washington Quarterly* 15, no. 1 (Winter 1992): 166.

11. Richards J. Heuer Jr., *Psychology of Intelligence Analysis* (n.p.: Center for the Study of Intelligence, Central Intelligence Agency, 1999), 21.

12. Rob Johnston, *Analytic Culture in the US Intelligence Community: An Ethnographic Study* (Washington, DC: Center for the Study of Intelligence, Central Intelligence Agency, 2005), 21–23; quotation on 22 (emphasis deleted).

13. Heuer, *Psychology of Intelligence Analysis*, 62.

14. Ibid., 14, 124, 74; Abraham Ben-Zvi, "Hindsight and Foresight: A Conceptual Framework for the Analysis of Surprise Attacks," *World Politics* 28, no. 3 (April 1976), 394–95; Betts, *Surprise Attack*, chap. 5; Ephraim Kam, *Surprise Attack: The Victim's Perspective* (Cambridge: Harvard University Press, 1988), 86–94.

15. Frank Stech, "Self-Deception: The Other Side of the Coin," *Washington Quarterly* 3, no. 3 (Summer 1980).

16. Commission on the Intelligence Capabilities of the United States Regarding Weapons of Mass Destruction, *Report to the President of the United States* (n.p.: March 2005), 174.

17. Heuer, *Psychology of Intelligence Analysis*, 51–52, 11, 15.

18. Jack Davis, "Combatting Mind-Set," *Studies in Intelligence* (unclassified edition) 36, no. 5 (1992): 33.

19. Michael R. Gordon and Gen. Bernard E. Trainor, *The Generals' War: The Inside Story of the Conflict in the Gulf* (Boston: Little, Brown, 1995), 4–6, 16, 25; quotation on 5. See also, Richard L. Russell, "CIA's Intelligence in Iraq," *Political Science Quarterly* 117, no. 2 (Summer 2002): 194–95.

4. INCORRUPTIBILITY OR INFLUENCE? COSTS AND BENEFITS OF POLITICIZATION

1. For example, Mark M. Lowenthal, "Tribal Tongues: Intelligence Consumers, Intelligence Producers," *Washington Quarterly*, Winter 1992, and Gregory F. Treverton, *Reshaping National Intelligence for an Age of Information* (New York: Cambridge University Press, 2001), 180.

2. Barry M. Katz, *Foreign Intelligence: Research and Analysis in the Office of Strategic Services, 1942–1945* (Cambridge: Harvard University Press, 1989), 196.

3. Amos Kovacs, "The Nonuse of Intelligence," *International Journal of Intelligence and Counterintelligence* 10, no. 4 (Winter 1997–98): 383; quotations on 394.

4. Arthur S. Hulnick, "Indications and Warning for Homeland Security: Seeking a New Paradigm," *International Journal of Intelligence and Counterintelligence* 18, no. 4 (Winter 2005–06): 597.

5. Joseph S. Nye Jr., "Peering Into the Future," *Foreign Affairs* 73, no. 4 (July/August 1994): 91.

6. Richard Kerr et al., "Collection and Analysis on Iraq: Issues for the US Intelligence Community," *Studies in Intelligence* (unclassified edition) 49, no. 3 (2005): 53.

7. *Intelligence and Policy: The Evolving Relationship* (Washington, DC: Center for the Study of Intelligence, Central Intelligence Agency, June 2004), 3.

8. L. Keith Gardiner, "Dealing with Intelligence-Policy Disconnects," in *Inside CIA's Private World: Declassified Articles from the Agency's Internal Journal, 1955–1992*, ed. H. Bradford Westerfield (New Haven: Yale University Press, 1995), 348.

9. This trade-off was recognized by Chester Cooper, "The CIA and Decision-Making," *Foreign Affairs* 50, no. 2 (January 1972): 236.

10. Quoted in Treverton, *Reshaping National Intelligence*, 180.

11. Robert M. Macy, "Issues on Intelligence Resource Management," in Commission on the Organization of the Government for the Conduct of Foreign Policy, *Appendices*, vol. 7 (Washington, DC: Government Printing Office, June 1975), 53.

12. Senate Committee to Study Governmental Operations with Respect to Intelligence Activities *Final Report*, (hereafter cited as Church Committee, *Report*), 94th Cong., 2nd sess., 1976, bk. I, *Foreign and Military Intelligence*, 48–53 and bk. IV, *Supplementary Detailed Staff Reports on Foreign and Military Intelligence*, 51, 70–71. See also Richard K. Betts, "American Strategic Intelligence: Politics, Priorities, and Direction," in *Intelligence Policy and National Security*, ed. Robert L. Pfaltzgraff Jr., Uri Ra'anan, and Warren Milberg (London: Macmillan, 1981), 247.

13. *Preparing for the 21st Century: An Appraisal of U.S. Intelligence*, a report by the Commission on the Roles and Capabilities of the United States Intelligence Community (Washington, DC: Government Printing Office, March 1, 1996), 31.

14. Church Committee, *Report*, bk. I, 84.

15. William Colby and Peter Forbath, *Honorable Men: My Life in the CIA* (New York: Simon & Schuster, 1978), 361; Church Committee, *Final Report*, bk. I, 83–84, 90–92, 347 (Schlesinger quotation), and bk. IV, 87.

16. "The term 'politicization' is nearly always applied to actions of which one disapproves." David A. Baldwin, *Economic Statecraft* (Princeton: Princeton University Press, 1985), 209n.

17. *Webster's Third New International Dictionary* (Springfield, MA: Merriam-Webster, 1986), 1755.

18. For other definitions see Harry Howe Ransom, "The Politicization of Intelligence," in *Intelligence and Intelligence Policy in a Democratic Society*, ed. Stephen J. Cimbala (Dobbs Ferry, NY: Transnational, 1987), 26.

19. See the discussion of these approaches, and the various other terms used to characterize them, in H. Bradford Westerfield, "Inside Ivory Bunkers: CIA An-

alysts Resist Managers' 'Pandering'—Part I," *International Journal of Intelligence and Counterintelligence* 9, no. 4 (Winter 1996/97): 409, passim.

20. Sherman Kent, *Strategic Intelligence for American World Policy* (Princeton: Princeton University Press, 1949), 195–201.

21. Willmoore Kendall, "The Function of Intelligence," *World Politics* 1, no. 4 (July 1949): 548, 550–51.

22. Robert Jervis, "What's Wrong with the Intelligence Process?" *International Journal of Intelligence and Counterintelligence* 1, no. 1 (1986): 39.

23. Jack Davis, "Facts, Findings, Forecasts, and Fortune-telling," *Studies in Intelligence* (special unclassified edition) November 2002, 96. See also Carmen A. Medina, "What to Do When Traditional Models Fail," *Studies in Intelligence* (unclassified edition) 46, no. 3 (2002): 27–28.

24. See, for example, Gardiner, "Dealing with Intelligence-Policy Disconnects" and David D. Gries, "New Links Between Intelligence and Policy," in Westerfield, *Inside CIA's Private World*, 346–47. For a detailed account of the shift, and the organizational changes that facilitated it from the perspective of the aggrieved, see John A. Gentry, "Intelligence Analyst/Manager Relations at the CIA," in *Intelligence Analysis and Assessment*, ed. David A. Charters, Stuart Farson, and Glenn P. Hastedt (London: Frank Cass, 1996), and John A. Gentry, *Lost Promise: How CIA Analysis Misserves the Nation* (Lanham, MD: University Press of America, 1993), chap. 10.

25. As academics often forget, models are more distinct in theory than in practice. While Kent warned of the danger of corruption from a relationship between intelligence and policy that is too close, he also warned "of the two dangers—that of intelligence being too far from the users and that of being too close—the greatest danger is the one of being too far." Kent, *Strategic Intelligence*, 195. Bar-Joseph uses "professional" and "realist" for what I call the Kent and Gates models. He identifies Michael Handel as one of the main proponents of the professional approach and cites me as a member of the realist school. Uri Bar-Joseph, *Intelligence Intervention in the Politics of Democratic States: The United States, Israel, and Britain* (University Park: Pennsylvania State University Press, 1995), 25–28. The fact that Handel and I were close friends and agreed more than we disagreed is a reminder that the models indicate only tendency and emphasis.

26. Bruce D. Berkowitz and Allan E. Goodman, *Best Truth: Intelligence in the Information Age* (New Haven: Yale University Press, 2000), 97.

27. Bar-Joseph, *Intelligence Intervention in the Politics of Democratic States*, 28.

28. Arthur S. Hulnick, "The Intelligence Producer-Policy Consumer Linkage: A Theoretical Approach," *Intelligence and National Security* 1, no. 2 (May 1986): 227 (emphasis in original).

29. Quoted in Sam Adams, *War of Numbers: An Intelligence Memoir* (South Royalton, VT: Steerforth, 1994), 80.

30. Yehoshafat Harkabi, "The Intelligence-Policymaker Tangle," *Jerusalem Quarterly*, Winter 1984, 126, 128.

31. Harold P. Ford, *Estimative Intelligence,* rev. ed. (Lanham, MD: University Press of America, 1993), 177.

32. Paul R. Pillar, "Intelligence, Policy, and the War in Iraq," *Foreign Affairs* 85, no. 2 (March/April 2006): 22.

33. Loch K. Johnson, "Decision Costs in the Intelligence Cycle," in *Intelligence: Policy and Process,* ed. Alfred C. Maurer, Marion D. Tunstall, and James M. Keagle (Boulder, CO: Westview, 1985), 186.

34. Kent, *Strategic Intelligence,* 205.

35. Church Committee, *Report,* bk. I, 80–81.

36. Henry Kissinger, *White House Years* (Boston: Little, Brown, 1979), 11, 36.

37. House Committee on Armed Services, *Report: Intelligence Successes and Failures in Operations Desert Shield/Storm,* 103rd Cong., 1st sess., 1993, 18–21; Michael R. Gordon and Gen. Bernard E. Trainor, *The Generals' War: The Inside Story of the Conflict in the Gulf* (Boston: Little, Brown, 1995), 334–36; Richard L. Russell, "CIA's Intelligence in Iraq," *Political Science Quarterly* 117, no. 2 (Summer 2002): 203; Brig. Gen. Robert H. Scales Jr., *Certain Victory: United States Army in the Gulf* War (Washington, DC: Office of the Chief of Staff, U.S. Army, 1993), 187–89; Rick Atkinson, *Crusade: The Untold Story of the Persian Gulf War* (Boston: Houghton Mifflin, 1993), 232–36, 345–47; quotation in Gen. H. Norman Schwarzkopf, with Peter Petre, *It Doesn't Take a Hero: An Autobiography* (New York: Bantam, 1993), 501.

38. Kay Oliver testimony in Gates hearings, quoted in Westerfield, "Inside Ivory Bunkers: CIA Analysts Resist Managers' 'Pandering,'—Part II," *International Journal of Intelligence and Counterintelligence* 10, no. 1, (Spring 1997): 19.

39. Ibid., 24 (Douglas MacEachin testimony).

40. Robert M. Gates, "Guarding Against Politicization," address to CIA personnel reprinted in *Studies in Intelligence* (unclassified edition) 36, no. 5 (1992): 9.

41. See the many examples cited in George W. Allen, *None So Blind: A Personal Account of the Intelligence Failure in Vietnam* (Chicago: Ivan Dee, 2001), especially the charge against Walt Rostow on 236–37. See also Richard K. Betts, *Soldiers, Statesmen, and Cold War Crises,* 2nd ed. (New York: Columbia University Press, 1991), chap. 10.

42. Lt. Gen. Phillip B. Davidson (ret.), *Secrets of the Vietnam War* (Novato, CA: Presidio, 1990), 64–65; Harold P. Ford, *CIA and the Vietnam Policymakers: Three Episodes, 1962–1968* (n.p.: Central Intelligence Agency, Center for the Study of Intelligence, 1998), 100; James J. Wirtz, *The Tet Offensive: Intelligence Failure in War* (Ithaca, NY: Cornell University Press, 1991), 158–62; T. L. Cubbage II, "Westmoreland vs. CBS: Was Intelligence Corrupted by Policy Demands?" in *Leaders and Intelligence,* ed. Michael I. Handel (London: Frank Cass, 1989), 133, 165. See also, Renata Adler, *Reckless Disregard: Westmoreland v. CBS et al.; Sharon v. Time* (New York: Knopf, 1986).

43. See especially paragraphs 32–37 of special national intelligence estimate 14.3-67, "Capabilities of the Vietnamese Communists for Fighting in South Viet-

nam," November 13, 1967 (declassified December 1, 1975), reprinted in House Select Committee on Intelligence (hereafter the Pike Committee), *Hearings: U.S. Intelligence Agencies and Activities*, pt. 5, *Risks and Control of Foreign Intelligence*, 94th Cong., 1st sess., 1975, appendix III, 1990–91.

44. Ford, *CIA and the Vietnam Policymakers*, 102.

45. Adams, *War of Numbers*, 105, 114–15. This is the lengthiest account of the dispute by the CIA analyst most involved in challenging MACV estimates. For the main points behind his position see especially chaps. 4–5.

46. Col. Gains Hawkins, George Allen, and George Carver cited in Ford, *CIA and the Vietnam Policymakers*, 91, 93–94.

47. Cable quoted by Samuel Adams in testimony in Pike Committee, *Hearings on U.S. Intelligence Agencies and Activities*, pt. 2, *The Performance of the Intelligence Community*, 684–85.

48. Ford, *CIA and the Vietnam Policymakers*, 94.

49. Cable from Saigon and Allen, quoted in Ford, *CIA and the Vietnam Policymakers*, 92, 97.

50. Davidson, *Secrets of the Vietnam War*, 34, 44, 66–67. Davidson's is the only published insider's account I have found that defends MACV's performance on the O/B estimate.

51. Adams's testimony in Pike Committee, *Hearings*, pt. 2, 685–86.

52. In other cases, policymakers can use secrecy to politicize intelligence by manipulating its dissemination. Analysis may retain integrity but be kept out of channels that could cause trouble. This can occur on behalf of policy views anywhere along the spectrum from hawks to doves or from conservatives to liberals. For example, in mid-1980, when Congress required that aid to Nicaragua "be contingent on a presidential certification that Nicaragua was not 'aiding, abetting, or supporting acts of violence,'" the Carter administration refused routine congressional staff requests to speak with the relevant CIA analyst. The embargo was lifted only two days before certification was announced. The committee staff reviewed the intelligence and found that it did not support the administration position. House Permanent Select Committee on Intelligence, *Staff Report: U.S. Intelligence Performance on Central America: Achievements and Selected Instances of Concern*, 97th Cong., 2nd sess., September 1982, 5–7.

53. Glenn P. Hastedt, "The New Context of Intelligence Estimating," in Cimbala, *Intelligence and Intelligence Policy*, 49–50, 56, 59–60, 64.

54. "We frequently fall into what I call the institutional view syndrome. For a long time in my career, we did not in actual practice foster a tradition of careful treatment of alternatives... . Rather than trying to lay out the threatening situation to the reader ... we routinely got bogged down in an internal contest as to whose views would win the institutional place." Douglas MacEachin testimony, in Senate Select Committee on Intelligence, *Hearings: Nomination of Robert M. Gates*, 102nd Cong., 1st sess., September-October 1991 (hereafter cited as *Gates Hearings*), vol. II, 271.

55. Senate Select Committee on Intelligence, Subcommittee on Collection, Production, and Quality, *The National Intelligence Estimates A-B Team Episode concerning Soviet Strategic Capability and Objectives,* February 1978; Anne Hessing Cahn, *Killing Detente: The Right Attacks the CIA* (University Park: Pennsylvania State University Press, 1998), passim.

56. Richard Pipes, "Team B: The Reality Behind the Myth," *Commentary* 73, no. 4 (October 1986): 40.

57. Cahn, *Killing Detente,* 127.

58. Pipes, "Team B," 29. Although Pipes's application of this insight was dubious, he had a point. Intelligence officers sometimes fail "to realize that facts and theory are not separable." Capt. Robert Bovey, "The Quality of Intelligence Analysis," *American Intelligence Journal* 3, no. 3 (Winter 1980–81). E. H. Carr made the point that "the facts speak only when the historian calls on them: it is he who decides which facts to give the floor, and in what context... . It is the historian who has decided for his own reasons that Caesar's crossing of that petty stream, the Rubicon, is a fact of history, whereas the crossing of the Rubicon by millions of other people before or since interests nobody at all." *What Is History?* (New York: Vintage, 1961), 9.

59. Howard Stoertz, cited in Cahn, *Killing Detente,* 174.

60. The report itself is *Intelligence Community Experiment in Competitive Analysis: Soviet Strategic Objectives, an Alternate View: Report of Team B,* December 1976. A declassified copy was obtained from the National Security Archive; see especially 9–16, 41–48.

61. Richard Pipes, "Why the Soviet Union Thinks It Could Fight and Win a Nuclear War," *Commentary* 64, no. 1 (July 1977).

62. Raymond L. Garthoff, "Mutual Deterrence and Strategic Arms Limitation in Soviet Policy," *International Security* 3, no. 1 (Summer 1978). For the later and definitive version of Garthoff's research and interpretation, see his *Deterrence and the Revolution in Soviet Military Doctrine* (Washington, DC: Brookings, 1990).

63. The salience of the difference between policy intent and strategic intent is my own view, not one emphasized explicitly by partisans in the debates of the Cold War. On the difference between public rhetoric and actual war plans in the United States, see Fred Kaplan, *The Wizards of Armageddon* (New York: Simon & Schuster, 1983), 326; Scott D. Sagan, *Moving Targets: Nuclear Strategy and National Security* (Princeton: Princeton University Press, 1989), 33–34, 52; Aaron L. Friedberg, "The Evolution of U.S. 'Strategic Doctrine,' 1945–1980," in *The Strategic Imperative: New Policies for American Security,* ed. Samuel P. Huntington (Boston: Ballinger, 1982), 54–56, 60–63, 75–84.

64. Quoted in Pipes, "Team B," 40n.

65. Melvin Goodman, testimony in *Gates Hearings,* vol. II, 143. See also testimony against Gates by Jennifer Glaudemans and Harold Ford.

66. Bar-Joseph, *Intelligence Intervention in the Politics of Democratic States,* 33.

67. Mark M. Lowenthal, *Intelligence: From Secrets to Policy* (Washington, DC: Congressional Quarterly Press, 2000), 91.

68. Graham Fuller, testimony in *Gates Hearings*, vol. II, 161. See also testimony in support of Gates by Charles Allen, Douglas MacEachin, Lawrence Gershwin, and Kay Oliver. Earlier, Jimmy Carter's DCI, Adm. Stansfield Turner, recounted instances of analysts who considered his editorial revisions of their work to be politicization, while he believed he was simply correcting misleading methods of net assessment on a subject about which he was more expert than the analysts—naval capabilities. Turner also dealt with the case of David Sullivan, an analyst who leaked his own work to anti-Soviet Senate staff because he feared that it would be suppressed by détentist leadership at CIA. Stansfield Turner, *Secrecy and Democracy: The CIA in Transition* (Boston: Houghton Mifflin, 1985), 122–23.

69. Memorandum by Carolyn Ekedahl, reprinted in *Gates Hearings*, vol. III, 84.

70. Ibid., 86.

71. Claire Sterling, *The Terror Network*, (New York: Holt, Rinehart, & Winston, 1981).

72. Bob Woodward, *Veil: The Secret Wars of the CIA 1981–1987* (New York: Simon & Schuster, 1987), 124–29.

73. Quoted in David C. Morrison, "Tilting With Intelligence," *National Journal,* May 9, 1987. See also John Horton, "Mexico, the Way of Iran?" *International Journal of Intelligence and Counterintelligence* 1, no. 2 (1986), and Horton, "The Real Intelligence Failure," *Foreign Service Journal* 62, no. 2 (February 1985).

74. *Intelligence and Polic:y: The Evolving Relationship,* 15.

75. For random examples of these episodic controversies, see Greg Miller and Bob Drogin, "CIA Feels Heat on Iraq Data," *Los Angeles Times,* October 11, 2002; John J. Lumpkin, "US Said to Twist Its Data on Iraq," *Boston Globe,* June 8, 2003; Walter Pincus and Dana Priest, "Some Iraq Analysts Felt Pressure from Cheney Visits," *Washington Post,* June 5, 2003; Mark Mazzetti, "Iraq Report Is Due in '07; Skeptics Want to See It Now" and Adam Nagourney, "Dispute on Intelligence Report Disrupts Republicans' Game Plan," *New York Times,* September 28, 2006.

76. Steven R. Weisman, "U.N. Nominee Is Accused of Seeking 2nd Dismissal," *New York Times,* April 17, 2005; Douglas Jehl, "Tug of War: Intelligence vs. Politics," *New York Times,* May 8, 2005; "The Bolton Standoff," *Newsweek,* July 4, 2005, 8.

77. Memo quoted in Elisabeth Bumiller, "Bush and Blair Deny 'Fixed' Iraq Reports," *New York Times,* June 8, 2005.

78. Democrats initially suspected Karl Rove, the president's main political strategist, of orchestrating the leak, but Deputy Secretary of State Richard Armitage later said that he had revealed the name in passing conversation with journalist Bob Woodward.

79. "Any time policymakers, rather than intelligence agencies, take the lead in selecting which bits of raw intelligence to present, there is ... a bias. The resulting public statements ostensibly reflect intelligence, but they do not reflect intelligence analysis. . . . On Iraq, the intelligence community was pulled over the line into policy advocacy—not so much by what it said as by its conspicuous role in the administration's public case for war." Pillar, "Intelligence, Policy, and the War in Iraq," 20.

80. Spencer Ackerman and John B. Judis, "The First Casualty," *The New Republic,* June 30, 2003, 17–18.

81. Kenneth M. Pollack, "Spies, Lies, and Weapons: What Went Wrong," *The Atlantic,* January-February 2004, 88.

82. Greg Miller, "Spy Unit Skirted CIA on Iraq," *Los Angeles Times,* March 10, 2004.

83. Senator Carl Levin (D-MI), *Report of an Inquiry into the Alternative Analysis of the Issue of an Iraq-al Queda Relationship,* October 21, 2004, www.levin.senate.gov.

84. The Commission on the Intelligence Capabilities of the United States Regarding Weapons of Mass Destruction, *Report to the President of the United States* (n.p., March 31, 2005) (hereafter cited as WMD Commission *Report*), 188, 189.

85. Quotations in Robert Dreyfuss, "The Pentagon Muzzles the CIA," *American Prospect,* December 16, 2002.

86. Pillar, "Intelligence, Policy, and the War in Iraq," 23.

87. Quoted in Greg Miller, "Spy Unit Skirted CIA on Iraq," *Los Angeles Times,* March 10, 2004.

88. See, for example, "The CIA's Insurgency," *Wall Street Journal,* September 29, 2004; Gabriel Schoenfeld, "What Became of the CIA," *Commentary* 119, no. 3 (March 2005): 44–51; David Brooks, "The C.I.A. Versus Bush," *New York Times,* November 13, 2004; Phillip Sherwell, "The CIA 'Old Guard' Goes to War with Bush," *Sunday Telegraph* (UK), October 10, 2004.

89. Douglas Jehl and David E. Sanger, "Prewar Assessment on Iraq Saw Chance of Strong Divisions," *New York Times,* September 28, 2004; Douglas Jehl, "Report Says White House Ignored C.I.A. on Iraq Chaos," *NewYork Times,* October 13, 2005; Jim Hoagland, "CIA's New Old Iraq File," *Washington Post,* October 21, 2002.

90. Mark Mazzetti and Scott Shane, "Fired C.I.A. Official Denies Role in Leak," *New York Times,* April 25, 2006. See also R. Jeffrey Smith, "Fired Officer Believed CIA Lied to Congress," *Washington Post,* May 14, 2006.

91. Quoted in Scott Shane, "Ex-C.I.A. Official Says Iraq Data Was Distorted," *New York Times,* February 11, 2006.

92. Carl Hulse and David D. Kirkpatrick, "Partisan Quarrel Causes Senators to Bar the Doors in an Unusual Closed Session," *New York Times,* November 2, 2005.

93. Alexander Bolton, "Dems Weighing Iraq Probe," *The Hill* 10, no. 66, (October 29, 2003), 1, 10; "Intelligence Update on Iran Is Requested," *Washington*

Post, May 20, 2006; Dan Balz, "Reid Seeks More Clarity in Nuclear Intelligence on Iran," *Washington Post*, June 11, 2006; Scott Shane, "Senate Panel's Partisanship Troubles Former Members," *New York Times*, March 12, 2006; Charles Babington, "Nothing Like a Good Infight," *Washington Post National Weekly Edition*, March 20–26, 2006, 13; U.S. Senate Republican Policy Committee, "Examining the Continuing Iraq Pre-War Intelligence Myths," (press release, February 8, 2006), http://rpc.senate.gov.

94. "Trends in Global Terrorism: Implications for the United States," April 2006, declassified key judgments section of the national intelligence estimate, www.dni.gov/press_releases/Declassified_NIE_Judgments.pdf; Mark Mazzetti, "Spy Agencies Say Iraq War Worsens Terrorism Threat," *New York Times*, September 24, 2006; Philip Shenon and Mark Mazzetti, "Study of Iraq War and Terror Stirs Strong Political Response," *New York Times*, September 25, 2006.

95. Some of the points below echo Ransom, "The Politicization of Intelligence," and Hastedt, "The New Context of Intelligence Estimating."

96. Tenet's continuation in office under Bush the Younger might be seen as the equivalent of McCone's service.

97. For example, see *Making Intelligence Smarter: The Future of U.S. Intelligence*, report of an independent task force (New York: Council on Foreign Relations, 1996), 8–19, and *In From the Cold: The Report of the Twentieth Century Fund Task Force on the Future of U.S. Intelligence* (New York: Twentieth Century Fund Press, 1996), 10–12.

98. Pillar, "Intelligence, Policy, and the War in Iraq," 26–27; Richard A. Clarke, *Against All Enemies: Inside America's War on Terror* (New York: Free Press, 2004), 252.

99. Hans Heymann, "Intelligence/Policy Relationships," in Maurer, Tunstall, and Keagle, *Intelligence: Policy and Process*, 63.

100. Lawrence Freedman, *U.S. Intelligence and the Soviet Strategic Threat*, 2nd ed. (Princeton: Princeton University Press, 1986), xi-xii.

101. Gates, "Guarding Against Politicization," 12.

102. Ibid., 1.

5. TWO FACES OF FAILURE: SEPTEMBER 11 AND IRAQ'S WMD

1. The main sources for September 11 are Senate Select Committee on Intelligence and House Permanent Select Committee on Intelligence, *Report: Joint Inquiry Into Intelligence Community Activities Before and after the Terrorist Attacks of September 11, 2001*, 107th Cong., 2nd sess., December 2002 (hereafter cited as Congressional Joint Inquiry, *Report*), and *The 9/11 Commission Report: Final Report of the National Commission on Terrorist Attacks upon the United States* (New York: W. W. Norton, 2004), especially chaps. 8, 11, 13. The main sources for U.S.

performance on Iraq are Senate Select Committee on Intelligence, *Report on the U.S. Intelligence Community's Prewar Intelligence Assessments on Iraq,* 108th Cong., 2nd sess., July 2004 (hereafter cited as SSCI, *Report*); Commission on the Intelligence Capabilities of the United States Regarding Weapons of Mass Destruction, *Report to the President of the United States* (n.p.: March 2005) (hereafter cited as WMD Commission, *Report*); and Iraq Survey Group, *Comprehensive Report of the Special Advisor to the DCI on Iraq's WMD,* 30 September 2004, 3 vols., (hereafter cited as Duelfer, *Report*). British and Australian perspectives on their intelligence failures regarding Iraq can be found in Rt. Hon. Lord Butler of Brockwell et al., *Review of Intelligence on Weapons of Mass Destruction: Report of a Committee of Privy Counsellors* (London: The Stationery Office, July 2004) and Philip Flood et al., *Report of the Inquiry into Australian Intelligence Agencies* (Canberra: Australian Government, July 2004).

2. Melvin A. Goodman, "9/11: The Failure of Strategic Intelligence," *Intelligence and National Security* 18, no. 4 (Winter 2003): 59.

3. Richard A. Clarke, *Against All Enemies: Inside America's War on Terror* (New York: Free Press, 2004), xxiv, 197–201, 229–32; Daniel Benjamin and Steven Simon, *The Age of Sacred Terror: Radical Islam's War Against America* (New York: Random House, 2003), 329, 382.

4. Richard Clarke testimony quoted in Congressional Joint Inquiry, *Report,* 90–91.

5. *9/11 Commission Report,* 254–60.

6. Quoted in James Risen, "U.S. Failed to Act on Warnings in '98 of a Plane Attack," *New York Times,* September 19, 2002.

7. Congressional Joint Inquiry, *Report,* 375; Walter Pincus and Dana Priest, "NSA Intercepts On Eve of 9/11 Sent a Warning," *Washington Post,* June 20, 2002; quotations in Bob Woodward, *Plan of Attack* (New York: Simon & Schuster, 2004), 215.

8. *9/11 Commission Report,* chap. 6, and 266–72, 352–54.

9. Jeff Gerth, "C.I.A. Chief Won't Name Officials Who Failed to Add Hijackers to Watch List," *New York Times,* May 15, 2003; David Johnston and Elizabeth Becker, "C.I.A. Was Tracking Hijacker Months Earlier Than It Had Said," *New York Times,* June 3, 2002; Elisabeth Bumiller and Alison Mitchell, "Bush and His Aides Accuse Democrats of Second-Guessing," *New York Times,* May 18, 2002.

10. Neil A. Lewis, "Superior Says He Didn't See Agent's Report on Moussaoui," *New York Times,* March 22, 2006. See also Neil A. Lewis et al., "F.B.I. Inaction Blurred Picture Before Sept. 11," *New York Times,* May 27, 2002.

11. *9/11 Commission Report,* 273–76; Congressional Joint Inquiry, *Report,* 96–97, 319–21, 366–67.

12. The acting director of FBI at the time, Thomas J. Pickard, was later asked what difference it would have made if he had known of Moussaoui's extremism, the presence of two Al Qaeda terrorists in the United States, and the Phoenix memo report of Middle Eastern men in flight schools and the danger of a hijack-

ing plot. "He replied that given the thousands of terrorism leads the bureau was evaluating in the summer of 2001, 'I don't know, with all the information the FBI collects, whether we would have had the ability to hone in on those three items.'" Neil A. Lewis, "Defense Tries to Undo Damage Moussaoui Did," *New York Times*, March 29, 2006.

13. *9/11 Commission Report*, 353–56.

14. WMD Commission, *Report*, 282; Congressional Joint Inquiry, *Report*, 49.

15. Congressional Joint Inquiry, *Report*, 46–48,

16. *9/11 Commission Report*, 341, 357.

17. Douglas Jehl, "'98 Terror Memo Disregarded, Report Says," *New York Times*, April 15, 2004.

18. Paul R. Pillar, "A Scapegoat Is Not a Solution," *New York Times*, June 4, 2004.

19. *9/11 Commission Report*, 344–45. See also Max H. Bazerman and Michael D. Watkins, *Predictable Surprises: The Disasters You Should Have Seen Coming and How to Prevent Them* (Cambridge: Harvard Business School Press, 2004), 18–33.

20. Paul Krugman, "A Can't Do Government," *New York Times*, September 2, 2005; Mark Fischetti, "They Saw It Coming," *New York Times*, September 2, 2005.

21. Bazerman and Watkins, *Predictable Surprises*, 6.

22. Roberta Wohlstetter, *Pearl Harbor: Warning and Decision* (Stanford: Stanford University Press, 1962), 3, 55–56, 130, 228, 387, 393.

23. Eric Lichtblau, "F.A.A. Alerted on Qaeda in '98, 9/11 Panel Said," *New York Times*, September 14, 2005.

24. WMD Commission, *Report*, 422.

25. *9/11 Commission Report*, 346–48. For example, although the possible use of aircraft as a weapon had been identified, the Counterterrorism Center did not analyze how this might be done, and "did not develop a set of telltale indicators for this method of attack" (347).

26. *Intelligence and Policy: The Evolving Relationship* (Washington, DC: Center for the Study of Intelligence, Central Intelligence Agency, June 2004), 8.

27. Richard A. Posner, "The 9/11 Report: A Dissent," *New York Times Book Review*, August 29, 2004, 9.

28. See James Chow et al., *Protecting Commercial Aviation against the Shoulder-Fired Missile Threat* (Santa Monica, CA: RAND, 2005) and Richard K. Betts, "How to Think About Terrorism," *Wilson Quarterly* 30, no. 1 (Winter 2006): 48–49.

29. *9/11 Commission Report*, 344.

30. It is not literally true that no WMD were found in Iraq. After 2003, according to a U.S. Army report, "approximately 500 weapons munitions which contain degraded mustard or sarin nerve agent" were discovered. These were decaying remnants of pre-1991 stockpiles, found in scattered "small numbers," not the types maintained in operational condition that were expected. Quotations in "Officials Discuss Report on Munitions," *New York Times*, June 23, 2006.

31. Richard Kerr et al., "Collection and Analysis on Iraq: Issues for the U.S. Intelligence Community," originally written in July 2004, reprinted in *Studies in Intelligence* 49, no. 3 (2005): 48. See also Paul Pillar, "Intelligence, Policy, and the War in Iraq," *Foreign Affairs* 85, no. 2 (March/April 2006): 16, 18–19. Given the number of questions and the complexity of the issues regarding Iraq, the record was of course mixed, and some saw the glass as half full; others, as half empty. See "Agencies Warned Bush Aides of Postwar Iraq Resistance," *Washington Post*, September 9, 2003; Michael R. Gordon, "Poor Intelligence Misled Troops About Risk of Drawn-Out War," *New York Times*, October 10, 2004. "The CIA in particular was not only wrong on WMD, but failed to identify the importance of the Fedayeen or to uncover the tons of arms that had been cached." Michael R. Gordon and Gen. Bernard E. Trainor, *Cobra II: The Inside Story of the Invasion and Occupation of Iraq* (New York: Pantheon, 2006), 498.

32. "I was in charge of coordinating all of the intelligence community's assessments regarding Iraq; the first request I received from any administration policymaker for any such assessment was not until a year into the war." Pillar, "Intelligence, Policy, and the War in Iraq," 18.

33. Quoted in Woodward, *Plan of Attack,* 249.

34. Robert Jervis, "Reports, Politics, and Intelligence Failures: The Case of Iraq," *Journal of Strategic Studies* 29, no. 1 (February 2006): 18. This article was based on an investigation of lessons led by Jervis (and in which I participated) for the Central Intelligence Agency.

35. Kenneth M. Pollack, "Spies, Lies, and Weapons: What Went Wrong," *The Atlantic,* January-February 2004, 81.

36. For details see the accounts by UNSCOM staff member Tim Trevan, *Saddam's Secrets: The Hunt for Iraq's Hidden Weapons* (London: HarperCollins, 1999) and UNSCOM Chairman Richard Butler, *The Greatest Threat: Iraq, Weapons of Mass Destruction and the Crisis of Global Security* (New York: PublicAffairs, 2000).

37. Pollack, "Spies, Lies, and Weapons," 86.

38. WMD Commission, *Report,* 155.

39. SSCI, *Report,* 22. See also Pollack, "Spies, Lies, and Weapons," 85, and WMD Commission, *Report,* 92.

40. Jervis, "Reports, Politcs, and Intelligence Failures," 24–25, 40.

41. WMD Commission, *Report,* 183. See also David Barstow, William J. Broad, and Jeff Gerth, "How White House Embraced Iraq Arms Intelligence," *New York Times,* October 23, 2004.

42. WMD Commission, *Report,* 49–50.

43. SSCI, *Report,* 11–13. As one of the outside consultants occasionally called on to review draft estimates, I must confess that I would probably have been part of the amen chorus, although I was surprised later to find how thin the base of direct evidence on the subject was.

44. Kerr et al., "Collection and Analysis on Iraq," 51.

45. SSCI, *Report,* 24–25.

46. WMD Commission, *Report*, 112–13, 116.

47. Some of the limitations on collection were due to the overall decline in intelligence resources following the Cold War. Kerr et al., "Collection and Analysis on Iraq," 49–50.

48. WMD Commission, *Report*, 117.

49. Douglas Jehl, "C.I.A. Chief Orders 'Curveball' Review," *New York Times*, April 8, 2005; SSCI, *Report*, 152–60; WMD Commission, *Report*, 84. See also Bob Drogin and John Goetz, "How U.S. Fell Under the Spell of 'Curveball,'" *Los Angeles Times*, November 20, 2005.

50. SSCI, *Report*, 161; WMD Commission, *Report*, 84–85; Drogin and Goetz, "How U.S. Fell Under the Spell of 'Curveball.'"

51. SSCI, *Report*, 20.

52. See Duelfer, *Report*, vol. I, and WMD Commission, *Report*, 121.

53. Jervis, "Reports, Politics, and Intelligence Failures," 42 (emphasis added).

54. Sherman Kent, "A Crucial Estimate Relived," reprinted in *Studies in Intelligence* (unclassified edition) 36, no. 5 (1992): 118.

55. The key judgments were declassified and made available to the public on July 18, 2003, and posted on the Internet at http://www.fas.org/irp/cia/product/iraq-wmd.html. One official document, *How the Intelligence Community Arrived at the Judgments in the October 2002 NIE on Iraq's WMD Programs* (National Intelligence Council, March 2004), cited in WMD Commission, *Report*, 197n3, will provide the public with a sober, detailed, and informative explanation of the process that produced the mistaken NIE, whenever it is declassified.

56. Kent, "A Crucial Estimate Relived," 115 (emphasis in original).

57. Ibid., 116.

58. Mark M. Lowenthal, "The Burdensome Concept of Failure," in *Intelligence: Policy and Process,* ed. Alfred C. Maurer, Marion D. Tunstall, and James M. Keagle (Boulder, CO: Westview, 1985), 43. See also Woodward, *Plan of Attack*, 196–97.

59. The president's summary reportedly did not contain the caveats or dissents found in the full NIE. Douglas Jehl, "White House and C.I.A. Withhold Document on Prewar Intelligence Given to Bush," *New York Times*, July 14, 2004.

60. Philip H.J. Davies, "A Critical Look at Britain's Spy Machinery," *Studies in Intelligence* (unclassified edition) 49, no. 4 (2005): 42. The official report, by a former cabinet secretary, was by Lord Butler of Brockwell, *Review of Weapons of Mass Destruction* (London: TSO, 2004).

61. The SSCI report "almost always equates reasonable, well-grounded inferences with those that proved to be correct. We can see the problem by asking the obvious counterfactual: Would the same report have been written if the estimates turned out to be correct? This is implausible, yet it is what SSCI implies." Jervis, "Reports, Politics, and Intelligence Failures," 14.

62. Ibid.

6. AN INTELLIGENCE REFORMATION? TWO FACES OF REORGANIZATION

1. Tim Weiner, "To Fight in the Shadows, Get Better Eyes," *New York Times*, October 7, 2001, Week in Review section, 1.

2. Matthew M. Aid, "The Time of Troubles: The US National Security Agency in the Twenty-First Century," *Intelligence and National Security* 15, no. 3 (Autumn 2000): 17–18.

3. See Scott D. Sagan, "The Problem of Redundancy Problem: Why More Nuclear Security Forces May Produce Less Nuclear Security," *Risk Analysis* 24, no. 4 (2004): 936–43; Robert Jervis, *System Effects* (Princeton: Princeton University Press, 1997), chaps. 1, 2, 7.

4. Quoted in Robert K. Ackerman, "Intelligence at the Crossroads," *Signal* 56, no. 2 (October 2001).

5. *Countering the Changing Threat of International Terrorism*, Report of the National Commission on Terrorism Pursuant to Public Law 277, 105th Congress, June 2001, 7–8.

6. Walter Pincus, "Spies are Called Essential," *Washington Post*, June 1, 2006.

7. Dan Eggen, "Lost in Translation," *Washington Post National Weekly Edition*, October 4–10, 2004, 31; Eric Lichtblau, "At F.B.I., Translation Lags as Does the System Upgrade," *New York Times*, July 28, 2005.

8. David Moore and Lisa Krizan, "Intelligence Analysis: Does NSA Have What It Takes?" *Cryptologic Quarterly* 20, no. 1 (Summer 2001): 17.

9. Ibid., 18.

10. See for example, "National Security Language Initiative," briefing by Assistant Secretary of State Dina Powell, January 5, 2006, http://www.state.gov/r/pa/prs/ps/2006/58733.htm; Senate Select Committee on Intelligence and House Permanent Select Committee on Intelligence, *Joint Inquiry Into Intelligence Community Activities Before and After the Terrorist Attacks of September 11, 2001*, 107th Cong., 2nd sess., December 2002, 343–44; "Senate Defense Bill Would Create Reserve Corps of Language Experts," *Inside the Pentagon* 21, no. 46 (November 17, 2005): 1, 12; Rati Bishnoi, "Council of High-Level Officials Proposed to Boost Language Training," *Inside the Pentagon* 22, no. 20 (May 18, 2006): 4.

11. House Permanent Select Committee on Intelligence, *IC21: Intelligence Community in the 21st Century*, 104th Cong., 1996, 224, 237–38; Intelligence Reform and Terrorism Prevention Act of 2004, Public Law 108-458, December 17, 2004, U.S. Statutes at Large 1188:3683, sec. 1053; James L. Quinn Jr., "Staffing the Intelligence Community: The Pros and Cons of an Intelligence Reserve," *International Journal of Intelligence and Counterintelligence* 13, no. 2 (Summer 2000): 159–170.

12. I first heard this idea proposed by former DCI William Colby during a dinner discussion with members of Congress in the late 1980s. He spoke of using "housewives," a politically insensitive choice of words that nevertheless conveys the essential idea behind a part-time corps.

13. Clancy ended his novel *Debt of Honor* (New York: G.. P. Putnam's Sons, 1994) with a Japanese pilot crashing his 747 into the Capitol during a joint session of Congress. This is the closest thing I have found to a scenario for what happened on September 11.

14. Martin V. Melosi, *The Shadow of Pearl Harbor: Public Controversy Over the Surprise Attack, 1941–1946* (College Station: Texas A&M University Press, 1977), chaps. 4, 6, 10.

15. Robert Pear, "Politics Can Get in the Way of Keeping Papers Secret," *New York Times*, April 10, 2004.

16. Clinton's discomfort with leaders of the intelligence establishment was a larger problem: "Responsibility for domestic intelligence gathering on terrorism was vested solely in the FBI, yet during almost all of the Clinton administration the relationship between the FBI Director and the President was nearly nonexistent." *The 9/11 Commission Report: Final Report of the National Commission on Terrorist Attacks upon the United States* (New York: W.W. Norton, 2004), 358.

17. Quoted in James Risen, "In Hindsight, C.I.A. Sees Flaws That Hindered Efforts on Terror," *New York Times*, October 7, 2001.

18. Herbert Kaufman, *Red Tape* (Washington, DC: Brookings Institution, 1977).

19. Richard A. Best Jr., *Proposals for Intelligence Reorganization, 1949–2004* (Washington, DC: Congressional Research Service, July 2004), 4–39; Michael Warner and Kenneth J. MacDonald, *US Intelligence Community Reform Studies Since 1947* (Washington, DC: DCI Strategic Management Issues Office and Center for the Study of Intelligence, April 2005), 7–40. These compilations do not count a number of legislative proposals that were put forward but not passed. See, for example, Senate Select Committee on Intelligence, *Hearings: S. 2198 and S. 421 to Reorganize the United States Intelligence Community*, 102nd Cong., 2nd sess., 1992, and Elaine Sciolino, "Lawmakers Unveil Spy Agency Plan," *New York Times*, February 6, 1992. Nor do they count numerous proposals from nongovernment organizations.

20. See examples in Richard K. Betts, "American Strategic Intelligence," in *Intelligence Policy and National Security*, ed. Robert L. Pfaltzgraff Jr., Uri Ra'anan, and Warren Milberg (London: Macmillan, 1981), 246–49.

21. Amy B. Zegart, "September 11 and the Adaptation Failure of U.S. Intelligence Agencies," *International Security* 29, no. 4 (Spring 2005): 85–88. See also Arthur S. Hulnick, "Does the Intelligence Community Need a DNI?" *International Journal of Intelligence and Counterintelligence* 17, no. 4 (Winter 2004–05): 716.

22. David W. Overton, "The DI 10 Years After Reorganization," *Studies in Intelligence* (unclassified edition) 36, no. 5 (1992): 48.

23. Rufus E. Miles Jr., "Considerations for a President Bent on Reorganization," *Public Administration Review* 37 (March/April 1977): 161.

24. Richard L. Russell, "Intelligence Failures: The Wrong Model for the War on Terror," *Policy Review,* February & March, 2004, 63.

25. Arthur B. Darling, *The Central Intelligence Agency: An Instrument of Government to 1950* (University Park: Pennsylvania State University Press, 1990), 138.

26. Ibid., 138–39.

27. "History of the Central Intelligence Agency," in Senate Select Committee to Study Governmental Operations with Respect to Intelligence Activities, *Final Report*, bk. IV, *Supplementary Detailed Staff Reports on Foreign and Military Intelligence*, 94th Cong., 2nd sess., April 1976, 12–15 (hereafter cited as Church Committee, *Report*).

28. Commission on the Roles and Capabilities of the United States Intelligence Community, *Preparing for the 21st Century: An Appraisal of U.S. Intelligence* (Washington, DC: Government Printing Office, March 1996), 47.

29. *9/11 Commission Report*, 353.

30. *The National Intelligence Strategy of the United States of America: Transformation through Integration and Innovation* (Washington, DC: Office of the Director of National Intelligence, October 2005), 4.

31. Harold L. Wilensky, *Organizational Intelligence* (New York: Basic Books, 1967), 58–62; Stephen G. Brooks, *Producing Security* (Princeton: Princeton University Press, 2005), 65–67.

32. "There is simply no way to provide 'one stop' intelligence analysis support to all departments. . . . An analogy with changes in computers is instructive: once microprocessors hit the market, large mainframe processors began to decline in usefulness. The DI has tried to be the 'central processor' for intelligence production, but distributed processing has taken the lion's share of the market." William E. Odom, *Fixing Intelligence* (New Haven: Yale University Press, 2003), 63–68; quotation on 68.

33. A contrasting view is Philip H.J. Davies, "Intelligence Culture and Intelligence Failure in Britain and the United States," *Cambridge Review of International Affairs* 17, no. 3 (October 2004): 513.

34. Richard A. Posner, "The 9/11 Commission Report: A Dissent," *New York Times Book Review*, August 29, 2004, 11. See also Richard A. Posner, *Uncertain Shield: The U.S. Intelligence System in the Throes of Reform* (New York: Rowman & Littlfield, 2006), 67.

35. *9/11 Commission Report*, 418.

36. Joshua Rovner and Austin Long, "The Perils of Shallow Theory: Intelligence Reform and the 9/11 Commission," *Journal of Intelligence and Counterintelligence* 18, no. 4 (Winter 2005–06): 627, quoting Charles Perrow, *Normal Accidents* (New York: Basic Books, 1984), 335.

37. Harold Seidman, *Politics, Position, and Power: The Dynamics of Federal Organization* (New York: Oxford University Press, 1970), 164–68.

38. See Senate Select Committee on Intelligence, *Hearings: S. 2198 and S. 421 to Reorganize the United States Intelligence Community*.

39. James Risen and Thom Shanker, "Rumsfeld Moves to Strengthen His Grip on Military Intelligence," *New York Times*, August 3, 2002; Thom Shanker and

Scott Shane, "Elite Troops Get Expanded Role on Intelligence," *New York Times*, March 8, 2006; Eric Schmitt, "Clash Foreseen Between C.I.A. and Pentagon," *New York Times*, May 10, 2006.

40. 1957 Senate testimony of an army deputy assistant chief of staff for intelligence, quoted in Harry Howe Ransom, *The Intelligence Establishment* (Cambridge: Harvard University Press, 1971), 116.

41. Richard Kerr, Thomas Wolfe, Rebecca Donegan, and Aris Pappas, "Collection and Analysis on Iraq: Issues for the US Intelligence Community," *Studies in Intelligence* (unclassified edition) 49, no. 3 (2005): 49. This was the third of a series of reports by former senior intelligence officers on the Iraq failure.

42. Albert Wohlstetter, "Racing Forward or Ambling Back?" in James Schlesinger et al., *Defending America* (New York: Basic Books, 1977), 111, 116, 118–19, 126–33.

43. Quoted in Mark Mazzetti, "Some in G.O.P. Say Iran Threat is Played Down," *New York Times*, August 4, 2006.

44. R. Jeffrey Smith, "Scrubbing Up at the CIA," *Washington Post National Weekly Edition*, March 10, 1997, 34; Tim Weiner, "For the U.S., a Bad Bedfellow in Guatemala," *New York Times*, May 12, 1996; Tim Weiner, "C.I.A. Severs Ties to 100 Foreign Agents," *New York Times*, March 3, 1997; James Risen, "Report Faults C.I.A.'s Recruitment Rules," *New York Times*, July 18, 2002; James Risen, "After Criticism, C.I.A. Eases Policy on Recruiting Informers," *New York Times*, July 19, 2002.

45. Paul R. Pillar, *Terrorism and U.S. Foreign Policy* (Washington, DC: Brookings, 2001), 231.

46. Kerr et al., "Collection and Analysis on Iraq," 51. A chorus of veterans echoing this lament is reported in Tim Weiner, "Langley, We Have a Problem," *New York Times*, Week in Review section, 3.

47. *National Intelligence Strategy of the United States of America*, 10.

48. Church Committee, *Report*, bk. IV, 16.

49. John A. Kringen, "How We've Improved Intelligence," *Washington Post*, April 3, 2006.

50. Bob Woodward, *Plan of Attack* (New York: Simon & Schuster, 2004), 196–97.

51. Quoted in "Top Spy's Deputy Testifies on Changes to Avoid Error," *New York Times*, July 29, 2005. See also Douglas Jehl, "Intelligence Briefing for Bush is Overhauled," *New York Times*, July 20, 2005.

7. WHOSE KNOWLEDGE OF WHOM? THE CONFLICT OF SECRETS

1. Edward A. Shils, *The Torment of Secrecy: The Background and Consequences of American Security Policies* (New York: Free Press, 1956), 22–23, 25. For surveys of

a wide range of government secrecy issues see Thomas M. Franck and Edward Weisband, eds., *Secrecy and Foreign Policy* (New York: Oxford University Press, 1974). For a post–Cold War liberal critique see Daniel Patrick Moynihan, *Secrecy* (New Haven: Yale University Press, 1998).

2. Michael J. Woods, "Counterintelligence and Access to Transactional Records: A Practical History of USA PATRIOT Act Section 215," *Journal of National Security Law & Policy* I, no. 1 (2005): 71 (emphasis added). USA PATRIOT stands for United and Strengthening America by Providing Appropriate Tools Required to Intercept and Obstruct Terrorism.

3. David Cole, "The Missing Patriot Debate," *The Nation,* May 30, 2005, 21.

4. Jeffrey Lax and Eric Richard contributed to my understanding of the *Korematsu* case, although neither necessarily endorses what I have made of it.

5. Tim Golden, "How a Trip to Film in Iraq Ended in a Military Jail Cell," *New York Times,* July 24, 2005; Neil A. Lewis, "Judge Is Urged to Intervene for Detainee Held in Iraq," *New York Times,* February 8, 2006.

6. Eric Lichtblau, "Two Groups Charge Abuse of Witness Law," *New York Times,* June 27, 2005; Neil A. Lewis, "Court Gives Bush Right to Detain U.S. Combatant," *New York Times,* September 10, 2005; Eric Lichtblau, "Detainee at Brig in Charleston Accuses His Jailers of Abuse," *New York Times,* August 9, 2005.

7. See the National Commission on Terrorism's criticism of the underutilization of the Alien Terrorist Removal Court and the recommendation on cleared counsel in *Countering the Changing Threat of International Terrorism,* Report of the National Commission on Terrorism Pursuant to Public Law 2777, 105th Cong., June 2000, 31–32 (hereafter cited as National Commission on Terrorism, *Report*).

8. "When the Army dropped six criminal counts against Yee . . . officials said they did so to avoid making sensitive information public—not because he was innocent." Laura Parker, "The Ordeal of Chaplain Yee," *USA Today,* May 16, 2004.

9. Philip B. Heymann, *Terrorism, Freedom, and Security: Winning Without War* (Cambridge: MIT Press, 2003), 95–96.

10. Senate Select Committee on Intelligence and House Permanent Select Committee on Intelligence, *Joint Inquiry into Intelligence Community Activities before and after the Terrorist Attacks of September 11, 2001,* 107th Cong., 2nd sess., December 2002, 96, 97, 319, 321, 366–67. The reasons for the FBI's failure to apply for the warrants reportedly arose from complaints that the FISA court and the attorney general had made about improper applications in the past. The trouble reportedly "prompted bureau officials to adopt a play-it-safe approach that meant submitting fewer applications and declining to submit any that could be questioned." Neil A. Lewis et al., "FBI Inaction Blurred Picture before September 11," *New York Times,* May 27, 2002. See also Neil A. Lewis, "F.B.I. Agent Testifies Superiors Didn't Pursue Moussaoui Case," *New York Times,* March 21, 2006.

11. A similar failure, if the allegation proves true, was the claim that, before September 11, military lawyers blocked personnel involved in the "Able Dan-

ger" program from informing the FBI of their discovery of a terrorist cell that included Mohamed Atta, who turned out to be the ringleader of the hijackers. The claim was that lawyers in the Special Operations Command feared that Able Danger would be criticized as an improper intrusion of military intelligence into domestic civilian affairs. Philip Shenon, "Officer Says Military Blocked Sharing of Files on Terrorists," *New York Times*, August 17, 2005. The Defense Department's inspector general, however, came to the conclusion that the stories of Atta's identification were not true. Philip Shenon, "Report Rejects Claim that 9/11 Terrorists Were Identified Before Attacks," *New York Times*, September 22, 2006.

12. National Commission on Terrorism, *Report*, 10–12.

13. Quoted in Scott Shane, "Experts Differ About Surveillance and Privacy," *New York Times*, July 20, 2006.

14. Lynette Clemetson, "Coalition Seeks Action on Shared Data on Arab-Americans," *New York Times*, August 13, 2004; Lynette Clemetson, "F.B.I. Tries to Dispel Surveillance Concerns," *New York Times*, January 12, 2006.

15. See, Senate Select Committee to Study Governmental Operations with Respect to Intelligence Activities (hereafter cited as Church Committee), *Final Report*, bk. II, *Intelligence Activities and the Rights of Americans*, 94th Cong., 2nd sess., April 1976; Church Committee, *Hearings*, 94th Cong., 1st sess., vol. 2, *Huston Plan* (September 1975); vol. 4, *Mail Opening* (October 1975); vol. 5, *The National Security Agency and Fourth Amendment Rights* (October 1975); and vol. 6, *Federal Bureau of Investigation* (November and December 1975). See also House Select Committee on Intelligence (hereafter cited as Pike Committee), *Hearings: U.S. Intelligence Agencies and Activities*, pt. 3, *Domestic Intelligence Programs*, 94th Cong., 1st sess., October, November, and December 1975; and John T. Elliff, *The Reform of FBI Intelligence Operations* (Princeton:: Princeton University Press, 1979), chaps. 3, 5, 6.

16. Senate Select Committee on Intelligence, Subcommittee on Intelligence and the Rights of Americans, *Hearings: Foreign Intelligence Surveillance Act of 1978*, 95th Cong., 2nd sess., July and February 1978.

17. Woods, "Counterintelligence and Access to Transactional Records," 40; Commission on the Intelligence Capabilities of the United States Regarding Weapons of Mass Destruction, *A Report to the President of the United States* (n.p., March 31, 2005), 335 (hereafter cited as WMD Commission, *Report*).

18. Neil A. Lewis, "Rule Created Legal 'Wall' to Sharing Information," *New York Times*, April 14, 2004; Steve Coll, "Legal Disputes Paralyzed Clinton's Aides," *Washington Post National Weekly Edition*, March 1–7, 2004, 9.

19. For a survey of legal changes see Donald F. Kettl, *System Under Stress: Homeland Security and American Politics* (Washington, DC: CQ Press, 2004), chap. 6. For a leftist critique see David Cole and James X. Dempsey, *Terrorism and the Constitution: Sacrificing Civil Liberties in the Name of National Security* (New York: New Press, 2002), chaps. 9–11.

20. Quoted in Douglas Jehl, "No. 2 Intelligence Nominee Testifies on Privacy Rules," *New York Times*, April 15, 2005.

21. Barton Gellman, "The FBI Is Watching," *Washington Post National Weekly Edition*, November 14–20, 2005, 7.

22. Woods, "Counterintelligence and Access to Transactional Records," 62. See also Eric Lichtblau's *New York Times* stories: "Libraries Say Yes, Officials Do Quiz Them About Users," June 20, 2005; "F.B.I., Using Patriot Act, Demands Library's Records," August 26, 2005; "Antiterrorism Law Defended as Hearings Start," April 6, 2005.

23. National Commission on Terrorism, *Report,* 29–31; Benjamin Orbach, "Tracking Students from Terrorism-Supporting Middle Eastern Countries: An Update," *Washington Institute for Near East Policy Research Notes*, no. 9 (December 1999); Michael Janofsky, "Plan to Gather Student Data Draws Fire," *New York Times*, May 27, 2005; Eric Lichtblau, "Plan Would Let F.B.I. Track Mail in Terrorism Inquiries," *New York Times*, May 21, 2005.

24. Woods, "Counterintelligence and Access to Transactional Records," 41–43.

25. See, "Counterterrorism Technology and Privacy: Report on the Cantigny Conference, Sponsored by the McCormick Tribune Foundation," *National Security Law Report* 27, no. 1 (February 2005): 1–16. "Under the old guidelines, surfing the internet for the sole purpose of developing leads was prohibited. . . . The bureau will also use commercial 'data-mining services' from companies that collect and analyze marketing and demographic information. . . . Businesses routinely use the information, but the bureau has been constrained." Don Van Natta Jr., "Government Will Ease Limits on Domestic Spying by FBI," *New York Times*, May 30, 2002.

26. Philip B. Heymann and Juliette N. Kayyem, *Protecting Liberty in an Age of Terror* (Cambridge: MIT Press, 2005), 78–79.

27. Victoria Toensing, "Terrorist on Tap," *Wall Street Journal*, January 19, 2006.

28. "Press Briefing by Attorney General Alberto Gonzalez and General Michael V. Hayden, Principal Deputy Director of National Intelligence," December 19, 2005, 2, http://www.dni.gov/release_letter_121905.html; David Johnston and Neil A. Lewis, "Defending Spy Program, Administration Cites Law," *New York Times*, December 23, 2005; Elisabeth Bumiller, "Bush Sees No Need for Law to Approve Eavesdropping," *New York Times*, January 27, 2006; Eric Lichtblau and David E. Sanger, "Administration Cites War Vote to Support Spying," *New York Times*, December 20, 2005.

29. Adam Liptak, "Little Help from Justices on Spy Program," *New York Times*, December 23, 2005, A21; David Johnston and Linda Greenhouse, " '01 Resolution is Central to '05 Controversy," *New York Times*, December 20, 2005; Eric Lichtblau and Adam Liptak, "Bush and His Senior Aides Press On in Legal Defense for Wiretapping Program," *New York Times*, January 28, 2006.

30. "Press Briefing by Attorney General Alberto Gonzalez and General Michael V. Hayden," 9.

31. Scott Shane, "With Access Denied, Justice Dept. Drops Spying Investigation," *New York Times*, May 11, 2006.

32. Robert Block and Jay Solomon, "Pentagon Steps Up Intelligence Efforts Inside U.S. Borders," *Wall Street Journal*, April 27, 2006; Dan Eggen, "Secret No More," *Washington Post National Weekly Edition*, October 31–November 6, 2005, 29; Walter Pincus, "Possibly Too Much Information," *Washington Post National Weekly Edition*, December 19–25, 2005, 30; Eric Lichtblau, "Tighter Oversight of F.B.I. Is Urged After Investigation Lapses," *New York Times*, October 25, 2005; Eric Lichtblau, "F.B.I. Watched Activist Groups, New Files Show," *New York Times*, December 20, 2005.

33. Heymann, *Terrorism, Freedom, and Security*, 147.

34. *Intelligence Reform and Terrorism Prevention Act of 2004*, Public Law 108–458, December 17, 2004, sec. 1011/103d and sec. 1061.

35. John M. Oseth, *Regulating U.S. Intelligence Operations* (Lexington: University Press of Kentucky, 1985), 94–95, 155–56.

36. WMD Commission, *Report*, 401.

37. *The 9/11 Commission Report: Final Report of the National Commission on Terrorist Attacks upon the United States* (New York: W. W. Norton, 2004), 418.

38. WMD Commission, *Report*, 26, 33.

39. *The National Intelligence Strategy of the United States of America* (Washington, DC: Office of the Director of National Intelligence, October 2005), 14.

40. John A. Kringen, "How We've Improved Intelligence," *Washington Post*, April 3, 2006.

41. Richard E. Neustadt and Ernest R. May, *Thinking in Time: The Uses of History for Decision Makers* (New York: Free Press, 1986), 143; Richard K. Betts, *Soldiers, Statesmen, and Cold War Crises*, 2nd ed. (New York: Columbia University Press, 1991), 158.

42. Church Committee, *Report*, bk. I, 348, 268.

43. Pike Committee, *Hearings: U.S. Intelligence Agencies and Activities*, pt. 2, *The Performance of the Intelligence Community*, 94th Cong., 1st sess., September and October 1975, 651.

44. Senate Select Committee on Intelligence, *Staff Report: U.S. Intelligence and the Oil Issue, 1973–1974*, 95th Cong., 1st sess., 1977, 3–4.

45. *Information Sharing: The Federal Government Needs to Establish Policies and Processes for Sharing Terrorism-Related and Sensitive but Unclassified Information*, GAO-06–385 (Washington, DC: Government Accountability Office, March 2006), 4.

46. See the list of recent cases in Michael A. Turner, *Why Secret Intelligence Fails* (Dulles, VA: Potomac Books, 2005), 135. Even this large compilation was incomplete, neglecting to list some known cases, such as that of State Department secretary Geneva Jones (Stephen Labaton, "U.S. Charges 2 With Espionage for Liberia Rebels," *New York Times*, August 5, 1993). Although some of the espionage cases, such as that one, involved matters of comparatively minor impor-

tance to national security, many were tremendously damaging, such as William Kampiles's selling of the KH-11 satellite manual, the Walker family's transmission of naval intelligence material to the USSR, and the betrayal by Edward Lee Howard and Aldrich Ames of the names of numerous U.S. agents in the Soviet Union, causing their apprehension and execution.

47. John Mintz, "U.S. Spy Prosecutions on the Upswing," *Washington Post*, July 12, 1985; Philip Shenon, "Navy Spy Case Propelling Efforts To Fortify U.S. Espionage Laws," *New York Times*, July 22, 1985; George Lardner Jr., "Panel Proposes Tougher Laws Against Espionage," *Washington Post*, May 24, 1990.

48. Senate Select Committee on Intelligence, *An Assessment of the Aldrich Ames Espionage Case and Its Implications for U.S. Intelligence,* November 1, 1994, 110.

49. Warren P. Strobel, "Clinton Orders Strikes on Terrorists," *Washington Times*, August 21, 1998; Martin Sieff, "Terrorist is Driven by Hatred for U.S., Israel," *Washington Times*, August 21, 1998; David E. Rosenbaum, "Bush Account of a Leak's Impact Has Support," *New York Times*, December 20, 2005. Other *Washington Times* columnists later disputed the account reported by the 9/11 Commission and President Bush. Bill Gertz and Rowan Scarborough, "Inside the Ring," December 23, 2005, http://www.gertzfile/ring122305.html.

50. Jeffrey T. Richelson, *The U.S. Intelligence Community*, 4th ed. (Boulder, CO: Westview, 1999), 201; Jack Anderson, "CIA Eavesdrops on Kremlin Chiefs," *Washington Post*, September 16, 1971; Scott Shane, "A History of Publishing, and Not Publishing, Secrets," *New York Times*, July 2, 2006.

51. Garrett Jones, "It's a Cultural Thing: Thoughts on a Troubled CIA, Part One," Foreign Policy Research Institute E-Notes, September 24, 2005, 7, http://www.fpri.org/enotes/20050628.americawar.jones.ciaculture.html.

52. WMD Commission, *Report*, 416.

8. ENEMIES AT BAY: SUCCESSFUL INTELLIGENCE

1. Amy B. Zegart, *Flawed by Design: the Evolution of the CIA, JCS, and NSC* (Stanford: Stanford University Press, 1999), 190–93, 208–12.

2. Robert Jervis, *System Effects: Complexity in Political and Social Life* (Princeton: Princeton University Press, 1997), 294.

3. Deborah G. Barger, *Toward a Revolution in Intelligence Affairs* (Santa Monica, CA: RAND National Security Research Division, 2005), 44, 96–97.

4. Max H. Bazerman and Michael D. Watkins, *Predictable Surprises: The Disasters You Should Have Seen Coming and How to Prevent Them* (Cambridge: Harvard Business School Press, 2004), 22–39.

5. Mark Fischetti, "They Saw It Coming," *New York Times*, September 2, 2005.

6. For elaboration and examples see Richard K. Betts, "How to Think About Terrorism," *Wilson Quarterly* 30, no. 1 (Winter 2006): 46–49.

7. Eliot A. Cohen and John Gooch, *Military Misfortunes: The Anatomy of Failure in War* (New York: Free Press, 1990), 40–43.

8. At the end of FY 2004 the market value of those three endowments totaled $45.3 billion. "College and University Endowments, 2004," http://www.info-please.com/ipa/A0112636.html. The aggregate U.S. intelligence budget in 2005 was $44 billion. Scott Shane, "Official Reveals Budget for U.S. Intelligence," *New York Times*, November 8, 2005. Normally only a small portion of that total goes to analysis and human intelligence collection; most goes to high-technology collection systems.

9. Thom Shanker, "Officials Reveal Threat to Troops Deploying to Gulf," *New York Times*, January 13, 2003.

10. Richard K. Betts, "Intelligence for Policymaking," *Washington Quarterly* 3, no. 3 (Summer 1980): 119.

11. For example, "17 in Terror Ring Arrested, Morocco Says," *New York Times*, November 21, 2005; "Saudis Say Raid Prevented An Imminent Terror Attack," *New York Times*, June 16, 2003; Daniel J. Wakin, "Lebanon Says Arrests Foiled Attack on the U.S. Embassy," *New York Times*, May 16, 2003; "U.S. Reports Plot to Fly a Plane Into U.S. Consulate in Pakistan," *New York Times*, May 3, 2003.

12. Richard W. Shryock, "The Intelligence Community Post-Mortem Program, 1973–1975," *Studies in Intelligence* 21 (unclassified edition) (Fall 1977): 16n.

13. Frank J. Stech, *Political and Military Intention Estimation: A Taxonometric Analysis*, final report to the Office of Naval Research (Bethesda, MD: Mathtech, November 1979), chap. 7.

14. David E. Sanger, "10 Plots Foiled Since September 11, Bush Declares," *New York Times*, October 7, 2005; Elisabeth Bumiller and David Johnston, "Bush Gives New Details of 2002 Qaeda Plot to Attack Los Angeles," *New York Times*, February 10, 2006.

15. "New Qaeda Cells and Links to Middle East Groups Revive Terror Threat to U.S.," *New York Times*, June 16, 2002. Since not all the attacks were executed by movements of concern to the United States (which meant that U.S. intelligence was not focused on them), the practical average was probably higher.

16. Daniel Benjamin and Steven Simon, *The Age of Sacred Terror: Radical Islam's War Against America* (New York: Random House, 2003), 30–31; quotation on 312. See also Richard A. Clarke, *Against All Enemies: Inside America's War on Terror* (New York: Free Press, 2004), 211–14. All three authors handled terrorism on the National Security Council staff.

17. Commission on the Intelligence Capabilities of the United States Regarding Weapons of Mass Destruction, *Report to the President of the United States* (n.p.: March 31, 2005), 4, 252–63.

18. Harold P. Ford, "Calling the Sino-Soviet Split," *Studies in Intelligence* (unclassified edition) (Winter 1998–99); David S. Robarge, "Getting It Right: CIA Analysis of the 1967 Arab-Israeli War," *Studies in Intelligence* (unclassified edition) 49, no. 1, (2005); Rep. Les Aspin, "Intelligence Performance on the China-Vietnam

Border," press release, March 26, 1979; Michael A. Turner, *Why Secret Intelligence Fails* (Dulles, VA: Potomac Books, 2005), 27; Michael R. Gordon and Gen. Bernard E. Trainor, *The Generals' War* (Boston: Little, Brown, 1995), 4–6.

19. Raymond L. Garthoff, "US Intelligence in the Cuban Missile Crisis," in *Intellligence and the Cuban Missile Crisis*, ed. James G. Blight and David A. Welch (London: Frank Cass, 1998), 29, 30, 32–33.

20. HPSCI Review Committee (Daniel M. Berkowitz et al.), "Survey Article: An Evaluation of the CIA's Analysis of Soviet Economic Performance, 1970–90," *Comparative Economic Studies* 35, no. 2 (Summer 1993); Douglas J. MacEachin, "The Record Versus the Charges: CIA Assessments of the Soviet Union," *Studies in Intelligence*, (semiannual unclassified edition), no. 1 (1997), 57–65; Bruce D. Berkowitz and Jeffrey T. Richelson, "CIA Vindicated," *National Interest* no. 41 (Fall 1995).

21. Richards J. Heuer Jr., *Psychology of Intelligence Analysis* (n.p.: Center for the Study of Intelligence, Central Intelligence Agency, 1999), 165–66.